The Snow Queen's Daughter

The
Snow Queen's Daughter

my life with aspergers,
a tale from the lost generation

•

Charli Devnet

Bramble Books

For information please contact:
Bramble Books
E-mail address: info@bramblebooks.com
Website, www.bramblebooks.com

Library of Congress Cataloging-in-Publication Data

Devnet, Charli.
  Snow Queen's daughter : my life with Aspergers, a tale from the lost generation / Charli Devnet.
     pages cm
  ISBN 978-1-883647-22-3 (alk. paper)
  1. Devnet, Charli—Mental health. 2. Asperger's syndrome—Patients—Biography 3. Asperger's syndrome—Social aspects. I. Title.

  RC553.A88D485 2013
  616.85'88320092--dc23
  [B]

ISBN 978-1-883647-22-3

Contents

•

Dedication

I would like to dedicate this book to the memory of Hans Christian Anderson whom, many scholars believe, was himself an aspie and who, like me, wanted only the things he could not get.

Acknowledgments

A debt of gratitude is owed to John J. Gochman, Esq. of Croton-on-Hudson, New York for allowing me the use of his computer to write this memoir, to Jessica Herman for technical support, to fellow Kykuit Guide Clare Feldman for pushing me to put my talents to good use, to Dr. Tony Attwood, world-famous expert on Asperger's Syndrome in girls and women, for his encouragement and support when this venture was new, to my publisher, Larry Bramble of Bramble Books, to Margaret Steele of Peekskill, New York, author and magician, for recommending me to him, and to my friend Jeanne Walter for driving me to Albany to attend Dr. Attwood's conference and later for introducing me to Margaret.

I would also like to thank those who stood by me and provided comfort and companionship in the darkest hours of my life, when the pain of loss, despair and isolation threatened to overwhelm me and I felt that I could not go on. I am particularly grateful to my guardian angels A and Bee, and all the friends I made through the bereavement support group at St. Patrick's Church in Yorktown Heights, New York. I would also like to thank my therapists, Susan Walton and Dr. Maureen Empfield of Mt. Kisco, New York, for helping me to unravel the mysteries of my past, and to all my colleagues at Kykuit, the Rockefeller Estate for accepting me as a member of their troupe despite my undeniable strangeness.

The Snow Queen's Daughter

A True Story

She really does come from another planet, but it is not one to be found in the far reaches of space. Rather it lies within the deepest galaxies of the human mind.

●

Here, in the kingdom of frost, it is always winter and most of the time it is night. There is a clearing in a deep forest. Gnarled and ancient trees form an impenetrable circle around a dark pool whose still waters have no bottom. High on a twisted bough, a snowy owl stands sentinel. The unnaturally bright light of a crescent moon illuminates the figure of a small girl who stands at the water's edge, wrapping her cloak tightly about her shoulders to guard against the ever present cold.

In the distance a wolf is watching. His eyes are crystals of ice and his breath can paralyze. The name of the wolf is Loneliness. He is tracking the little girl and always will. Thankfully, she does not yet realize this. She thinks she is the huntress, but she is only the prey.

Morning of a Misfit

●

*L*ong, long ago in the small riverside village of Croton-on-Hudson, (pop. 7700), thirty-four miles due north of Manhattan, there lived the heroine of this tale, a spunky inquisitive child that we will call the Real Me. She was a tomboy and a mischief-maker, but brave and curious and un-ashamed. She might have lived by the motto later proclaimed proudly in a country song: "I'm perfectly normal; everyone else is just a little mixed-up!"

To her classmates, her teachers and her family, she was bright, but quirky and strange, atypical in a way that was neither deci-pherable nor explicable. There was no specific word for it at the time. People just called her a misfit.

Perhaps it was because the Real Me's Mom was a goddess or, more precisely, a demigoddess, more than human, but less than divine. She was tall with dark hair and high cheekbones and exceptionally slender, as beautiful as a snowflake and just as hard to hold. Her attire was composed exclusively of navy blue, black and white. Whenever she walked out in the sun, she would don a pair of sunglasses (a habit that the Real Me would also adopt at an early age, finding that the brightness hurt her eyes). Her name was Jacqueline, like the First Lady, whom she did indeed look like. In fact, the resemblance was so strong that many years later, when Jackie Onassis passed away, her daughter would be shaken by grief, although, at the time, her own mother would still be alive and well. Not only was the Real Me's Mom the best-looking woman in town, but poised and sophisticated in a way that caused people to break off conversations and turn their heads when she walked into a room, brandishing a long cigarette holder like a forties movie star. The Real Me was intensely proud of her glamorous elusive mother and delighted in showing her off, or would have, had it not been damn near impossible to get her to abide in the company of mere mortals. The Snow Queen did not socialize with the other kids' moms, the sole exception being Hazel from the house next door. Hazel was exempted from the general rule by being older, cultured and employed, and, most notably, the mother of Alexis, the Real Me's best friend.

When the Real Me was in 7th grade, the entire class spent a week roughing it at Camp Rainbow near the Croton Dam. It was a wonderful adventure, made most memorable by a mysterious illness which swept through the cabins and struck down most of the campers. Even the usually hearty Alexis succumbed and had to leave early. At the end of the week, only the Real Me, her teachers, and a few fortunate survivors were left standing.

Various activities had been planned for the week. The teachers were accompanied by the other kids' parents, mostly mothers, but some fathers, too. Only the Real Me was unrepresented. Then, on Thursday morning, the campers were taken on a nature hike to Storm King Mountain and there, right alongside the other grown-ups, was her Mom. The Real Me fairly beamed. At last! However, within an hour, her mother had vanished, not a trace left behind. The Real Me knew better than to ask questions. That evening, one of the teachers came to her and explained that it had been her Mom's "time of the month." The Real Me buried her disappointment deep inside and nodded as if she understood. You cannot expect a demigoddess to follow the same rules that bound mere mortals.

The Real Me's mother had grown up in Ossining, the next village down the Hudson. It is Ossining, and its legendary prison, Sing-Sing, that gave birth to the phrase, *being sent up the river*. She rarely spoke of her childhood except to say that she had gone to school with the actor Peter Falk or, wistfully blowing smoke rings in the air, she would describe how, as a little girl, her family had been quite wealthy and lived in a big house on a hill with a maid. It is true that her father, Charlie G. had once been a successful restaurateur, and undoubtedly a bootlegger as well, but by the time the Real Me arrived on the scene, her grandparents were anything but well off. They owned and operated a bar and grill two blocks from Sing-Sing and lived in a one-bedroom apartment around the corner. The family business was referred to as *the saloon*, as though it came out of a Western movie. Well, yes, it did have swinging doors and it was indeed patronized by gunslingers aplenty (correctional officers coming off shift at the prison), but the jukebox did not play country music and there were no honky-tonk angels in sight.

The Real Me knew Charlie G. as a handsome, laconic and taciturn man. She was his first grandchild and his namesake as well. You might have supposed that he would make a fuss over her, but no. He would walk right by her as though she was a complete stranger. *What's this little imp doing in our saloon?* Nevertheless, the Real Me was fascinated by her refrigerator grandfather, and loved to tag along behind him. He told her that nothing in life was free. "What about birthdays?" piped up the Real Me. "No, not even birthdays." One day she followed him as he walked down toward Sing Sing. He paused before the forbidding walls of the prison and turned to her. "This is where you'll wind up if you're not a good little girl." Experts say that Asperger's Syndrome and other forms of autism are genetic in origin. If so, this was certainly where the Real Me got her aspietude, not from vaccines, or toxins in the environment, or living near a highway, but from a former bootlegger and cynic. In fact, Charlie G.'s words proved oddly prophetic. Thirty years thereafter, his granddaughter was to fall in love with a handsome young desperado within the confines of Sing-Sing, all doom and disaster and highly inappropriate.

The Real Me's Mom was beautiful and intelligent, and you would suppose that, given her obsession with lost wealth and status, she would have married above herself. Nothing could be further from the truth. In fact, she did not even try to land a millionaire. Instead, she wed her childhood sweetheart, one of ten children of a dirt poor Italian immigrant. She was fourteen and he was sixteen the day he walked into the saloon with his underage buddies to test the waters. Opposites attract, they say, and here was living proof. The boy was everything she was not, warm, friendly, gentle, unabashedly blue-collar and thoroughly neurotypical. One look and they were soul mates. He adored her, he was besotted with her, and if she ever, in her entire life, so much as glanced at another man with desire, it was a secret she took to the grave.

Croton-on-Hudson was his hometown. Just go to the top of Ossining and walk north across the narrow bridge.

The first recorded visit of white men to these parts occurred in late summer of 1609 when Henry Hudson's crew anchored the *Half Moon* off Croton Point and traded with the locals, the Kitchawank Indians, a branch of the Mohicans. Fifteen years later, Peter Stuyvesant came to Manhattan Island, and not long thereafter Dutch colonists had flooded the east bank of the Hudson, from New Amsterdam to Albany. The Dutch were merchants, not *conquistadores*, and took great pains to purchase their land from the tribes that were residing there, in legal and proper fashion. The terms of these transactions were always favorable to the Dutch, however, as the Native Americans did not quite grasp the European concept of land conveyances. How could anyone buy and sell the earth which had been given by the gods to all living things? Be that as it may, busy little villages soon crowded the shores of what the Indians had named *the river that runs both ways*.

A Dutch family called the Van Cortlandts founded a village where the Croton River empties into the mighty Hudson. One of their scions, Pierre Van Cortlandt, became the first lieutenant governor of the State of New York and gave his name to the Croton middle school which the Real Me attended, and which is still in operation today. In the mid-nineteenth century the railroad arrived and, with it, an influx of Irish workers. The Italians came later, in the early 1900's. The necessity had arisen to build a new dam along the Croton River, no trifling matter, for its purpose was to insure an adequate water supply to the folk in New York City. It was to be the largest hand-hewn structure in the world, and a call went out for the best stonemasons in the world. Where are such stonemasons to be found? Why, in Italy, of course! Ever since the Romans built their aqueducts and their coliseums, the Italians have been reputed to be the finest stonemasons of all.

One of the stonemasons who answered the call was a young man with red hair and blue eyes, from a village south of Naples called Ariana del Irpino. Because he was a hard worker, and perhaps because he did not really look *Italian*, he did well in his new country, so well that he sent back to Italy for his bride and infant son to join him in a rented house on Grand Street. When his first wife died and left him with five children to bring up, he wrote home again and summoned the beautiful Mari-angela who tended the sheep on the family farm in Italy. She came to America, and soon the five children became ten. No. 8 was named Dad; he had two older sisters, Aunts Carmela and Rose, and two younger brothers, Uncles Spence and Ralph, not to mention the five grown half-siblings. Uncle Ralph, the baby of the family, was born just as the Great Depression settled in, ending with a crash his parents' first American Dream. By the time the Real Me came along, the eager young stonemason had turned into an elderly weather-beaten man, bald and swilling cheap wine in his faded leather armchair, worn out from decades of hard work and from husbanding his large family through good times and bad. He would take the Real Me on a tour of his backyard chicken coops and call her "*Bella*," which means something good in Italian.

Although their sojourn in the New World had begun with promise, the tribe had fallen into abject poverty by the time the Real Me's Dad was old enough to run. All the boys slept in one room, the girls in another. When Pearl Harbor was attacked, he dropped out of high school, along with half his male classmates, to sign up for the war. Life was not easy for a seventeen-year-old Marine. Buddies died in his arms at Okinawa, he himself went under the boat at Iwo Jima and barely survived. Later, he was assigned to mop-up duty in Nagasaki. Sometimes he was sent as a scout to reconnoiter the Japanese positions. Sure, he had a rifle, but his superiors instructed him not to fire lest he give himself away. That was the scariest of all his wartime experiences. It is one thing to march bravely into battle when there are comrades to the right and the left of you, and covering your back. It is quite another thing to be alone and afraid in the shadow of a hidden enemy. At the end of the war he had left those horrors behind, and returned to marry the girl who was waiting for him. To give his bride the new start she was hankering for, he gave up his own plans for law school on the G.I. Bill. They moved to California where one of his older half-brothers had settled. From there, they traveled to Virginia and dwelt for several years in a town high up in the mountains called Roanoke, always spoken of by the Snow Queen with a sad reverence. In the end, whatever youthful dreams they had shared had come to naught, and the two returned to his hometown. There, they took the well-worn path that most young couples trod in the 1950s. They bought a house and settled down to raise a family. He went to work with his brothers in construction. It was not his wife's true desire, but because she loved him, she bided her time and did her temporary best to play the part of suburban mom and housewife.

Many years before, after the Croton Dam was completed, Grandpa had found work with Colonel Tom Harmon, the local version of Howard Hughes. Colonel Harmon was an aviator and adventurer and the developer of a tract of land along the Croton River which he named after himself. He also had a yen for beautiful, celebrated women. The colonel had fallen in love with Madame Lillian Nordica, a famed and exquisite diva, a star of the Metropolitan Opera. In the hope of luring her to his hometown, he built a row of cottages and a playhouse which he hoped would become a summer colony for performing artists from New York City. To this very day, a street runs along the Croton River named *Nordica Drive.*

The summer colony never quite caught on, and by mid-century, Colonel Harmon's tract had been subdivided into single family homes and offered for sale to returning veterans and their pint-sized baby boomers. The modest but comfy two story stucco on a wide shady street, known thereabouts as No. 13 Franklin Avenue, was purchased by the Real Me's Mom and Dad.

The Real Me's bedroom window overlooked the kitchen patio of the L-shaped ranch house next door in which her best friend, the golden-haired sprite Alexis, dwelt with her two older sisters (although the eldest soon married and moved away), her sophisticated, piano-playing mother Hazel, her father Artie who possessed Mephistophelian good looks and intelligence, and their boxer, Ony (a dog, that is, not a prizefighter). Their cellar had a wood shop in it where Artie crafted for Alexis useful things such as stilts, a bow for archery and a ping-pong table. To add to their allure, Hazel had a job outside the home. She worked part-time for the local pharmacist. Alexis was blessed to be a latchkey kid without her parents constantly underfoot. When the Real Me knelt to pray, she faced the House Next Door. It was her Mecca, land of marvels, where she always wanted to be.

If Alexis was the best part of growing up in Harmon, there were other benefits, as well. The Real Me had two sets of grandparents and a plethora of aunts and uncles, many within shouting range. They were always glad to see her, invariably treating her as if she were someone special, and providing plenty of tiny cousins for her amusement. In fact, the Real Me was forever being dragged off to coo and awe over a newborn member of the clan when she would much rather have been out riding her bike or playing stickball with the kids down the street. All in all, her extended family was a good thing. It provided the Real Me with a sense of community. It made her brave, it allowed her to thrive.

The Real Me also derived strength from companions of her own age. No need, in those days, for play dates or such modern conceits which imply, after all, a certain amount of commitment, just open the front door, hop over the fence, knock on the door and say, " *Can Alexis come out to play?*" If, by chance, Alexis was not at home or was otherwise unavailable, it was not the end of the world. The neighborhood was filled with other children her age, or near to it, kids across the street, down the block and around the corner, kids riding their bikes, kids hanging from the monkey bars, kids sitting at the soda fountain. Deride, if you will, this *Leave it to Beaver Land*, but it was a good time to be a child, especially for a socially challenged tomboy who might today have had no playmates at all. At that age, no distinction is drawn between friends and acquaintances. When the kids need another warm body for a pick-up game of stickball in the vacant lot, or a session of hide-and-seek, or when all the gang is tobogganing on the hill behind Alexis' house, it matters little if you are a bit quirky and strange, especially when you bring the ball.

It was in school, where life was more structured, that the problems first began, and oddly enough, they began not with other kids, but with her teachers.

You see, the Real Me was a gifted child with behavioral issues. She was already an accomplished reader in first grade while the rest of her class was struggling with the alphabet. It was common practice at the time for such a scholastically advanced student to be allowed to skip a grade or even two. However, the Real Me never qualified for such treatment because she was tagged early on as "emotionally immature." This was 1960s speak for what is today called Asperger's Syndrome.

It takes a pretty wicked first-grader to be labeled "emotionally immature" and the Real Me did not disappoint. Right off the bat, her teachers recognized that she was not a proper little girl at all but rough and tumble like a boy. Relegated to her own age group, she was restive and bored, and when the Real Me was bored, there'd soon be hell to pay. She fiddled, she disrupted, she spoke out of turn, and she cut up, or, in modern parlance "acted out." With increasing regularity, she was sentenced to stand by herself out in the hall (the "sensory break room" of the day), or drew time in the principal's office, a more feared sanction. No one ever uttered the phrase "special needs child" back in those days. The term was "problem child," placing responsibility squarely upon the student rather than upon those charged with care of the student. For a couple years, the Real Me was treated by the school speech therapist—perhaps she really did talk funny as people said—but that was the only indulgence she received.

Now in the Real Me's village, as in most, there dwelt a group of schoolyard bullies. Oh, they did not think of themselves as bullies. They thought of themselves more as guardians of what was right and proper, self-appointed enforcers of community values, bouncers at the nightclub of life. Their mission was to make life hell for any kid who differed from the accepted norm in looks, words or deeds.

No doubt, the bullies would have targeted the Real Me in any event, and begin to mock her, to chase her around the school-yard, to rip her papers apart and try to steal her lunch. They were buoyed when they witnessed their teachers' treatment of the Real Me. Here was one target they could harass with im-punity. Her other classmates, those who were not natural-born bullies, saw what was going on and joined in. After all, what kid will contravene the common wisdom? Before she knew it, the Real Me was embattled on all sides and each day faced a constant struggle to keep her social standing in the class from falling through the floor.

It was a battle the Real Me was left to fight alone. At that time, the Croton-Harmon School District had two classes in each grade: two first grades, two second grades, and so forth. Her best friend Alexis was invariably assigned to the class across the hall, even though the two were next door neighbors and exactly the same age. The Real Me ascribed this to some malevolence on the part of the powers that be to deprive her of her strongest ally. More likely, some quirk in the scheduling department caused them to be placed in different homerooms.

Nor could the Real Me rely on her parents to be in her corner. The Real Me's Dad was a good man, a warm man and one with a strong capacity for contentment, unshared by either wife or daughter. That he loved the Real Me, there was no doubt. Had he not taken her fishing as a tot, to petting zoos, and pony rides and for short "dips" at Silver Lake on summer evenings? Had he not annoyed her to no end with his soulful rendition of *Daddy's Little Girl* when she just wanted to go out and play? Yet, for some mysterious reason, he would never stand and fight. When she most needed his support, it was nowhere to be found.

"I'm just like President Kennedy," the Real Me's Dad would oftentimes declare.

Both men, after all, were from large Catholic families, had fought on ships in the war and married beautiful women named Jacqueline. Didn't JFK have a daughter, too, whose name likewise began with a "C" and didn't Caroline also have a baby brother? That the Kennedys also had money and power was beside the point. His message was that he was lucky, lucky as JFK, so lucky that he would run like blazes from any confrontation or any bitter truth that might cast doubt upon the good fortune that had finally smiled upon him.

The Real Me's Dad rarely spoke of his time in the Marines. What the Real Me learned, she gleaned in dribs and drabs from her Aunt Rose who was not half so reticent. Unfortunately, what she learned she failed to appreciate. Like most small children, the Real Me saw only the here and now. Whatever had transpired before her birth might as well have occurred in the Stone Age. She only saw a father who would slap you on the shoulders and make small talk, but would also make light of your troubles or say "Talk to your mother," whenever a serious issue arose. As the Real Me's life became increasingly one of challenge and struggle, her relationship with her Dad began to founder. She viewed her Dad as a wimp because he so studiously avoided conflict. She much preferred his younger brother, her dashing, dynamic and brawling Uncle Spencer. Uncle Spence would play rough and tumble and let her ride in the back of his pickup truck, her hair blowing in the wind as she held on to the rail. If you can remember Billy Martin of the Yankees, you understand the Real Me's Uncle Spence.

Once the Real Me's little cousin John got into trouble in school and, was, in addition, misdiagnosed as mentally retarded. The school authorities called in his parents and suggested they send him to a special school for developmentally disabled children. Instead of quaking in his boots and deferring to the experts, as her parents would surely have done, Uncle Spence puffed out his chest and roared, "How *dare* you say that about *my* son!" And *that* was the end of *that!* When the Real Me heard the story, she fairly beamed with pride and jealousy. Why couldn't she have been born with a father like Uncle Spencer!

Even worse, the Real Me's Dad took to lying. Suppose, for example, that the Real Me and her Dad went to the store and the Real Me spied something on the shelf that she wanted. *Something that she just had to have.* The Real Me would then importune her Dad in a rather vociferous fashion that here was something *they just had* to buy. Instead of just saying, *No!* in an equally determined manner, the Real Me's Dad would resort to an underhanded strategy. He might declare, "Your Mom bought that yesterday. It's waiting at home." Or, he might announce, "I forgot my wallet. We'll come back this afternoon and buy it." The first few times he resorted to this foolery, the Real Me believed him and felt betrayed. Even after this game had lost all credibility, her Dad insisted on playing it, and each time he dishonored himself a bit more in the Real Me's eyes.

To tell the truth, the disillusionment ran both ways. Alone in the dark on some infernal atoll, the young Marine had dreamt of a daughter who wore frilly pink dresses and pigtails and was sugar and spice and everything nice. Instead, what he got was a visitor from another star, all tantrums and scraped knees and fireflies, who spoke a language he never quite understood, and asked questions for which he had no answer.

The riddle of the baby brother likewise could not be untangled. When the Real Me was small, she was an only child, and it was one of the factors which made her stand out from the other kids. Alexis had two big sisters. Paulie across the street came with a sister, Diane (and a model railroad in their playroom). Her first grade class included two sets of twins. One day in art class, all the students were instructed to draw pictures of their siblings. The two other "only children" in the class were allowed to submit drawings of their pets. The Real Me was the only one without either pet or sibling, and, boy, did that make her angry. She came right home from school and commenced a campaign. Her Mom would not bend where a dog was concerned. Unlike the Real Me's Dad, she had no trouble putting her foot down. Nevertheless, she seemed quite willing to listen to pleas for a baby brother or sister. Lo and behold, shortly thereafter, her Mom announced there would soon be a new addition to the family. The Real Me was proud as can be. Wherever she and her Mom went, she would keep score. "My Mom is five months pregnant! My Mom is six months pregnant!" Cute coming from a six-year-old, I suppose, but the Real Me's Mom always greeted these proclamations with a sheepish grin. One Saturday morning, her Dad met her at her grandparents' saloon and said, "Guess what? You have a baby brother!" The Real Me happily anticipated a new buddy, but, three days later when she walked home with Alexis from the school bus stop, there was her Mom holding a very tiny infant. The size of her new sibling was disappointing. "Aah," exclaimed the Real Me. "He's so small, he'll never amount to anything!" Her mother burst into tears and the Real Me was mystified. Had she said something wrong?

Still, the Real Me was elated to have a sibling at last, one step closer to being like everyone else. She took her brother's infant photos to school and proudly displayed them for "Show and Tell." In truth, the promise of a baby brother turned out to be the falsest of false promises. Instead of the little pal she expected, what the Real Me got was a faerie changeling, even stranger than the Real Me herself. No sooner did the tot learn to talk, than he began to sing jingles from TV commercials, every hour of the day and night. The Real Me fought down the urge to wallop him one, at least when their parents were looking. When he jingled himself out, he would throw himself on the living room couch belly-down and wiggle for hours. He would play with the shiny new top her Dad had bought her. Even worse, as they grew older, he would pilfer her record collection with seeming impunity. An album she had purchased *with her own money* would vanish from its shelf and reappear in his room. When she ran straight to her parents and complained, they refused to punish the little urchin. "Why can't you share with your brother?" they asked. The Real Me did not want to share; she wanted him to keep his grubby little hands off her stuff.

The Real Me prized honesty above all other attributes and always stood by her word. In the Real Me's childhood, there were beaches on the Hudson River, but the preferred swimming hole was Silver Lake on the Croton River. Today it has gone to rack and ruin, but in the Real Me's day Silver Lake was well-maintained, with a sandy shore and a play area for the kids which included board games and a ping-pong table. There were rafts out in the water and, at the far end of the lake, a diving board. The diving board, as you might suspect, was a favored gathering place for the older kids and a place of great merriment and derring do. Early in the summer before the Real Me's ninth birthday, she decided that she was a sufficiently accomplished swimmer and asked the lifeguards, no more than teenagers themselves, if she was ready for the diving board. They asked her how old she was. "Eight, going on nine." "You can use the diving board when you turn nine," the lifeguards replied. The Real Me found these terms reasonable and agreed. All through that summer she watched with envy as the other kids, including Alexis who had not thought to ask permission, trudged happily along the path to the diving board. Yes, it would have been easy to give the lifeguards the slip. They could hardly keep their eyes on everyone, but the Real Me was not made like that. She kept her word and waited the summer through. On the morning of her birthday she proudly took that first plunge off the end of the diving board.

Her honesty sometimes brought her misfortune. Once, when the Real Me was barely six, her Aunt Rose took her shopping in White Plains. On the way home, they were cruising down Route 9A, when a policeman pulled them over. "How fast were you going!" he asked Aunt Rose. "No more than 35, officer." "We were going sixty!" the Real Me piped up, proud that she could read an odometer at such a tender age. That earned her a tongue-lashing and a lifetime of Aunt Rose's laments. She would evermore point at the Real Me and wail, *"My only speeding ticket."*

When the Real Me walked down the street in Croton, perfect strangers would approach her and exclaim, "Don't you look *just* like your father?" causing the Real Me to cringe. It was meant as a compliment, no doubt. Her Dad was reputed to be quite handsome. Like most of his family however, he was inclined to be short and stocky, fair skinned with green eyes and a thick shock of reddish-brown hair that turned prematurely white. (Of all her father's clan, only Aunt Rose and Uncle Ralph sported the olive skin that betrayed the family's origin in southern Italy. The rest of them were all redheads. Her Dad said there must have been an Irishman in the woodpile back in the day. Now, whatever did that mean?)

The Real Me dreamed of becoming the image of her mother, tall and slender with high-cheekbones and as graceful as a dispossessed queen, her beautiful mother whose ancestors came from a province far, far to the north called Aspergia where people are aloof, enchanted and alluring, made of snowflakes and starlight and just as hard to hold, where they appear to be descended, not from great apes, but from big cats.

The Real Me's Mom was exceptionally proud of her gifted child, and let the world know about it. She taught her daughter to read at the age of four and then decided that her job was done and it was time to rest on her laurels. She bragged constantly of how the Real Me could recite the Presidents of the United States, in order, backwards and forwards, as well as the Kings and Queens of England and the gods of Mount Olympus, while her classmates were still struggling with their ABC's. It was the kind of pride that goeth before a fall. Those ill-advised boasts would come back soon enough to haunt her when her little savant fell flat on her face.

In fact, she vastly over estimated her daughter's precociousness. That December when the Real Me was five—only five!—

the Snow Queen sat her down on the living room couch and casually remarked, "You do realize that there is no Santa Claus." The Real Me was shocked. No Santa Claus! Come again? *You and Dad?* Who would have thought? Yes, now that you mention it, that part about flying all over the world in a sleigh delivering presents to all the boys and girls in one night, sounds a bit shaky but . . . As the Real Me sat there in stunned disbelief, her mother smiled smugly and said, "I knew you had figured it out." For the next two years the Real Me had to smile and bite her tongue until Alexis and her other playmates had likewise been apprised of the sorry truth.

For the life of her, the Real Me's Mom could not understand why her prodigy insisted on acting like a little kid. She even had a special word for tantrum. It was "act," as in, "Are you going to put on another act?" and "Here goes another of your acts." The Real Me was astonished when she discovered that the word "act" was not a synonym for tantrum at all, but possessed another meaning altogether. Acting took planning and forethought whereas tantrums came naturally and on the spur of the moment.

The Real Me's mother strongly believed in the primacy of reason. She thought a person with a high intellect should have no problems reining in her emotions. Willpower was everything in her book. You could fry bacon or bake bread right under the nose of the Snow Queen and she would not even salivate. When the Real Me complained of difficulty in turning a cartwheel or keeping a tune, she would receive a lecture about a child who had broken his spine, spent years in a wheelchair and grown up to run a three-minute mile, all by dint of an unbreakable will. Her mother did not know the Real Me had Asperger's Syndrome, of course, but, had she known, it would probably have made little difference. The Real Me would no doubt have received the following lecture: "Albert Einstein had Asperger's and *he* learned to tie his shoelaces, now didn't he?

Her mother gave her suspect advice, too, on the proper way to deal with bullies. "Just ignore them," her Mom said." Hold your head up high, and just walk right by. They only want to get a rise out of you. Don't give them the reaction they expect, and they'll soon tire of chasing you about and go away."

These rules of engagement never sat right with the Real Me, but her Mom was a demigoddess, and presumably knew whereof she spoke. For years the Real Me stifled her own impulses and duly held her tongue and walked on by. Of course, a victim who refused to fight back was a bully's delight, and only spurred her tormentors on. Finally, the Real Me had had enough and did what came naturally.

Now kids had survival skills in those days. They knew that the proper retort to mockery was, "Sticks and stones can break my bones, but words will never hurt me." They walked or biked everywhere and never wore a helmet. Bruised knees and elbow scabs and going *kerplot* on the hard, cold pavement were just part of being a kid.

Unless you lived in the sticks, there was no school bus service after the third grade, and even then, you had to make it on your own to the bus stop around the corner. There were playgrounds with see-saws and real monkey bars, things you're not likely to see today. There was dog poop everywhere; it was legal in those days. You stepped around it and if you happened to get it on your shoes, you wiped off in the grass and proceeded on your way. So much independence carried with it its perils. Walking home from school alone was the prime opportunity for bullies. If you were wise, you kept one eye over your shoulder all the way,

She must have been ten or eleven when she finally put the bullies in their place. One day when she was walking home from school, the bullies surrounded the Real Me. They began taunting her and calling her names, as usual, but this time, she did not turn the other cheek. No, indeed. She shrieked like a banshee and launched her book bag at them. That sped them on their way. A few more such incidents, and the Real Me had figured out the proper way to deal with bullies.

The Real Me did not believe she was a gifted child or especially intelligent and wished people would not speak of her that way. Sure, she knew all those Kings and Queens of England and all the gods of Mount Olympus and their jurisdictions. But it was not as if she was Karnak the Magnificent and acquired her knowledge by magic! The library was there for all to use, and chock full of books and charts and maps. One read books and learned stuff, no mystery there. What the Real Me lacked were the useful skills that came easily to other kids. It had taken her forever to learn to tie her shoelaces, she couldn't whistle or keep the hula hoop around her waist, and the art of balancing herself on her bike once the training wheels came off proved a challenge. Did she feel like a "gifted child" in second grade as she pedaled once, pedaled twice, and fell squat on the blacktop while all the other kids in the neighborhood went speeding by on their two-wheelers? No, she felt like a real *dummy!*

Despite all the disciplinary problems with her teachers and the trouble fitting in with her classmates, the Real Me kept up her grades at school. Her favorite subjects were history and geography. She could not understand why other kids hated these subjects. Recalling names and dates was easy for her. History was a collection of stories about kings and queens and cowboys and Indians, heroes and villains. The truth was more thrilling than half the novels she borrowed from the library. However, she also liked sports, and that was where she found her real challenge. She wished so very much that she could excel at them. The Real Me had heart, speed, strength and smarts and that sufficed for many childhood sports, but acrobatics were her downfall. It's called "dyspraxia," a fancy word that means *"bull in a china shop."* When she and Alexis were five, their mothers enrolled them in ballet class at a local dance school. The Real Me flunked out in three weeks, but Alexis went on to complete a full year of ballet, followed by two years of tap dancing. Alexis had perfect motor skills coordination and constantly amazed the Real Me with perfect somersaults and handsprings executed on their front lawns. The Real Me would have gladly traded in all her book-learning for one respectable cartwheel.

The popular image of a child targeted by bullies is of a misunderstood meek and mild lamb. The Real Me was misunderstood, sure enough, but not meek or mild and more like a lion than a lamb. Truth to tell, she was capable of some pretty wicked behavior of her own.

Her Mom told her that, as a toddler, she had bitten other children in the sandbox. The Real Me scoffed at the notion. She would never have done anything like that! But those times when she turned coat and joined the bullies in pursuing a new target could not be denied nor could the complaints from other mothers with their allegations of hair-pulling and push-downs.

The worst thing the Real Me ever did: when she was eight she hit a kid half her age with a rock on his brow. This was a little boy who lived across the street. He was not a bad tyke, not at all, but he did make a nuisance of himself by forever pestering the older kids to play with him. As if the Real Me did not have better things to do than spend her time with a toddler! Generally, she ignored him, but he caught her one evening feeling out of sorts. Unable to find anyone of her own age to hang out with, she and the tyke began playfully flinging pebbles and small rocks in each other's direction. Then, she began lobbing her missiles closer to his head, accidentally on purpose, you might say. Maybe she could frighten the baby and send him scurrying back to his mama! One stone landed just above his left eye, and not only did he cry out in anguish, but blood poured down his little face in buckets. The Real Me, astonished that she had caused so much damage in an off hand sort of way, hastened to make herself scarce.

After her son had been attended to by the doctor and stitched up, the tyke's mother hunted the Real Me down. The Real Me's heartfelt apologies were not accepted.

"Do you know what the word *vicious* means?" the tyke's mother thundered. "You're a smart kid. Look up the word *vicious*. That is what you are."

The Real Me protested heartily. Not me! Not at all! She had not intended to hurt the tyke, not really. Put the fear of God into him, as they say, but no more.

Now, the Real Me was not vicious, but she had a propensity for recklessness. Reckless conduct is a step down in culpability from the intentional infliction of harm. It's what changes murder to manslaughter. Reckless implies full speed ahead with risky behavior and the possible consequences be damned.

The moral of the story? The tyke's mom was the Real Me's third-grade teacher. It should not have come as such a surprise. They lived just across the street, the family's name was right there, on the mailbox, and she probably passed their driveway six times a day. The Real Me who, at the age of eight, understood the meaning of the term "*vicious*," was not mature enough to grasp the fact that her teacher might have a life outside the classroom. She was blindsided, and she should not have been. If her name had not already been mud in the local school, that sealed her fate.

Like most children of the sixties, the Real Me was accorded freedoms unknown in the modern world. Her parents did not expect to know where she was each moment of the day. If she left in the morning and returned by dinner time, that was good and sufficient. Freedom helped her cope with the vagaries of life. If she was on the outs with the other kids, she did not have to stay around and mope. She could get on her bike and head over to the public library where she could bury herself in the stacks and be transported to another place and time. The Oz books were her favorite. At the age of ten she read them all, one by one. She could visit one of her many aunts and uncles who would lend her a shoulder to cry on. Or she could head over to the What-Not Shoppe and check out the latest comics on the rack. She was partial to Superboy. After all, she too, felt like a visitor from a distant planet, and, furthermore, was not her hometown a lot like Smallville with a river instead of a cornfield?

The Real Me was an extremely picky eater. She had a good appetite, but ate a few favorite foods over and over and over again. As adventurous as she might have been in other areas, she had no desire to taste anything new, especially if it were sticky or slimy or green or had a funny smell. For a while there, her Mom had tried to force her to eat her veggies, as mothers will. Unless you consider popcorn a vegetable, the experiment was a failure. The Real Me would push her peas or carrots or lima beans around her plate hoping that they would fade away. When all else failed, she would close her eyes and hold her nose and try to force them down so that she could go back outside and play. The taste and texture was so off-putting. It just would not go down the hatch.

The Real Me's aversions extended beyond healthy foods to treats the other kids pined for, strawberry shortcake, caramel fudge and peanut butter and jelly. Her taste in candy was quite limited as well. Although she and Alexis went trick or treating all around the village each Halloween, the Real Me would end up giving most of her booty to her Dad. All she really wanted was the thrill of the chase. Nonetheless, she was painfully aware that her inability to partake in the usual childhood food fests was one of the factors that set her apart from the others.

One day when the Real Me was four or five, she heard the kids on the block discussing something called "pizza," reputed to be a kind of delicacy. The next time her parents took her out to dinner, she ordered a "pizza." However, when the waiter delivered it, the pizza proved to be too gooey and sticky and weird-looking to be appealing. The Real Me let her parents eat the pizza and ordered a burger instead.

Fifth grade was a welcome respite from the disciplinary problems at school. That year the Real Me was assigned the best teacher that the Croton-Harmon School District ever produced. Her name was Miss Livingston, she was young and inventive, and unlike all the teachers that had gone before her, Miss Livingston actually treated her students as if they had a brain. She would sit the class in a circle and begin a reasoned discourse on the United Nations or the trouble with Cuba and invite the class to share their ideas. Now most ten-year-olds do not have informed opinions on foreign policy, but the Real Me did and she was delighted to discuss them. Miss Livingston never belittled her or called her immature, but treated her and her classmates like little adults. Once when the Real Me tiptoed up to her teacher's desk she saw that her ledger was open and that the column labeled *"Problem Children"* was completely bare. No names were listed, none at all! From that moment on the Real Me adored Miss Livingston and did her best to please her.

Miss Livingston was homesick for a town called Plattsburgh, located up near the Canadian border and spoke about it wistfully from time to time. Miss Livingston would talk of Plattsburgh in the same soft tone of voice that the Real Me's Mom employed when speaking of her childhood in that big house on Cedar Lane.

One weekend the Real Me accompanied her parents on a visit to the Brewster Game Farm in *Patterson,* New York, a fun spot where there were pony rides and a petting zoo. On Monday morning, the Real Me proudly walked into class and advised Miss Livingston that she had visited her hometown. Miss Livingston asked the Real Me a few questions about the trip, and then exclaimed, "But you couldn't have been to Plattsburgh. That's 300 miles away!" The Real Me was crestfallen and did not understand why her teacher had impugned her credibility out of hand. Why would she lie?

Miss Livingston was marching to a different drummer of her own which may have made her more tolerant of quirky kids like the Real Me. She was harboring a secret which, back in the 1960s, could have ended her career. Miss Livingston, you see, was gay and shared a lifelong love affair with another female elementary school teacher. Not that anyone knew it at the time, no, of course not! Back in those days, kids called each other "faggot" and "queer" as put-downs, with no conception of their meaning.

The Real Me looked these words up. Faggots were used to kill Joan of Arc, and why kids would fling that epithet around was indeed a puzzlement. Queer, on the other hand, meant odd, eccentric, out of the ordinary, and, yes, the Real Me might cop to that one. Despite all her book-learning, the word lesbian had not yet entered her vocabulary.

Now Miss Livingston lived to see the dawn of a new millennium, and in later years, when she and her partner had retired from teaching, they lived together openly. Everyone knew the nature of their relationship, and no one batted an eye, so much had the world changed in just a few decades. However, when the Real Me was in fifth grade, discovery would surely have brought the roof tumbling down about them.

If fifth grade was the best of times, the worst of times followed hard on its heels. Sixth grade brought Mrs. Thomas, an older, no nonsense harridan of a teacher. She was a neighbor as well, and lived around the corner from the Real Me. No doubt aware of the incident with the third-grade teacher's toddler, she determined to break the spirit of the Real Me right then and there. In her crusade, she resorted to tactics that would not be allowed today, such as spanking the Real Me in front of the entire class, setting aside a special desk for her, right under the teacher's nose, and ordering her to eat lunch at the faculty table instead of with her friends. Sixth grade was a trial and a tribulation, but unexpected benefits flowed from such abuse. Classmates, who had hitherto mocked and tormented the Real Me, now witnessed such unfair treatment bestowed upon her, that their hearts softened. The Real Me had won the sympathy vote.

Her experience in the sixth grade caused the Real Me to lose respect for *The Rules*. Whereas she had once believed that strict adherence to *The Rules* was the proper strategy for creating order out of chaos, she now realized how arbitrary they could become in the hands of an authority figure with no brakes. *The Rules* were a two-edged sword. Still, Mrs. Thomas' tough love approach did teach the Real Me to toe the line, and after sixth grade there were no more disciplinary problems.

It was in junior high that life turned around. Now you were nearly a teenager, and, in the sixties, teenagers ruled. All the teachers treated you with respect, not only the rare gem like Miss Livingston. In junior high, one did not stay in the homeroom all day. Your classes might well include Alexis and the kids across the hall, formerly seen only at recess, and on Thursday afternoons when all the Catholic kids trudged together to catechism class at Holy Name of Mary. Now advanced classes with upperclassmen were available in your favorite subjects. No longer did you have to be weighed down by the slowpokes. Seventh grade meant branching out. For the first time, the Real Me had a chance to play an instrument, and, in fact, played second violin in the school orchestra. (Alexis, of course, was chosen for first violin). She went out for girls' softball and floor hockey and the teams were chosen by the coach and not by the other kids. There were the Friday afternoon hops, as they were still called. Twelve and thirteen-year-old boys were not much inclined toward dancing and the girls ended up partnering themselves, like as not. Nevertheless, there was music and exercise and free eats and companionship. Junior High also meant coming home to the old, comfy right-in-the-village school building where the Real Me had spent the early grades before the antiseptically modern elementary school was opened. Junior High students were allowed to walk into town for lunch and hang out with the older kids at Scoop 'n' Judy's. Best of all, the bullies had been dealt with in a way they understood.

Scoop'n'Judy's was a popular luncheonette in the Village and a favored hangout for the older kids, being located near the junior high and high schools and right next to the Catholic school which the Real Me's Cousin Lou attended. The Real Me and Alexis were not quite eleven when they first discovered Scoop 'n' Judy's and, while Alexis fit right it, the Real Me had a problem. The gang at Scoop 'n' Judy's all drank either hot fudge sundaes or Coca-Cola. The Real Me did not like sundaes and she had never tasted Coca-Cola. What to do? Drastic measures were in order lest she lose her best friend to the lure of Scoop'n'Judy's and find herself out in the cold again. Remembering too well the incident of the pizza, the Real Me biked into town on a Saturday morning when she knew that the luncheonette would be half empty. Striding briskly up to the counter, she demanded a Coke. When it arrived, she stared at the cup for a few moments and idly swizzled her straw around. Then she bravely took a swallow. Lo and behold, it was good! She drank the whole glass and then ordered another. When Monday came, she returned to the luncheonette and slid into a booth as casually as if she had been born there. She had made her bones at Scoop 'n' Judy's, and become *one of the gang.*

Now that the corner had been turned, the Real Me began to wonder if her Different Drummer had all along been leading her astray. Whenever she had asked her mother why she never quite fit in, her Mom had fallen back on the *gifted child* idea, smugly declaring "they are all jealous of you." Now the Real Me did not believe this, not consciously, but a wee bit of a superiority complex had seeped into her unbidden. After all, her Mom was a demigoddess, and that made her—what? A quadroon, perhaps? Could it really be true that they resented her simply because she was a cut above?

Nevertheless, the Real Me began to entertain the notion that the fault might lie with her and not with her classmates. First, she consulted her best friend. Why, she asked Alexis did the bullies chase me and call me names? Why, when we were choosing sides, was I picked toward the end even though I was a good player? Why don't the other girls invite me to their parties and sleepovers? Why aren't I popular like you? Alexis thought a moment and the best answer she could come up with was, "Well, you were always a bit overweight. "

That confused the Real Me. In those days, fat meant *visibly* fat, falling over your own feet fat, and that did not describe the Real Me. She was no svelte pixie like Alexis, and that was the truth, but she had never been called names like "Hippo" and "Fatso" like the chubby kids had. Just for good measure, she checked out library books on diet and calories and for several weeks she went to school armed with weight charts. "Look at this!" she would say to anyone she could corral. "See, I'm not overweight, not really. Here I am, right in the range of normal."

The lack of interest her arguments evoked convinced the Real Me that her instincts had been correct. It was not her weight, not anything so easily decipherable that kept her from truly belonging. She was dealing with a much deeper enigma.

At that point, she consulted a guidance counselor. He was not a neighbor like Mrs. Thomas. He was a professional from another town who could be counted on to give her an objective viewpoint. After speaking with her and pouring over her records, he delivered his verdict. "You seem like a typical 12-year-old to me."

The Real Me fairly beamed. Aah, sweet normalization! All her struggles and persistence had paid off, the enchantment that had bound her was dispelled. *She belonged.*

Even as the Real Me, anticipated a happy future as a typical teenager, the sands of the hourglass were running out. While she had been fighting her own battle for acceptance, her beautiful tragic mother had been watching her own youth ebb away. This was no life for a demigoddess, sitting at the kitchen table, her nose in *Photoplay* magazine, blowing smoke rings from a long black cigarette holder, passing the time in coffee klatches with the mom next door and longing in vain for a kingdom of her own.

The Real Me's parents loved each other fiercely as only opposites can do, yet her Mom bore a slightly disguised contempt for her brawling, blue-collar ethnic in-laws, and their hometown. Now, before overdevelopment reared its ugly head, Croton-on-Hudson was a picturesque storied village, and even today people often remark on what a wonderful place it is to live. Many famous people, from artists to anarchists, have left their imprint, including the aforementioned Madame Nordica and John Reed, the subject of the Warren Beatty film *Reds*. Nonetheless, life in Croton seemed most irksome to the Real Me's Mom. It represented a failure to regain her rightful station in life. While they dwelt in Croton, she remained hopelessly mired among the peasantry. She suffered, too, from the assumption of the day that a woman's highest calling was to be a homemaker. It was not that she disliked kids, but she did not understand them, her own or anyone else's. She herself must have been a kid at some point, but no sign of that remained. The Real Me instinctively knew this, and, for that reason, she preferred to pass her time at Alexis' home or out in the village.

It troubled her Mom as well, that her husband remained a laborer. Not only was construction work demeaning in her eyes, but it was a part of his life that she could not share. Had she married a teacher, she could have helped correct his papers; had her husband been a junior executive on his way up the corporate ladder, she could have thrown parties for his bosses and smoothed his way, had she wed a lawyer, he might have practiced his closing arguments before her. Her parents had worked together as business partners, and she had grown up viewing it as part of the marriage contract, but you cannot make pillow talk on the price of paint or the best method of mixing cement. Furthermore, construction work entailed a measurable risk of injury. Already, in his thirties, the Real Me's Dad had been laid up twice with his back. There was no union, no disability benefits, and no workers compensation. What would they do if he were hurt? Not to mention, of course, her heartfelt desire to protect him from harm.

When the opportunity arose to purchase a crumbling rundown Gothic Estate further north on the Hudson, the Real Me's Mom leapt at it. This was something *she had to have*. Here it was, gifted to her by fate, a chance to leave behind the humdrum *petit bourgeois* life that so ill became her. In no time at all, she conceived a plan, a good plan, the sort of a plan any adult could applaud. There was an untapped need back then for modern state-of-the-art, skilled nursing homes in the State of New York, and federal loans were widely available to build such facilities. Why not place one of these sparkling high-tech skilled nursing homes on a down at the heels once-splendid Estate? (Today it is called *adaptive reuse*; the Snow Queen was ahead of her time). As sponsors and administrators of the proposed multimillion dollar facility, she and her husband would at last be business partners as well as lovers. She would keep the books while her more people-friendly husband would deal directly with the patients and their families. If things turned out as imagined, there would be money, too, enough for the finer things of life and tuition at the sort of Ivy League college that befitted her savant of a daughter. Furthermore, if the Real Me proved to be chronically unable to rise before 9 a.m., if she was supersensitive to cold and would go about raising thermostats in every building she entered, if her behavior was a bit off-putting and if she could not work and play well with others, no problem. She would never have to pound the pavement or send out hundreds of resumes to line hundreds of trash cans in several different states. No need to sit at home, take a low-paying job or go on the Government dole. No, there would always be suitable work waiting for her as the next Administrator of the Far North Nursing Home.

No, it was not just the chance to regain her birthright in the landed gentry or any such selfish impulse that prompted the move upstate. It was a misguided attempt to benefit the Real Me as well, leave the bullies behind in the dust and outdistance the disciplinary problems that had dogged her at school. It did not occur to her that her daughter had no desire for a change of scenery. After all, she herself was prey to the constant craving for a fresh start. How was it that the Real Me preferred life as she knew it? The Snow Queen did not intend to destroy her firstborn, but she was blind. She could not see the fault line.

You see, The Real Me was not just a bright, quirky but emotionally immature tomboy. She was an autistic child. The people around her would have been amazed to have known that, and as bewildered as, say, the folks in Smallville to discover that the Kent's mild-mannered son Clark was a refugee from the planet Krypton. Back in the sixties people knew what autism was, and they knew what extraterrestrials looked like. A space alien's body was tall, thin and elongated as if it had stepped out of an El Greco painting; he sported an enormous head, green scaly skin and antennae sprouting where its ears should be. An autistic child spoke little, if at all, sat in the corner with a blank expression, rocked back and forth and played with the sunbeams on the floor.

But things are not always as they seem. Like extraterrestrials, autistic children are as varied as snowflakes in a storm. There is one characteristic, however, that most of them share. Few on the autism spectrum welcome change, and the Real Me welcomed it not at all. For change meant only loss—loss of her home, her friends, her neighbors, her school, all the safe and familiar things that had kept at bay the twin monsters of loneliness and despair that are the bane of the child with Asperger's. Without them, she had no defense and the monsters rushed in.

The Kingdom of Frost

●

ife as I knew it ended the summer I turned thirteen. Against my will, I was transported to a crumbling estate far up the Hudson, a gathering place for shadows, howling winds and endless winter. Alexis had vanished, along with my childhood home, village, neighbors, grandparents, aunts and uncles, playmates and school. Suddenly I had no one to talk to—and I mean *no one*. There was no where to go and nothing to do to while away the interminable hours. It was not only loneliness, boredom and homesickness which caused my soul to shatter into fragments; it was the sheer terror of abandonment. By day I wandered the haunted ruins aimlessly, searching for signs of life where none could be found. Occasionally I spoke to the grizzled old handyman who swore he saw the specter of a long-ago chatelaine riding a ghostly coach and four when the moon was full. Sometimes I wandered down by the river, huddled up on a rock, my arms about my knees, crying bitter tears of loss and despair. I hung a sign on my bedroom door, quoting a passage from Lord Tennyson:

Sorrow's crown of sorrow is remembering happier days.

At night, I lay in my bed, frightened of the impenetrable darkness and nights so dense they were almost tangible. I remembered how the light from the street lamp had gently illuminated my bedroom at home and calmed me so that I might fall asleep. Here there were no street lamps to pierce the dark and no one to watch over me. The wind screaming through the woods seemed to me to be the cry of a wolf. No, not a real wolf, but a shadow wolf whose hunger was not for the body, but for the soul. His name was Loneliness and, from that point on, he would never cease to track me. His eyes were made of ice and his gaze could paralyze the heart. His breath chilled me even in high summer. Thenceforth, there would never be a time when I was not lonely and rarely a day when I was not cold.

The travelogues call it the Great Estates Region of upstate New York, a name that conjures up images of Dutch patroons and the barons of the Gilded Age who had taken their place, wide, sweeping views of the Hudson, private railroad cars, masked balls, wrought iron gates and landscaped gardens with bridle paths. By the mid-to-late 1960s, however, this genteel life had become a thing of the past. Although many of the estates were still inhabited by descendants of their founders or by other wealthy families—these Old Money types were always spoken of in hushed tones and reverent whispers by us *arrivistes*—others had fallen prey to developers. Some had simply been abandoned and left to crumble into rack and ruin. The historical preservation movement was only in its infancy back then; withering away was still the rule, dust to dust, as the years march relentlessly by.

Some of the estates had been converted to contemporary uses. Ours had been a private school for girls before my parents bought it. Except for the first few months when my parents played country squire, and we bunked down in the big house, the mansion itself was put to use as a convalescent home for out-patients from the nearby veterans' hospital. That was my parents' actual business. The Far North Nursing Home was, and would remain, a *proposed* business. Had it ever materialized, it would have been built in the cow pasture out front. We lived in the caretaker's cottage in the back, so cramped that the four of us were always falling over each other. When the trains sped by along the river below, the floor shook, and the TV went to static. I spent most of my time outside, no matter the weather—and it always seemed to be January—exploring the deserted sheds, run down barns and corn cribs and half-heartedly digging for buried treasure.

Lonely thirteen-year-old girls and spooky old estates where things come out of the shadows and go bump in the night are never a good combination, but for a child on the autism spectrum it spelled regression. I spiraled down, down, down into an abyss of dysfunction from which I would not fully recover for forty years—if, indeed, I ever did. I called it *The Fall*, as if I had been one of the rebel angels, or *The Exile*. It was the end of the line for the Real Me. All the coping skills that she had so painstakingly acquired vanished in the blink of an eye and my heart was enclosed in ice. The Real Me did not go quietly, she died hard. That first summer was all rage and tears, all sobs and shouting, flapping arms and flying objects. I threw myself on the ground, I screamed, I stimmed, I beat my head against the wall. I tore my clothes and ran sobbing out into the dark. One night my mother even called the police; I was acting like such a psycho.

That night was an anomaly. For the most part, my parents stood back and watched me founder. To my mother, it was all make-believe, an act put on to punish her from tearing me away from Alexis and my childhood world. My Dad preferred to ascribe it all to a mysterious medical problem. Indeed, there were physical signs of distress. I stopped growing. The Real Me had consistently been one of the tallest kids in her class. By junior high she had attained the height of 5'4" and wore a size six and a half shoe. I never grew a smidgeon more. My parents would view this with surprise and admonish me forevermore, "You stunted your growth." As if I would have been six feet tall, but for a bad attitude! Well, I never gave much credence to that. The cessation of my menses was more alarming. My periods had begun six months before we moved north. With *The Exile*, they stopped dead.

At first people from our old life would come to see us, but they did not find a warm welcome. My mother refused to entertain visitors in the caretaker's cottage, and she would force them to wait for her at the mansion while she took her own sweet time to get ready. Sometimes she would just send her regrets. After a few doses of this treatment, most visitors got the hint.

My parents no longer brought me along to family gatherings, which ran the gamut from Aunt Rose's wedding, birthday parties, graduations and grandparents' funerals. They would tell me I was not invited, but it was a lie. I was left behind for fear that I would make a scene and embarrass them. Of all my "acts," the one that my parents hated most of all was the one they called *fishing for sympathy*. Any adult who wandered onto the estate witnessed my undisguised despair. I was not particular about whose shoulder I cried upon. I would pour my heart out to total strangers. As if they cared.

For the same reason, apparently, I was discouraged from finding a part-time job. Back in Croton, all the teenage girls earned a few dollars from babysitting the younger kids, and I had imagined that I would one day do so as well. However, when the time came, my parents were afraid I would go to other people's homes and burden them with my tale of sorrow. They put roadblocks in my way, and without any transportation or connections of my own, I eventually abandoned the idea.

I did learn the route to the nearest village, three miles away, and began to bike there almost on a daily basis. The sole attraction was the public library, such as it was. It was very small, smaller than the one in Croton, and as dimly lit as a funeral chapel. I devoured everything in it. The librarian treated me with kindness and might have been my friend, but I was scared of her, as scared as I would have been of Charon, the ferryman on the River Styx. To my mind she was ancient. In truth, she was probably no more that forty-five when we first met, but with her horn-rimmed glasses, tightly curled hairstyle and long dresses which seemed vaguely Victorian, she might have been a visitor from a bygone past, like that spectral chatelaine our handyman spoke about.

My parents sent me to school, of course, and they were glad to do so, hoping that I would make new friends there and forget Alexis. Unfortunately, the nearest high school was not a *school* at all, as I had previously understood the term. It was a modern, impersonal education factory to which two thousand students from all the surrounding towns were bused. The baby boom had invaded even this backwater, and hence the need for this new centralized facility. However, to a young person with sensory problems, it was forbiddingly large and overwhelming. The building was made of steel beams and thick glass, antiseptic, cold and radiating unwelcome. As I walked through the door, I was immediately swallowed up in a crowd of bullies and strangers. There were good teachers there who might have taken me in tow, under ordinary circumstances, but they were frazzled, overworked and far too busy to favor any one student with personal attention.

Being required to ride the school bus again as I had not done since the age of eight was a humiliation in itself. It was another sign of my lost independence. In Croton school buses were associated with the very young and those who lived out in the hinterlands. After the third grade, you walked or biked to school. Even in the first three grades, you were responsible for making your way to the bus stop around the corner where the neighborhood kids were gathered. There was no door-to-door service as there was up north. Now I waited alone in the early morn at the end of the driveway, sleepy and shivering, for a bus that I dreaded to board. The bus, when it came, was filled with bullies. These were unlike the schoolyard bullies that had filled the Real Me's life with trouble, chased her down the street and attempted to throw her books in the mud. These new age bullies could neither be avoided nor confronted. They simply acted as if I was not there—and, in a way, I suppose I was not. They refused to remove their legs from the aisle when I walked to my seat. They looked right through me. They spoke over me, and sometimes about me, as if I were deaf and invisible.

My reputation as a gifted child had unfortunately, preceded me, and, without any prior notice or warning, I found myself as a freshman assigned to all advanced classes. Furious, I protested that I was really quite a dummy, but found that I had to go through channels to seek reassignment to the general population. There were plenty of obstacles in my way. All my tears and pleas and arguments fell upon stone ears; the school officials had my records and they insisted I belonged in the advanced group, no matter how much I wanted otherwise. My one small victory came when I was demoted from solid geometry to plane geometry. In my gratitude, I aced plane geometry and walked away with a perfect grade. However, as a rule, I just coasted through high school. I no longer cared about making the honor role or achieving straight A's. All I wanted was to close my eyes and seek refuge in the Land of Nod.

It was only in my dreams that the Real Me lived on. Each night I'd fall asleep and go back home. I'd attend classes at Croton High, as I had been meant to do, I would hang out with Alexis and the rest of the gang at Scoop 'n' Judy's, do my homework, go to parties, dances and football games and learn to drive. Nothing special happened in those dreams, just the life of an ordinary teenager not abandoned in the Kingdom of Frost. Roy Orbison must have known what I was going through. He explained it so well in a song called, *In Dreams*.

These dreams were so vivid and so real that it came as a physical shock each morning at 6:30 when my mother called to me to get up. I always awoke cold and shivering as well, for my mother had adopted a practice of turning the thermostat down at bedtime. It amazes me that many people do this; I do exactly the opposite. It is when I am lying down and not moving, that I need to be wrapped in warmth most of all. Invariably I burrowed into the covers and did my best to recapture sleep, but my mother would be persistent. Finally, with the greatest of efforts, I would drag myself out of bed, heavy lidded, and slowly go through the motions of dressing and getting ready for school. I never rubbed the sleep out of my eyes in those days; it was easier that way to keep the waking world from encroaching into my private realm of sorrow. I would have slept 24/7 if that had only been possible.

My constant pining for Alexis and the world we had left behind was, to my mother, most irksome and, apparently, a puzzlement that defied understanding. Alexis' mom, Hazel, had been her own best friend, or so it had seemed, but once the ink had dried on the deed to our home in Croton, it was as if Hazel had never been born. "Best friends?" She would exclaim scornfully in her Snow Queen fashion. "That's only for children in grade school. Once girls become teenagers, their friendship turns to rivalry. They are only interested in competing for boys." Yes, she really did say this to me, and at first, I was even inclined to accept it, a mountain of evidence notwithstanding. Who was I to believe, a demigoddess or my own lying eyes? When I witnessed teenage girls walk through the school corridors arm in arm, whispering secrets in each other's ear or chatting away in some private language, I averted my glance and pretended not to have noticed.

For a while, I had a horse to assuage my loneliness. The Real Me had learned to ride at a local dude ranch day camp when she was eleven and, like many young girls, became a little horse-crazy. When the move north was looming, my mother promised to buy me a horse, to ease the poison pill. I never quite believed her, and afterward, she did indeed attempt to weasel out of her promise. One day she pointed to a rabbit I was chasing playfully about, laughed and said, "There's your horse!" It was my Dad who, for once, stood up to her and insisted on carrying through. It was my Dad who took me to an auction one day where we purchased a gelding named Perhaps. His name was a family joke—perhaps he will go and perhaps he will not. He was black and he was gentle and he responded well to me. I owned the horse for a year and a half and, while he could not replace Alexis, he did provide me with some comfort.

We fixed up an unused stall in one of the old, tumbling-down barns. There was no riding ring on the estate and no bridle trails. However, it was such a backwater in those days that I could ride him up and down the road without much fear of danger. Sometimes we rode down by the railroad tracks which run along the river, and sometimes we cantered across meadows or blazed our own path through the woods. I even rode Perhaps bareback and once, when I fell off, I did what was wise and proper and hopped right back on.

The second winter was exceptionally harsh and snowy. I could not ride for months. By that time, I was battling not only homesickness and despair, but what I now know as anorexia. My mother came to me one February afternoon and suggested we give Perhaps away to a local horse farm where he would have equine companions and grassy pastures, and be able to live out his life in peace. That sounds cruel, and I suppose it was. There was some merit, though, in what my mother said to me. At that point, I had neither the energy nor the maturity to take care of a horse. From the beginning, I had let the weather beaten handyman feed him, groom him, turn him out and tack him up. I rode him when the mood took me, but when it turned bitterly cold, I lacked even that desire. For weeks I had hardly even visited. Furthermore, a horse is a herd animal. Solitude is more distasteful to a horse than even to a teenage girl. Perhaps could not have been happy living alone in our old barn, and, dying of loneliness myself, I could never wish that fate on an animal who had given me a measure of solace.

I nodded and voiced no objections. I never spoke of Perhaps again but the black gelding haunted my dreams for decades to come. During the rest of my adolescence, I gulped and choked down the ache that rose up in my throat whenever I saw other kids riding their mounts along the country roads, but I never forgot. As an adult, I took up western trail-riding. Forty years after Perhaps had been given away, with both my parents dead; I came into a little money. I knew exactly how to spend it. I bought a pony.

It was when I stopped eating that someone finally blew the whistle on me, and my parents were galvanized into action. Fasting did not come naturally. My mother was more practiced at that form of self-chastisement. She could go all day on half a bagel, starving herself to be fashionably thin and then some. I never had that particular conceit or that strength of will. Although I am an exceptionally picky eater, I have a healthy appetite for the foods I love, and you are not likely to find me in the size four department. Still there came a point where I lost interest in food. The tale of Persephone and the pomegranate may have been weighing on my mind. Moreover, I had latched onto the notion that if I went on a hunger strike, and things got bleak enough, my parents would send me back home to live with Uncle Spence or Aunt Rose.

The plan back fired. One afternoon, without prior warning, my parents appeared at the high school and pulled me out of class. I was driven to a hospital and involuntarily admitted. No, it was not a mental hospital; just a local medical hospital, but being left there alone frightened me out of my wits. There was a desk by my bed and in the top drawer there was a paper. I found that the first evening. The paper said, among other things, that one had to be twenty-one to check oneself out of the hospital. I had just turned fifteen. The experts call it *catastrophizing*, and it's a tendency to which autistic people are prone. In a few moments, I had become convinced that I would be confined to the hospital for the next six years and I could see myself, like a prisoner in the state penitentiary, marking the days off the wall. I freaked out, began shrieking wildly and the nurse had to give me a sedative.

In reality, I stayed at the hospital for only one week and not six years. During that week, blood was drawn daily and I was subjected to a battery of tests. My father believed, and perhaps wanted to believe, that my problems were due to a physical ailment, one that could be cured with a pill. I remember Dad telling the doctors to be sure to check for *sugar*, apparently, meaning diabetes. One of his many relatives had *sugar*, and he imagined that might be the cause of my despair.

I was examined from head to toe, and all that the physicians could discover was an underactive thyroid gland for which thyroid supplements were prescribed. A mental health doctor also spoke to me and he prescribed a psychotropic medication which was probably Ritalin. I was not told why I needed it or what good it would do. I took it for a time without noticing any beneficial effects, and my mother agreed. She said it was only making me act like a zombie—or rather, *more like a zombie*— and the prescription was not refilled. The thyroid supplements did act as intended, though. My appetite returned and so did my menstrual periods. My Dad was satisfied, at least temporarily, that he had done right by me.

My Dad was a real conundrum. He had all the attributes that should have made him an excellent father. Perhaps he would have been so to a typical child. Everyone remarked on what an easygoing, good-natured and warm-hearted man my father was. It was so true. I saw with my own eyes his kind treatment of the disabled veterans who resided in the mansion. As a caregiver, he was nurturing and solicitous; each night he held court in the office for the staff and those patients who were ambulatory. He listened sympathetically to their problems and tried to help. He advanced money to employees who were not doing so well. He advocated for the veterans to their doctors or the V.A. However, like the carpenter's daughter, I was left to build my own house.

There was no doubt that he loved my mother passionately and unconditionally, body and soul. Perhaps she sucked all the love out of him. Or perhaps he preferred to hold me at arm's length, look away and pretend that I was the kind of daughter he had dreamed about, the little girl made of sugar and spice and everything nice. Even so, Dad was not completely blind to my distress, and, from time to time, did try to help me out. His attempts, however, were so inept and bizarre that they only made it worse. Every now and then he would bring home an animal to amuse me. Then, just as I was beginning to bond with the new pet, I would come home from school one day and it would be gone. Ran away, Dad would say. Or shot by hunters. Or eaten by a fox. I would be shaken to the bottom of my boots by these gruesome tales. Later on I found out that many of our animals had simply been given away on impulse. When they failed to instantly lift my spirits, my father lost interest, and if someone came along and offered to provide a better home, that was that. Embarrassed by his own behavior, my father blamed the foxes who could not speak up for themselves.

Another time Dad brought home an old junker he had gotten from Uncle Spence. He was going to teach the kids to drive, he announced. Now the baby brother was far too young, even to conceive of it, but I was of an age to learn and as eager to take the wheel as any teenager. We had the car awhile and took a few spins along the back roads. Then one day, it too, was gone, never to be spoken of again. I took driving courses, but without an automobile to practice with, I had no hope of earning a license. When I was an adult my Aunt Rose taught me how to drive.

Strangely enough, I gave my mother a pass although there was never any doubt in my mind that she had been the engine of my destruction. My mother was more like me, not on the surface, but deep down inside. She had seen the Gothic Estate and *just had to have it*. Was I not like that too, repeatedly brought down by a treasure which dazzled me but hung just out of reach? In my mother's case, it was not friends she craved, but diamonds and furs and a place among the landed gentry. When I finally realized she was not, after all, half a goddess, I nonetheless saw her as a tragic heroine, *the Snow Queen*. In pursuit of the prize her heart desired, she not only sacrificed her daughter and damaged her son, but damn well near destroyed her own life as well. You see, the move north had not brought my mother joy. Even before the nursing home project went belly up, she was as restless and discontented as before. Each afternoon, I would return from school and find her sitting in the kitchen of our cottage, flicking ashes from her long cigarette holder and staring out at the falling snow. On Wednesday she would go to the hairdresser and have her hair perfectly styled, but then find herself with no where to go, stranded like myself in the frozen tundra. Many days she did not even bother to get dressed and remained in her "knocking around" clothes as she called them—well worn baby doll pajamas. My Mom did the books for the business, and did them well. She was very meticulous. There was no cutting around the corners, no fudging at the edges, no grey areas here and there. Every entry was checked once, twice and once again. Afterward, she would bury herself in a novel or curl up and watch TV. You had to be quite hungry for TV to watch it up there. We only received two stations, and even these were faint and indistinct as though the signal were coming from another world, the land of the living that we had left behind.

No, I placed the blame squarely on my father for not having talked some sense into her. *He* had never needed a country seat to feel fulfilled. *He* would have been perfectly content to remain in Croton and manage a little shop. I knew that my Dad continued to have lunch with Uncle Spence and made regular trips back home to see his own family and friends. Aunt Rose had already whispered to me an instructional tale. When the siblings were young, and the Depression had eroded their way of life, Grandpa decided to pack up his brood and move back to Italy. The kids had banded together in insurrection. "Leave our home? Leave our friends? Hell, no! Not us!" The fate my Dad would not have suffered himself, he nevertheless allowed to be visited upon me. For that I resented him mightily and I shut him out of my heart.

Near the end of his life, when he was widowed and close to eighty, Dad consulted a psychiatrist from the Veteran's Administration. He was diagnosed with partial Post Traumatic Stress Syndrome stemming from his experiences in World War II, sixty years before. It was at that time that he began, for the very first time, to speak about the things he had witnessed as a young Marine. These were horrific indeed and certainly left a lasting imprint on his heart. By then we had reconciled and I had forgiven him for not watching my back in the long ago. I listened to what he had to say, and I tried my best to understand, and not to demand more from him than he was willing to give me. Maybe there really were foxes.

In the end my soul was kept from dying, not because of anything my parents did or my teachers did or through any medical treatment. No, it was what the U.S. Government did which roused me from my stupor.

When I was in high school, the U.S. was waging war in a faraway place called Vietnam, a military action that was seen in many quarters as imperialist and oppressive. Nowhere, however, was it more unpopular than in my own heart.

During the week I spent confined to the hospital, I passed the time by reading newsmagazines in the solarium: *Newsweek, Time, U.S. News & World Report*. In one issue, I came upon a story that hit home. It told of a young Vietnamese woman who worked in the rice paddies. One day as she headed home to her village, tired to the bone, and, without a doubt, looking forward to a warm bowl of stew and the chance to sack out on her straw pallet, American warplanes zoomed by overhead. Although she ran as fast as her legs would carry her, she was too late. The village was strafed, the huts set ablaze and her family literally blown apart. I sat bolt upright and my eyes flew open. Wasn't that *exactly* what had happened to me? Had I not lost everything I cared about through no wrongdoing of my own? Had not life as I knew it been destroyed in one fell swoop?

I have heard it said that persons with Asperger's Syndrome (or "aspies," as we call ourselves) have a great concern for social justice. I would like to think that is what motivated me, and that a pure and altruistic flame was lit in my soul. Rather, I suspect, because of my own experiences, the plight of the innocent Vietnamese peasants, caught up in this conflict, resonated in my heart. I felt like one of them. I would never shake this sensation. All through my life, whenever the bombs began to fall, I instantly identified with the *bombees* and not with those who dropped the bombs. My protest was more self-advocacy than philanthropy.

The young woman in the news story had taken up arms and joined the Viet Cong. I raised my voice and joined the antiwar movement. Before long I was hiking a mile up the street for the bus to Poughkeepsie, the nearest large town, to join in peace marches. I proudly held protest signs or stood solemnly outside the courthouse and sheltered candles from the wind. Many of my high school teachers were likewise opposed to the war and came to respect me as sage and precocious. A political science club was organized after school where kids could debate current events. I gave impassioned speeches. I wrote articles for the student newspaper which earned praise. In the end, I did find a few—well, no, not *friends,* but sympathizers and companions in arms. Through my participation in the antiwar movement, I encountered others with whom I shared an interest, and in whose company I attained a certain comfort level.

It was also during these years in the Kingdom of Frost that I came to realize that I did not, in fact, have a kid brother. My parents had a son, but I was still an only child. In contrast to imaginary friends who are all substance and no form, I had a brother in form but not in substance.

It had begun with such promise. His first words were not "Mama" or Dada," but "Yar, Yar!" an infant's attempt to call my name. I was proud of that. However, I was a child myself at the time and paid him no great mind. It was not until after the move north, when there were no neighbors or friends or relations or anyone else about, that I turned in desperation to the one person I had supposed would always be there. In place of the little pal I had happily anticipated, there stood a shy, sullen stranger who candidly lacked any interest whatsoever in me or anything I might say or do. Already, at a tender age, my brother had drawn about him the parameters of his world and I was left on the outside, banished then and forever. The door was shut and I had no key. I could knock and knock and plead for entry, but I would never be let in.

After I had become adult, relatives and acquaintances would often ask me, "How is your brother doing?" This question always astonished me. Was I expected to know? At first, I would honestly reply that I had not a clue. Eventually, I realized that some further explanation was called for, and I learned to say, "We're not close." *Not close* is a term that neurotypicals seem to understand. Of course, *not close* does not begin to tell the story. *It's as if we never met.*

I understand why parents of autistic children claim that they *grieve* for their offspring. All my life I have grieved for the brother I might have had. At first, I was certain that it must be something that I had done and no longer recalled. Perhaps I had abused him in some forgotten way. Year after year, I racked my brain for the long-ago transgression that had caused him to shut me out of his world. Each time I came up empty.

In truth, I saw my brother in childhood as a small figure of pathos. Mom had named him after Brett Maverick, a character in her favorite western. Brett Maverick, the TV character was a gambler and a risk-taker. Our Brett was neither. He exhibited none of the spunk and feistiness that had characterized the Real Me. He did not get on his bike in the morning and take off, not to return until dinnertime. He did not climb trees or run about, hooting and hollering in the game of Cowboys and Indians. He neither fought nor played with other kids, not that I could see. Each day he returned from school and, without a word, retreated to his bedroom, put his records on the spindle, and closed the door. Sure, I, too, lived in a world of my own, but at least I looked out the window.

My mother, who maintained official neutrality, found Brett much preferable to me, and I understood why. My brother seemed as different from me as July is from January. He was neither insubordinate nor disruptive. With Brett, there were no midnight tantrums, no frantic calls from teachers or other parents, no barrage of protest when faced with a parental order. He was a welcome change from the whirling spitfire that had been me. While I bounced cheerfully from one obsession to another, Brett had but one consuming interest from the day he could first mimic jingles on TV. His only love was music, modern music, that is, not Beethoven-style music, and he loved it very much. It could be a cereal ad with a catchy tune. It could be the Beatles. It could be an underground garage band that no one else had ever heard of. Mom would gladly sit with him for hours, talking albums, artists and the latest variation of rock'n'roll. Her eyes, on the other hand, always glazed over whenever I expounded upon my special interest of the moment, be it the politics of some obscure third-world nation or the characteristics of ancient Greek deities.

My brother may not be inquisitive, but I doubt he is unintelligent. Not that I have ever had enough of a conversation with Brett to judge, but my parents told me the names of the schools he attended, and they do not open their doors to just anyone. Mom never raved about his alleged near-genius as she had about mine, but that was due, I presume, to a lesson finally learned.

My adolescent pity was wasted on Brett. My brother adapted much better than I, never having known anything but frost and solitude. He was not haunted by memories of happier times. He had no Alexis walking through the shadows of his mind, nor were there shards of the Real Me piercing his heart to cause him pain. Brett found shelter and solace in his cocoon. He did not expect as much of life as I did, and so, in the end he received much more.

When I was finally bundled off to college, my parents sent Brett away to private school "so that whatever happened to you will not happen to him." These words did not make me angry. Instead, I was glad that my parents had seen the light, and that one of us might still be saved. However, rather than appreciating my sacrifice, Brett only sailed further out of my life. My father, well-intentioned but without a clue, chose a military type academy for his shy, sensitive, introverted son. After the inevitable disaster, he was allowed to transfer to more suitable prep schools. Eventually, Brett landed at an upscale college in Amherst, Massachusetts where he fell in with a clique of students whose lives, like his, revolved around music. My brother had found his niche, and upon graduation, he moved to Boston where, as a music journalist, he achieved the status of a minor celebrity. Indeed, he made a good interviewer, having so little personality of his own.

Like me, Brett, has never married, but he has had a proper series of live-in girlfriends that he duly paraded before our parents. All of them were polite and well-behaved young women, not a druggie or robber girl among them. He also stands six foot, three, no stunted growth *there*. By the time we were both adults, it was more or less accepted family wisdom that he was the one who had overcome his early challenges and done well.

I, on the other hand, was perceived to be suffering from some vaguely defined and untreatable mental illness which prevented me from finding a steady job, pursuing a normal life or achieving emotional stability. If I protested that Brett was far from O.K. and that it was extremely weird and unacceptable for a boy—and then a man—to treat his only sister as if she were a total stranger, even when seated at the same table, I was told to hush up. My complaints were ascribed to jealousy of my more successful in-all-facets-of-life sibling.

My mother would always say, "If your brother wants nothing to do with you, leave him alone. Don't try to force yourself on him." It was the exact same advice she gave me in regard to the young men I stalked. Perhaps in her mind there was really no difference. Dad, in contrast, saw my point very well, but he was reluctant to go against my Mom's opinion. Eventually, he attempted to step in and patch things up between us, but as was generally the case with my Dad's good intentions, it was too little and too late.

As I had foreseen, our parents' death erased the tenuous ties between us and my brother, as a matter of course, has now vanished entirely from my life. Even so, from time to time I feel an overwhelming need to dial his telephone number. When I do, I get a recording that says: "This is Brett. You've reached me, except that you haven't."

Did I try to keep him from slipping through my fingers? Yes, I suppose I did, awkwardly, half-heartedly and then earnestly and with sincere regret. Each time I ran up against the same barrier of sheer indifference that had always stood between us. Once, in Baghdad, I witnessed a bird kill itself by flying headlong into a glass wall outside the Al-Rashid Hotel. Trying to reach my brother made me feel a lot like that bird.

Three years ago when I was diagnosed with Asperger's Syndrome, I pondered once more the puzzle of the brother I almost had. I encountered autistic males in support groups for adults on the spectrum who were dead-on ringers for Brett. Like him, they were withdrawn, passive and shy and spoke little, if at all.

Surprisingly, we female aspies, although always outnumbered, tend to be more outgoing, aggressive and dominate the conversation. *Autism runs in families*, so it has been written and I know it is true. It simply manifests itself differently in males and females. Perhaps that is why four times as many boys as girls are diagnosed with an autism spectrum disorder. Despite my mother's later protestations, it had been quite evident, and not only to me, that as a child there was something a little *off* about Brett. Whereas I was left to fend for myself, Brett was sent to school therapists and counselors and later off to private school. Even without a proper diagnosis, Brett received the individualized care and attention that would so have benefited me. *He* was never accused of *just pretending*.

After a lifetime of resentment which nibbled away at my soul, I've tried to forgive Brett for never having loved me. Just as I was never able to become the daughter my Dad had wanted, Brett lacked the capacity to be a real brother to me. Perhaps, if I realized the truth earlier in life, I could have found a way to keep him from drifting completely out of my life. As it is, he will remain in my memory as the promised baby brother who turned out to be only one more reminder that no one belongs to me in this world of strangers.

Lost Girl at College

•

My mother was the first to admonish me with that old lie, "Time heals all wounds." She strenuously insisted, and apparently her belief was sincere, that on the day I left for college my troubles would suddenly evaporate like spring snowflakes. I would be as good as new, only better. This conviction served to justify her in ignoring my teenage anguish. After all, if my problems were deemed temporary, transient and ephemeral, their importance would be diminished. Soon they would all be gone and forgotten like last week's bellyache.

When I was skeptical, she would point to examples in the animal kingdom. Look at the mother bird. She warms the eggs with her body, she hunts and brings home food for the hatchlings, but when the season is over, she pushes them out of the nest. See how the barn cats behave. The mama cat licks life into her kittens, nurses them and watches over them, but the day will come when they bid her goodbye and set off to seek their fortunes.

The Snow Queen's parables were based on logic, but there was one step she always left out. Before the mother bird pushes the fledglings out of the nest, she makes darn sure they can fly, and the mama cat takes care to impart to her kittens the skills that are needful in the feline world. By contrast, I had been given no training whatsoever in the ways of an adult. In fact, I had been more *grown-up* at 12, than I was at 18.

It had always been expected that I would attend college. From early childhood, it was spoken of as a matter of course, as certain as night giving way to dawn. When the time approached, however, I resisted the whole idea. High school had been so full of misery and pain that I had no desire to repeat the experience. Instead, I made rather bizarre plans for my future. I would pick sugar cane in Cuba, write poetry in a garret in San Francisco or back pack across Europe. All of these proved to be pipe dreams. I had no more hope of carrying them through than I had of sprouting wings. In the end I duly trundled off to college for much the same reason that my mother had given birth to me— it was expected, and there appeared to be no feasible alternative. College turned out to be an unmitigated catastrophe.

Even at this point, school or college was not necessarily associated in my mind with *education*. I thought education was the purpose of the public library. I had become well-read in many fields, and conversant with a plethora of obscure facts and ancient deities, by spending many an afternoon among shelves of books, hiding in some cozy nook and burying my nose in charts, maps and old magazines. My teachers had mentioned a few things along the way that had piqued my interest, but I only gained real knowledge by pursuing the matter on my own. Of course, neither school nor the public library had ever taught me what other people call *common sense*.

Nor did I have a clue as to the proper way of choosing a college. My father wanted to enroll me in what he called a *finishing school*. "Finishing school?" I cried with disdain, "I haven't even been started!" In fact, Dad had selected an exclusive girl's college with excellent academic credentials in nearby Millbrook, New York. I would certainly have fared better there than I did where I ultimately wound up. However, the very phrase *finishing school* raised my hackles, and I refused to entertain the notion.

My freshman year was spent at a university in New Orleans. I imagined I could run toward the summer and outdistance the Wolf of Loneliness. In my naïveté, I supposed that he was bound, like a medieval serf, to our haunted estate way up the Hudson. Too late, I realized that, where so ever I fled, he would be waiting there for me like my shadow.

During my second semester, the school officials encouraged me to consider a transfer. I had not gotten on with my roommate. I did not fit in on campus and my left-wing political opinions were not appreciated down South. In retrospect, I should have planted my feet and stood my ground. New Orleans was not bad even if I did have to attend Mardi Gras alone. At least it was warm, and it had something that always appealed to me, a colorful sense of history.

I decided to seek a transfer to Washington D.C. where I fancied I might find a few kindred spirits. The Vietnam War had not yet ended, and I wanted to be part of the movement to stop it. We *did,* in fact, stop it, but its cessation did nothing to quell my hungry heart.

At the first university in D.C. where I enrolled, I did not even survive orientation. The exact transgression for which I was bounced is long forgotten, but I do recall that a conflict arose when I discovered that I was expected to share a dormitory suite with, not one roommate, but five other girls. Such an encroachment upon my private space could not be borne. Then, too, there were the revolutionary slogans I went around muttering in a menacing tone of voice. Mom and Dad quickly shipped me across town to another college where the administration, dazzled by my high grades and perfect SAT scores, was willing to take a chance on me. Much, I might add, to its later regret.

For, ironically, I had now landed at the only urban university in the 1970s which did not have its share of hippies, radicals, counter-culturists or freethinkers. I stood out like the proverbial black swan in the midst of a student body which was homogenous in the extreme. It was nearly all white and absolutely all from the bourgeoisie, well-dressed, well-behaved and ready to hunker down for a serious education and future career. This university did, in fact, have a renowned academic program which was famed throughout the country. I only wish I had been mature enough to take advantage of it.

Truly, I did my best to be sociable and make friends, but my classmates did not take to me. It was not in a bullying way; they simply thought I was weird, and with reason. These were the days when I behaved much stranger than ever before.

Seven days I week I sported an oversized khaki jacket which I had bought from army and navy surplus. My hair fell in bedraggled strands to my waist and was rarely combed. At times I forgot to take a shower or brush my teeth. I plastered the walls of my dorm room, for at last I had a private one, with controversial posters including one of Che Guevara and another entitled *Satan Overlooking Paradise*. The poster of Satan, which I had purchased from a head shop in Georgetown, had nothing to do with witchcraft or the occult, even though I had acquired a passing knowledge of both. It was an artistic rendering of a scene from John Milton's poem, *Paradise Lost*. Satan, like Che, was one of my revolutionary models; in fact, the *original* revolutionary. Satan and I had something else in common. We both knew the pain of homesickness. Did he point at heaven and muse that once there walked an archangel who was known as the Real Me? Did he, like myself, weep tears of bitter sorrow whenever Linda Ronstadt sang *Blue Bayou*?

The dorm supervisor demanded that I take the posters down. I refused.

Despite their hands-off ways, my parents had at least provided some structure to my life. They had dragged me out of bed in the morning, sent me on my way to school, decently dressed and groomed, put reasonably healthy food on the table, washed my laundry, reminded me to do my homework and provided me with a modicum of companionship, often the only social life I had. Now that they were no longer there to pull on the reins and with public transportation easily available, I did what was right in my own eyes. I ran wild in the streets.

Feeling unwelcome on campus, I rarely attended class that first year and a half. Instead I spent most of my time in downtown D.C., taking part in rallies, protest marches and demonstrations. There was one almost every day. We called it simply the Movement, and like a magnet it drew students from all the nearby colleges, although not every one in the Movement was a student or even young. We had come together to stand against the war, first and foremost, but there were other issues, too:

civil rights, women's rights, police brutality, the plight of the poor, the plight of the immigrant worker and the widespread abuses of corporate capitalism. I found it all very exciting and, for a while, the Movement provided me a feeling of community, a sense of exaltation. When I was striding proudly down the street—and, in those days, you could march defiantly right by the White House—holding a sign and chanting to the music of clapping hands and tambourines along with thousands of other young dissidents, I was on fire with a sense of high moral purpose. I could almost forget that I had no friends.

Once I was arrested on a charge of *Parading Without a Permit*. A mass demonstration was breaking up, and I noticed that the police had arrived and were harassing the marchers across the street. Putting down my sign, I hurried to be of assistance. Before I knew it, I was grabbed and thrown into a police van with a dozen other protestors. I was driven to the Women's House of Detention and ushered into a cell with several other women. My cell mates were all older than I, many of them veteran activists and used to these experiences. Several were former freedom riders, and for hours they regaled me with war stories of Selma and Martin Luther King. So absorbed was I in these tales of legendary struggles and days gone by, that it took me some time to realize that we were, in fact, locked in. I could not get up and leave. No key. Then I freaked.

I might well have freaked. I knew very little about the legal system in those days. From *Perry Mason* and *Ironsides*, I had gleaned that, upon arrest, one had the right to a single telephone call, but there was no one I could phone. I could hardly call my parents. I had no friends who might post my bail in Washington D.C., or anywhere else, for that matter, and I was already on the outs with the college administration. Fortunately, a convention of progressive lawyers was meeting in a nearby hotel that very night. They put up our collateral. One of the older women gave up her place in line so that I might go free ahead of her. From then on, whenever the police appeared at a protest, I gave them a wide berth.

Eventually, the sense of camaraderie with the other demonstrators wore thin. I formed no lasting relationships in the Movement. In fact, the more radical student groups that I tried to join, such as the Weathermen, viewed me as immature and undependable and fobbed me off. With the war winding down and feeling a bit queasy over squandering my parents' tuition money so lightly, I vowed to return to campus and devote myself to my studies. This sounds laudable, I know, but like so many of my best conceived plans, it backfired. The more the college officials saw of me, the more convinced they became of my undesirability and concluded that I was a very bad influence indeed on the student body.

Incendiary political rhetoric was widespread on campuses in those days, even relatively sedate ones such as mine. For most adherents of the *New Left*, as it was called, it was all talk. Unfortunately, in my case, the talk knew no bounds. Like most aspies, I am prone to obsessions. Once I have latched onto an interest, it consumes me, and I do not know when to change the subject.

There were other young people around at the time who did more than just talk, who set off bombs and fired shots and robbed banks in pursuit of political goals, individuals such as Bill Ayres, Joanne Chesimard, Kathy Boudin and Patty Hearst, to name a few. Would I have ever emulated them? I think not. For all my recklessness, I had better sense than that.

One night in jail had taught me that I was not cut out to be a domestic terrorist. Yes, I might make wild-eyed speeches, but that is as far as it went. Yes, I could be reckless but I lacked the talent for cold-blooded violence. Once, soon after the move north, my mother grew so angry at what she perceived to be my willful obstinacy, that she stormed into my bedroom, began rifling through my record collection, placed my favorite albums across her knee and smashed them, one by one. Then she tossed the pieces against the wall as if to say, "See, I can throw tantrums, too!" I stood there horrified at the violence of it all, although, of course, broken records are not like broken hearts. They feel no pain.

Nevertheless, the *concept* of armed insurrection seemed unbearably romantic to me, the storming of the Bastille, the rising of the moon, the Abba song *Fernando*. Revolution offered all the elements I found attractive: a quest for social justice, a sense of solidarity and the opportunity to seek revenge against bullies and tyrants. For the more I was rejected and tossed aside, the more quickly that early idealism which had won me kudos in high school devolved into full-blown anarchism. Like Samson in the temple of the Philistines, I could bring the whole unforgiving world crashing down with me.

Looking back on those years, from a post-diagnosis vantage point, I can clearly see the role I was playing. I was trying to make myself appear big and purposeful rather than small and powerless. I did not want to be seen as a *victim*. The Real Me had never thought of herself as a victim not even when she was tormented by bullies, taunted by her peers and disciplined by her teachers. She ascribed these troubles to the vagaries of life, and imagined that she would one day overcome these obstacles. However, at the age of thirteen, all alone with my childhood support system stripped away, I felt utterly powerless and learned to internalize my victim hood. At the same time, I grew desperately unhappy. Being a victim and being unhappy went together. I wanted to be happy again, so I adopted the role of a non-victim. Throughout the 1970s, radical activists were in the news, and I pretended to be one. Revolutionaries are not victims; they do not sit and nurse their grievances, they take matters into their own hands. Their methods may be questionable, but their goals are laudable. Even when revolutionaries come to misfortune, like Che Guevara or Leon Trotsky, they are not seen as victims but as *martyrs*. Martyrs are brave while victims are objects of pity. Martyrs die with their minds at peace, while victims survive only to weep and tear their clothes.

I was all bark and very little bite, but it was an obsessive aspie bark, and given the temper of the times, the college officials might reasonably have drawn the conclusion that they had a budding terrorist on their hands.

There were also the drugs. Actually, there were no drugs, but the administration believed that there were, and as I would later learn in law school, it is impossible to prove a negative.

Illegal substances were rampant on college campuses in the seventies, and probably still are. It was logical that my weird behavior would be attributed to them. It is well known that druggies behave strangely, but I was never a druggie. I had no money to buy drugs, no idea of where to obtain them and I was distrustful of them. My foothold in the real world was tenuous at best; I needed no LSD or angel dust to feel myself slipping away.

Yes, I did smoke marijuana from time to time. Pot was so plentiful in those days that even if you were not in the loop, you could score an occasional toke. If I saw a joint being passed around, I would willingly partake. It had a calming effect on me much like the anti-anxiety pills I take now. However, I scrupulously avoided the hard stuff, even when offered a sample.

Nevertheless, the college officials suspected that I must be on drugs, and soon rumors began to spread that I was not only taking drugs, but selling them. I laughed off these allegations when they were laid at my doorstep. Could I even imagine myself as a trafficker? Where would I get the stuff? Was I a member of a cartel? Was I in the mafia? Who would I sell drugs to, as I had no friends? Would I have risked imprisonment for such a dishonorable motive as filthy profit when I preached so raucously against the evils of capitalism? Yet despite my protestations of innocence, the college persisted in searching my dorm room for contraband or for proceeds of illegal sales. They came up empty each time, for neither existed.

In the end, my downfall was caused by neither drugs nor politics, but by sex. At this university there was an exceedingly handsome young man whose favors I much desired. He was not only supremely good looking, but clever and artistic as well. He attended the school of architecture, and was charismatic, popular and well-respected on campus. In fact, he was the president of the student body. This one boy embodied all the qualities which I lacked and would have liked to acquire.

Perhaps I hoped that, as his girlfriend I might absorb some of these magical qualities by osmosis. Perhaps I thought that if I were seen at his side I would no longer be an outcast, that I too would be sought after and respected.

Now I had no clue as to the proper way to approach a boy and I was totally unversed in the arts of seduction. So I took to following him about campus, lurking in the street by his apartment and waiting for him after class. If he were lunching with his friends in the college rathskeller, I would sit down at their table uninvited and begin to talk about the upcoming revolution. You might say that I was stalking him.

For a while, the boy took it in stride and, out of kindness, I suppose, let me join his hangers-on. It was in the spring of my junior year that I enjoyed a brief respite from the relentless loneliness that had tracked me since I turned thirteen. I was buoyed by what I imagined was my newfound acceptance. It seemed that I had been welcomed into his inner circle, if not as a lover, than as a friend. Too soon I learned the bitter truth.

The young man was dating a girl named Betty who was my polar opposite. She was a sorority sister from an affluent family in Florida, dark-haired, petite, not a hair out of place. She did not walk like a swaying ship. Her grades were good, her poise, impeccable, her politics, liberal but conventional. She was the kind of daughter my father would have been proud of, that, indeed, any father would have been proud of. I was jealous of Betty, true enough, but I was also in awe of her as a peasant girl might be in awe of a queen even when they are rivals for the same man. In fact, if you had asked me during those weeks, I would have claimed that Betty was my friend as well. The pangs of unrequited love were a fair price to pay for the new social status that I foolishly believed I had attained.

A story made the rounds that I was plotting an injury to Betty. It was whispered that I had been overheard making threats against her. In another version of the tale, I had been seen hiding in the bushes under Betty's window. Truly bizarre rumors were circulated that I had been seen following Betty with an ice pick or pouring some unknown substance into her drink.

When I was first confronted with this nonsense, I shrugged and tried to ignore it. I had loudly and indignantly proclaimed my innocence against the drug dealing accusations, but now I did not know what to say. These rumors hit closer to home because they unveiled my forbidden secret. Was there a kernel of truth in this folderol? Had I not harbored envy of Betty in my heart? Could I have, in some unguarded moment, given voice to my darkest desires? Like many aspies, I am completely incapable of making small talk. Many times I have sat and twiddled my thumbs while people made casual conversation back and forth above me. Yet, when the conversation turns to a subject that interests me, I tend to talk what my mother called a *blue streak*. Careless words fly out of my mouth with a will of their own. Then there were my inept attempts to be witty and amusing like one of the gang. I had noted that college students frequently make jokes which are in very poor taste but are nonetheless met with shouts of merriment, laughter and back-slapping. Unfortunately, whenever *I* spoke in jest, there was dead silence.

Perhaps, indeed, I had once made an offhand remark such as, "Not to worry, Betty, if anything happens to you, your boyfriend will be safe with me," intending it all in fun. Could it be that such a silly comment had been stolen, misconstrued, twisted out of proportion, and spread throughout the college community by those hoping to see the last of me? I bit my tongue and hoped that the storm would pass.

One afternoon near the end of the semester I came home to find that the locks had been changed on my dorm room. I was not allowed in, not even to retrieve my belongings. I sprinted frantically across the campus to find the Dean of Women. There was a new Dean of Women at the time. She was very young, not much older than a college student herself, and had seemed friendly and sympathetic. I had trouble locating her; she was not in her office and no one would tell me where she might be. This threw me into a panic. When I finally tracked her down, it was at a faculty party. She may have been drunk;

she was certainly cruel. When I desperately poured out my distress and begged her to intervene, she laughed and taunted me like a schoolyard bully. I stood there in disbelief that any adult, and one in a position of responsibility at that, would behave in such fashion.

I ran this way and that throughout the university searching for someone who would help me. No one would come to my aid, not a professor, not a member of the administration, not a fellow student. I called my parents and their response was to wire me the train fare home. They spoke to the dorm supervisor and asked her to pack up my things and ship them north C.O.D. Despite her promise to do so, most of my personal property simply vanished.

The only one to show me the least kindness was the young man who had been the cause of it all. Through his good offices, I was permitted to camp out in the student lounge for the next two weeks until exams were over. I made an attempt to take my finals, but I was so shell-shocked that I ended up with an Incomplete in most of my courses.

The way the college officials dealt with me was neither legal nor moral. The answer was right there in the university manual, although I did not discover it until much later. As a student, I was guaranteed *due process.* I was entitled to a hearing, to see the evidence against me, to make my accusers come forth and testify as to what they claimed to have seen or heard. At the time I knew nothing of this and my ignorance made me as helpless as a lamb in a colony of wolves.

The school refused to readmit me unless I underwent a psych evaluation. That was fine with me. I had had no desire to ever return there, ever again, under any terms. I was determined to transfer once more. My mother warned me that no one would accept me under this cloud, and apparently, she was right. All summer I searched in vain for any college which would overlook my troubles. I had slunk back to my parents' home in disgrace. Once again I was stranded in the middle of nowhere, nursing my betrayal, without public transportation or anyone to talk to. A few months of this and I was ready to submit to anything.

My parents drove me to the office of a local psychiatrist. He asked me a few cursory questions, the only one of which I recall is, "Do you masturbate?" to which I scornfully replied, *"Sure. Wouldn't you?"* If he reached a diagnosis, I was not informed of it. He did not suggest a course of treatment. He did clear me so I could complete my degree as my parents had requested. The degree, when I finally received it, was as worthless as that psychiatric consultation.

The college permitted me to attend classes, but I was not allowed to live in the dormitory. I spent my last two years in D.C. holed up in an off-campus apartment, listening to the radio and gorging myself with comfort foods. I took the bus to class, but I did not even try to socialize. My papers were shabbily done and always turned in late. My grade level fell precipitously. I wandered the streets of the city and peered in the windows. I frequented the D.C. public library and checked out books on my favorite subjects. Although I never abused illegal drugs as had been alleged, I did overdose on the thyroid supplements I had been prescribed. I reasoned that if they were good for me, taking more than directed might be even better. As a result, my appetite grew ravenous. I ate and ate and still my hunger went unsatisfied. One day I stepped on the bathroom scale and it topped 200 pounds. Two hundred pounds did not sit well on my five foot four frame. In fact, I now had rolls of fat falling over my belly and my legs rubbed together when I walked. Here was another reason for self-loathing. Alexis' comment of ten years before about my weight had been untrue at the time, but had acted like a prophecy.

I had purchased a small coin bank at a five and ten in downtown D.C. which sported a papier-mâché teddy bear, a knick-knack of little value, real or sentimental, but I became attached to it. It was kept on the bathroom counter of my apartment. One day I went to use the bathroom and my arm inadvertently knocked the bank to the floor. The head came off the bear as neatly as if it had been guillotined and rolled across the floor. I began to shake with fright. I stood there transfixed for an hour before I could summon up the courage to pick up the pieces of the bear and carry them out to the garbage disposal. I emptied the bank and threw the base away as well, yet for weeks thereafter my sleep was disrupted by visions of bloody bears with severed heads. I had become that dysfunctional.

My parents paid my rent and sent me an allowance for food and essentials. The check arrived each Wednesday, and I spent every penny of it. By Tuesday evening, I had not one cent in my pocket. On occasion the check failed to arrive in Wednesday's mail. Sometimes it came on Thursday or Friday, and once it did not show up until Saturday. At these times I was thrown into a panic, remembering that I was alone in Washington D.C. with no money or bank account, and that I knew not one sole person to whom I might turn in an emergency. On the one occasion that I did not receive my allowance until Saturday, I broke down. I went to the university bursar and begged for a few dollars. She gave me a loan to tide me over, but not before barreling into me with embarrassing questions, such as why someone bright enough to attend college did not know the meaning of *budget*.

As I aimlessly wandered the streets of Washington D.C., I pondered the enigma that was my life. Was it merely the exile to the Kingdom of Frost which had caused my regression, or had some part of me failed to develop? Other people grow from children into adults, but I had gone the other way. It was a riddle with no answer. As a sophomore, I had endured several visits with the campus psychologist at the strong urging of the administration. (This was a separate person from the shrink that my parents brought me to for a cursory examination). The school psychologist let me rant and rave and pour out my despair. He listened as I described the unbearable loneliness of high school, and my inability to accept the loss of Alexis and my childhood friends. He sat there and nodded his head while I trashed my parents and lamented my failure to form new relationships. However, he never offered an opinion on why I was not like other people or what might be done to remedy my heartache. One day I asked him why he never gave me any advice. He just looked at me straight-faced and said, "What is it you want of me?" I stared at him aghast, stunned into silence. That was our last session.

When I finally made senior, I tried again. This time I consulted my faculty advisor. He was a professor of medieval history, young, eager, friendly and imaginative. I liked him immensely and signed up for his classes whenever possible. Indeed, had he not been on sabbatical at the time I had the troubles, he might have been the one person on campus to stand up for me.

The faculty advisor invited me into his home, introduced me to his wife and dog, served me cookies and a soda, and talked with me for two hours. He did give me pointers, although most of them were rather obvious, such as, dressing like the other girls, and having my hair done up in the current fashion. At the end of our visit, he undercut all his credibility by one offhand remark. "You are the most intelligent person I have ever met," he said to me. I quickly responded, "How can you be so wrong?"

The university eventually awarded me my diploma, not because I had earned it, but because it was the only way to get rid of me. I did not attend the graduation ceremonies, nor did I feel in the least festive. I picked up my diploma from the registrar's office, mailed it home to Dad and never looked at it again.

I knew only too well what was expected of me then. Grown-ups work for a living. Indeed, in this society, one cannot attain true adulthood without a job. In fact, if everyone ever needed a job, it was I, and not just for the wages. I needed to be productive and put my skills and intellect to use if I was ever to regain any pride in myself. Employment would also fill the void in my life where a social life should have been. Unfortunately, I had no clue as to how to *find* a job, or what kind of work I might be suited for. The very prospect of submitting to an interview was terrifying. If none of the people I had considered friends had been willing to defend me against false accusations, why would a perfect stranger offer me a place in his company? Any prospective boss would surely disparage me as too weird, too slovenly, too fat, or he might regard me mockingly and burst into laughter as the Dean of Women had done.

When the Real Me was nine, her father had managed a bait and tackle shop in Harmon. For a penny a throw, the Real Me had folded cardboard boxes to hold the bait. She was very proud of this job and her expertise thereat, displaying the perfectly folded boxes to everyone who came into the store and smugly pocketing her pay. Now, at twenty-three, armed with an undeserved college degree, I was unemployable.

It was not possible to stay in Washington D.C. without a source of income, nor did I particularly want to remain there. There would always be a place waiting for me in the Kingdom of Frost. My parents would not turn me away. They would take care of my basic needs, food, clothing and housing, as they had always done. They might even provide me with employment of a sort, using me to do the typing for their business. What they would *not* do is teach me the skills I needed to live in the outside world.

There's an old proverb about the difference between giving a person a fish and teaching him how to fish. It goes something like this: if you give a person a fish, he has a meal tonight, but if you teach him to fish, he will never go to bed hungry. My parents would always be there to give me a fish, but they would never, ever, teach me how to cast my own net. In order to learn that skill, I would have to look elsewhere.

The Real Me had had a maiden aunt to whom she had been close, who had taken her shopping and taught her to fry bacon and bake bread. That was her Dad's older sister, Aunt Rose. One day in early autumn, Rose took the pint-sized Real Me down to the Village Democratic Headquarters and pinned her with a *JFK for President* button, sparking a life-long fascination with politics, and upsetting the Real Me's Mom. Jacqueline might bear the same name and look like Mrs. Kennedy, but her sympathies definitely lay elsewhere. Not that the Snow Queen would ever do anything so pedestrian as *vote*, you understand, but she had a rooting interest in the Republicans, inherited, no doubt, from Grandpa Charlie, the onetime bootlegger, who had never forgiven FDR for the repeal of Prohibition. After the

Real Me had been taken to the Kingdom of Frost, Aunt Rose had married, but she had not forgotten her favorite niece. She had driven up several times to visit, but she was one of those to whom my mother invariably sent regrets. Now, when I had hit rock bottom, I sought rescue from my Aunt Rose.

The Toy Garden

•

Once upon a time there was a small town newspaper called the Croton–Cortlandt News. Before it went belly-up in 1987, it featured an article by local reporter Phyllis McQuillan about my Aunt Rose and her unique method of landscape design. It was entitled *Toy Garden Yields Full Harvest*. This is how it went:

People driving past the Grand Street home of Rose and James Carvelas often do a double-take. Some even turn around and drive by again just to make sure they aren't seeing things.

They aren't.

You see, the Carvelas home is not much different from other homes in Croton. It is the yard that sets it apart—more than 1000 plastic toys peer from poles there, catching the eyes of both drivers and pedestrians alike.

The *Carvelas Toy Garden* (as is spelled out by toy blocks in the back yard) started out innocently enough. Mrs. Carvelas was tending to her garden in May or June 1982 when she realized she would need poles to control her wandering peonies.

"The bare poles looked so ugly," she remembers, "So I happened to find a few old toys and stuck them at the end of the poles. It just snowballed from there."

Snowballed isn't the word. Mrs. Carvelas estimates that more than 300 *friends* crowd her front yard, the site of the original unruly perennials. Today each toy is placed somewhat scientifically in the yard, some in their own little *categories*.

"Here is my business section," said Mrs. Carvelas, pointing to the side of the house where plastic typewriters and cash registers are held aloft on poles. She also has similar themed sections for Indians, prehistoric animals, fast food (with replicas of a Pizza Hut and Mc-Donald's), a traffic section and a water scene with everything from sharks to boats to frogs.

"There are my bowling alleys," said Mrs. Carvelas, referring to several sets of bowling pins. Then she points to an assortment of dolls, animals, trucks and boats that are not on poles—they are lined up on the ground.

"I ran out of poles," she explains with a smile. "I have boxes of toys just waiting for new poles."

However, once the poles are attained, an even bigger problem looms—how to attach the toys to the poles. Since some of them are made of hard plastic and plaster, they would shatter if holes were opened in their bottoms. Mrs. Carvelas solves that problem by either hanging the toy or developing a special stand. "Some of them are so cute that I just cannot put a hole in them" she says, pointing to an "E.T." ball that has been tied to a tree.

For the rubber toys, Mrs. Carvelas has devised a collection of pipes that she heats in order to make a hole in the bottom of the toys.

A great deal of preparation is taken before the toys are placed outside. First, Mrs. Carvelas takes great pains to clean them, since many have been long-forgotten by their original young owners and have gathered considerable dust.

After cleansing, Mrs. Carvelas shellacs the toys to help preserve them from the sun and the elements. "Nothing can protect them from the strong ultra-violet rays," she notes, pointing to a sun-faded kangaroo in the front yard.

How do people react to the yard?

"Everyone really likes it," Mrs. Carvelas reports, adding that the neighbors' children frequently visit to check out any new residents.

"Mrs. Carvelas says people always stop and chat and look at her unusual garden which, along with the toys, harvests pretty flowers and beautiful flowering trees, including what Mrs. Carvelas calls her *paradise tree*. This tree, located in the front yard, has a wide variety of very authentic-looking fruit nestled among its leaves. "The only place you would ever find a tree like this is in paradise," she explains.

Visitors are always invited into the yard for a tour, which is usually given by Mr. Carvelas. Other than the tours, Mr. Carvelas says he tries to avoid yard-decorating. "It's Rose's project," he observes.

People touring the yard are never disappointed, whether walking through *Frogville* or visiting Bozo, the almost life-sized St. Bernard with the top hat on the front stoop.

Out of all the seasons, though, Mrs. Carvelas said she is partial to the Christmas season because then she can add a holiday motif to her existing decorations.

But looking at the Carvelas' yard, it almost seems as if every day is Christmas.

There is an old proverb that goes: *One man's trash is another man's treasure*. I cited that proverb in the eulogy I gave for Aunt Rose. She rescued me as surely as she rescued Bozo or the residents of *Frogville*. She plucked me from the trash heap on which I had fallen and raised me up on a pole, like the toys in her fantasy garden, so that I might have some semblance of a productive life.

Rose was the seventh of Grandpa-in-Croton's *ten little Indians* and the youngest daughter. Dad was the next to arrive in the house on Grand Street, and a special bond was forged between the two in childhood that persisted throughout their lives. They also became, for a little while, the last two survivors of the tribe.

Aunt Rose had a sharp mind. Perhaps, that was what drew her to the Real Me. When she eventually married, she wed an introverted, socially awkward geek, who may have been an undiagnosed aspie himself. She also had a wealth of energy and a firm, athletic frame although, she lacked what in those days was considered essential to the happiness of every young girl. Aunt Rose did not have a pretty face. All her life, she suffered by comparison to her ravishingly-red-haired-older sister, Carmela, to whom all good things seemed to come, including the boy that Aunt Rose would have liked to marry. In the absence of physical beauty, Rose developed quite a strong personality and a defiant take on the world. "I'll outlive you all!" she promised her more favored siblings, and indeed she did.

Aunt Rose was a star basketball player at Croton High. One of her old teammates recalled how she would swing her handbag at the coach whenever he made a bad call. That was something the Real Me could appreciate! Rose had her heart set on college and even won a scholarship, but her parents were so poor there was no money for books. Still, she put her foot down at quitting high school like Aunt Car to help support the family. During the war she went to work in the defense industry and earned the title *Rosie the Riveter*. Less laudable, was her claim to have killed FDR.

It happened like this: World War II was a burden for Grandpa's household although it had finally lifted them out from the poverty the Great Depression had brought. Several of the sons were taken for soldiers. Even the family dog was drafted, and gave his life for his country. One day a present arrived for Aunt Rose in the mail. My Dad had sent her a snow globe from his camp in the Pacific. It had broken in shipping and all the confetti had seeped through the package. To Aunt Rose, this was a bad omen. She cried and cried, and that night she uttered a prayer: "Dear God, please strike dead the person who began this horrid war!" The next morning a radio announcer declared that President Roosevelt had passed away.

Although Aunt Rose had no children, she was blessed-or-cursed with a myriad of nieces and nephews. She was in her early forties when she married, an advanced age in the 1960s, and her only pregnancy ended in miscarriage. When she felt the baby slipping away, she grabbed frantically onto the first sacred object she could find. It was a medal of Saint Dymphna, the protectress of those who suffer with mental disorders, and she prayed like hell. As was said about the Oracle of Delphi, the saints reply in mysterious ways.

During my exile, I lost touch with Aunt Rose as I did with most of my relatives. By the time I was sixteen, I had begun to take the train to Croton on weekends. My main purpose was to hunt down Alexis, but it provided an opportunity to reconnect with Aunt Rose and my paternal Grandma, Mariangela. Aunt Rose had married by then, but she had not left home. Instead, Uncle Jim had moved in with her and Grandma.

One afternoon I even ventured to voice, in a timorous voice, what my heart desired above all things: *"could I possibly, would you perhaps consider, is there a chance* that I could live here for my senior year in high school?" Aunt Rose did not make a firm commitment—she said it was up to my parents—but I knew that she would go along. Not only was Aunt Rose the type who took in stray dogs and relatives, but she was unlikely to pass up an opportunity to one-up my Mom whom she thought unbearably stuck-up and aloof.

On the train ride north, I was in ecstasy. My head was filled with visions of football games, and Scoop'n'Judy's and dances at Croton High. When I burst through the front door and breathlessly broached the subject to my mother, she looked at me as incredulously as though I had asked her to take me to London and fix me up with Prince Charles. And that was *that*—one more flickering hope snuffed out like a candle. Although I cried myself to sleep that night, there was nothing to be done.

My mother quashed that dream, but she could not prevent me from returning to my hometown as an adult. Aunt Rose found me curled up on her doorstep one morning. *"Hello. I was sent by St. Dymphna . . ."*

I was not Aunt Rose's first kinfolk rescue, nor would I be her last. My Cousin Pete had preceded me; his mother died when he was young and his father had been unable to care for him. Following upon his heels were Aunt Rose's father-in-law and mother-in-law, though not at the same time. On occasion, another cousin, too, would have cause to use the spare bedroom off the kitchen, but I was the one who came to stay.

So I moved into the old house on Grand Street, where my Dad had been born, the house that Grandpa and his first wife had rented when they came over from Italy at the dawn of the twentieth century. Aunt Car had purchased the house from its former landlords, and then conveyed the title to Aunt Rose as a wedding gift. It was our ancestral home, the one remaining place on earth where I felt safe, the only place I had ever called *home* since junior high. It was there that Aunt Rose would spend the rest of her life trying to bring me back to what I had been. Turning me into a functional adult was no easy chore. On the day I arrived on her doorstep, I had all the social skills of one of those jungle boys depicted in the campy old movies, *Raised by Wolves*. Yeah, I may as well have been.

Even when I was not physically residing with her, I would keep her address on my driver's license and all my legal papers. Every car I ever owned until my present Yaris was registered there (and that, only because the Toyota dealer frowned upon registering a car to a house now owned by strangers.) Aunt Rose's home became what we call in the legal profession, my *domicile*—the place to which I always intended to return.

There was a spirited little ditty that circulated among the junior high crowd back in the day and was always sung with great gusto at the Friday afternoon hops the Real Me attended. It was called *The Cat Came Back the Very Next Day,* and involved a farmer's frantic, but futile attempts to rid himself of a stray cat that had taken up residence under his front porch. Well, that sure proved prophetic. Aspies are a lot like cats.

In the end, Aunt Rose became more of a parent to me than either of my own. She was certainly the diametrical opposite of my beautiful, tragic Mom, the Snow Queen. You would never approach Aunt Rose with feelings of awe and reverence nor fall upon your knees and worship her. People could not curry your favor by calling you her spitting image. She did not wear her hair perfectly coiffed nor did she sport clothes of black and white and navy blue which were fitted to a T. Instead, she wore earth colors like tan and salmon and peach, hues that neither my mother nor I would have been caught dead in, often riddled with stains and cigarette holes and two sizes too big or too small. As a British tabloid once declared, when comparing Camilla Parker-Bowles to Don Quixote's fair Desdemona, "Not so fair, perhaps, but more tangible."

Aunt Rose was certainly tangible. She brought me inside, picked me up by the scruff of the neck, and brushed the dirt and the muck off my pants. She bought me new clothes and took me to a hairdresser. She made an appointment with a doctor who specialized in metabolic disorders and he adjusted my thyroid medication. I slowly began to lose the extra weight. I had my Grandmother, and I again had neighbors on either side of me. Aunt Rose had friends of her own and I adopted them as my own. All of them were older than I, of course, but that does not matter when you have been stranded in a universe of one.

I felt happy to be back in my hometown although Alexis and the rest of my childhood playmates had moved on and Scoop'n'Judy's was history. When I walked down the street, people would wave and call me by name. "How are you feeling?" they would say, or "What about this weather?" I would nod and wave to them in return. Aunt Rose covered her walls with photos of all her siblings and her nieces and nephews, including many cousins I had never heard of or forgotten. She received Christmas cards from many of them and they, too, were posted on the wall. Furthermore, her conversation was liberally sprinkled with names and dates, births and weddings and graduations. She seemed to know whenever a member of the tribe fell sick and the nature of the ailment, which baby belonged to which parents, who lived in this town or that one, who worked on the railroad and who owned one. This knowledge I would never have acquired on my own and it turned out to be of no practical value, but it provided a measure of comfort, and an illusion of belonging. It was indeed only an illusion, albeit a warm and fuzzy one. Immediately upon Aunt Rose's death, thirty years thereafter, my paternal cousins would band together and cast me out of the clan. I should have foreseen it, but in my eternal naïveté, I was blindsided.

Aunt Rose also taught me to drive and lent me her old Volvo. Three days after passing my road test, I wrapped it around a telephone pole. To the end of her life, she would point at me and wail, "Where's my Volvo?" much in the way Caesar Augustus was alleged to have evermore cried "Where are my legions?" after one of his commanders blundered into a German ambush.

My grandmother's name was Mariangela, *Mary of the Angels*, and it suited her well. She may have been a saint. Grandma had no formal education to speak of, she spoke in broken English, but she was wise in an earth-mother way that a dozen college degrees could not confer. In her village near Naples, it had been the custom for orphans or illegitimate children to be adopted into the families of more affluent peasants as companions to their own children or helpers on the farm. Little Mariangela had qualified. Great-Grandma had worked as a chambermaid in a household of wealthy barristers and one of the sons had left her in the family way. The child was put to work as a shepherdess on my future Grandpa's family farm. For the rest of her life, she refused to eat lamb in memory of her days tending the flocks. Not that she was flawless, by any means. On the way to market one day, the little shepherdess had laughed at another young woman who had taken a tumble in the local creek. The girl in the creek turned out to be a witch, and, for the rest of her days, Grandma was subject to furious bouts of hiccups. She called me her little *communiste* and expressed the hope that I would return to school and marry another *communiste*. One day a small red automobile was parked outside our home and my Grandma, recognizing how much I wanted a car of my own, asked Aunt Rose if it was a gift for Charli. Well, no, of course not, that auto belonged to a total stranger. However, when I finally purchased a car of my own, you know it would be small and you know it would be red.

Aunt Rose did not share the negative attitude that my mother had toward the acquisition of pets. (*They had muddy paws and you had to clean up after them. Then they ran away or died and caused you to weep bitter tears*). One Thanksgiving eve, my Uncle Jim picked me up at the train station and remarked, "By the way, we have a houseguest." I thought, "oh, no, one of those pesky cousins." Little did I expect the wonderful surprise which awaited me upon opening the front door. I was greeted by the sight of a small white shaggy dog making himself at home on the sofa. I squealed with delight. He was a Lhasa Apso, a Tibetan temple dog that Aunt Rose had adopted from the pound. She called him *Lucki* and he certainly was, because for the next ten years our lives revolved around him. Lucki loved to go for walks. All you had to say was, "Where's my shoes?" and he would come running like a bat out of hell. He had a good trick, too, of lying on his back with his legs spread, testicles pointed toward heaven. We called that a "doggy vision." We told each other "doggy stories." After Lucki died, there would be three more Lhasa Apsos. Calliope was our one dog of color, almost pure black. I bought her from a breeder in South Salem shortly after we lost Lucki. Six months later I happened upon a pet store at a mall where a half-grown Lhasa was shoved into a puppy cage much too tiny for him. His brown lipid eyes reached out to me. I stepped up to the counter and put my money down. He was named *Gorbi* after the then leader of Russia. For weeks Gorbi could hardly balance himself on his hind legs, having been crammed into that tiny cage for God-knows how long. Aunt Rose patiently walked him on a leash around the neighborhood until he found his strength. Gorbi's most excellent trick was standing upright with his paws extended as if in supplication, begging for love. The fourth, acquired some years later, was another shelter dog. When we adopted him, Newt Gingrich was serving as Speaker of the House of Representatives. The new pup bore an uncanny resemblance to Newt, sported the same haircut and jumped up on his hind legs, and barked incessantly. Aunt Rose named him Buffy, but I called him *Mr. Speaker*.

I had hoped that the move back to Croton would afford me the opportunity to reunite with Alexis. Unfortunately, that did not happen. We had actually met up on several occasions during our late teens and early twenties. These visits, which I always initiated, were bittersweet. In a few short years she had changed, as adolescents often do. My childhood best friend, the impish pixie tomboy, had been replaced with a sophisticated, artsy young woman, rather like her own mother. How did that make me feel? Remember that scene at the end of *Peter Pan* where Peter goes back for Wendy and discovers, to his shock and puzzlement that she has turned into a married woman with children of her own? Is it not the saddest scene in movie history? So it was with me and Alexis. She had grown up while I was still, well, Peter Pan. Nevertheless, I kept knocking on her door. Yes, we had good times together, but it was never the same. Still I nourished in my heart the belief that someday we would be best friends as adults, just the way we had been as children.

Alexis had gone away to college, as I had, but I assumed she would be coming back to Croton, if not to live, then certainly for Christmas and on family occasions. I planned to be here waiting for her when she did return. But, as fate would have it—and I believe it is called *irony*—a few months after I moved in with Aunt Rose, Hazel and Artie retired, sold their house in Harmon and moved south. Fate plays tricks like that. People find their hats after they have lost their heads. Before her parents left town, I learned that Alexis had married an opera singer twenty years her senior and the couple had built a house down in the Carolinas. That was the last I heard of her until last summer. In my dreams at night we would meet, at her parents' home, at the train station, walking down the village streets. In reality, she had left me behind and gone off to live a grown-up life as surely as the adult Wendy had forgotten Peter Pan.

Living with Aunt Rose was not an unmixed blessing. Despite her big heart and all her wonderful attributes, she had other qualities which could only be deemed *wicked*. She had a short fuse and would grow very angry with you at the least provocation. Although Aunt Rose was quite capable of administering the *silent treatment* for weeks on end, she was better known for her big mouth. She would nag, nag, nag and rant, rant, rant, and it was not uncommon for her tirades to be spiced with language that was uncouth, vulgar and lewd. She referred to African-Americans as *niggers* long after that word had become forbidden, If you put your hands over your ears and said, "Aunt Rose, please stop," she would deliver a dissertation on the River Niger and how it all derived from the French word for *black*. Gay men were *fruits*, and the term never failed to evoke in my mind pictures of human-size peaches, grapes and tangerines waving their hands as they pranced down the street. All this came from the daughter of immigrants who, in her own youth, had been subjected to ethnic slurs such as *wop* and *guinea*. Eventually I realized that it was all for shock value. Aunt Rose was, in reality, a fairly tolerant person. "There is some good in everyone," she would declare. How else could she have put up with me for thirty years?

Most annoying was her practice of *rubbing it in*. If there was some area of your life about which you were supersensitive—if you were overweight or going bald or had a minimum-wage job, for example—she would find a way to work it into every conversation. She would then cackle while you squirmed. Likewise, if there was something in your past which was better forgotten—an abortion, a bit of thievery, a sorry love affair, a fight with a cop that resulted in a broken nose—Aunt Rose would see that it was engraved in stone. She knew everyone's secrets and none of them were safe with her.

This particular form of torture was reserved for those relatives who had disappointed her, and we all did disappoint her sooner or later. My cut was the deepest, however. It had not taken long for Aunt Rose to discover that she had opened her home to a pretender. The bedraggled niece who had shown up on her doorstep and invoked the name of Saint Dymphna was not the Real Me, as she had first supposed, but a shadowy rag doll semblance of her former self. Time and again she would point out that I did not have her fooled. She knew me for an imposter. She would reminisce about the night when she had watched the Real Me take a turn on the flying swings at the Firemen's Bazaar. "You took my breath away," she would tell me. "You were as graceful as a bird. Now here you are—*a bull in a china shop*." I pointed out to her that I had always been *a bull in a china shop*, and that perhaps she had been watching Alexis by mistake. Or maybe the magic of those flying swings had invested the Real Me, if for only a moment, with the grace of an angel. The mere thought of it caused my heart to ache.

Not that Aunt Rose would ever give up on me, not ever. All her days she recounted how Saint Monica had prayed for her profligate son Augustine until, one day, *voila,* he saw the light. She would continue to pray for me until I did likewise. Her very last words were for me. Before she died, she looked at me and said, "Why are you crying? You know I will always be with you."

Aunt Rose tried her best to put me on the path to adulthood, but the one thing she was unable to do was to find me steady work. It was not for lack of trying. She called up all her friends, relations and casual acquaintances. She cashed in her markers and pulled out all the stops. Finding me a foothold in the work-place proved to be an almost insurmountable task.

It is a sad reality that the majority of people on the autism spectrum are either unemployed or underemployed. The stereotype of the highly paid scientist with Asperger's Syndrome in Silicon Valley is the exception, not the rule. It is a great accomplishment for most of us to simply have a job. Regardless of our intellects, education or talents, we are the last to be hired and the first to be let go. Nearly all employers are neurotypicals; they feel most comfortable with their own. Many persons on the spectrum have such negative experiences early in life that they never develop the self-discipline to persevere. Neurotypicals go through hard times as well, but somehow they hang onto hope. They develop what people call a *thick skin*. Aspies, on the other hand, learn never to expect good things. How many potential Einsteins or Emily Dickinsons have been dragged down to despair too early? How many, with paralysis in their souls, have watched helplessly as their talents withered to dust, never to bloom? As for me, a nightmarish image of what a job entailed was planted in my mind early on.

There was much excitement in the town where I went to high school when IBM decided to locate a branch of its headquarters nearby. The folks who worked for IBM were paid a much higher salary than anyone else in that backwater region, and had more material goods and status. It was tacitly assumed that scholastically advanced students—and I was still included in that group—would be aiming for such a career, if not at IBM itself, then in a similar corporate environment.

I never really learned what it was that the IBM employees actually *did*, but I knew what they looked like and where they worked. Their offices were situated in the midst of a vast corporate park, isolated from the world beyond by an electric gate. We were taken to visit on a field trip. The buildings were large and foreboding, giant structures of concrete and steel. There was glass aplenty, but none of the windows opened. In fact, the building was so tightly sealed that not a whisper of wind from the outside could enter. The people that worked there, men and women, all looked alike in their gray flannel suits. They pushed papers around in windowless cubicles, drank coffee and sported phony, plastic smiles on their immaculately scrubbed faces. For recreation they got drunk at inane Christmas parties, attended office picnics and entertained the boss at dinner. (*This last I gleaned from watching TV*). My entire life would be like high school without the possibility of parole. Here you would not graduate in a few years. You would be trapped in this ice palace until you turned sixty five and, to my adolescent eyes, ready for either a nursing home or the graveyard.

College was seen as the prerequisite to such a career. Perhaps that is why I entered into it with such a bad attitude.

I wonder how someone as well read as I could have been so blind. People work in zoos, on ranches, in theatres, on boats, in small boutiques. Some have jobs in historic house museums as I do today. Others become wedding photographers or D.J.s and spend their life attending parties even if they do not have friends to invite them. A little guidance might have spared me from wasting what should have been my most productive years vainly trying to hammer a square peg into a round hole. It would have been better to search for a square hole.

Neurotypicals seem to judge the worth of a job primarily by its paycheck. When my Cousin Jan signed on with a new employer, the first question Aunt Rose asked was, "How much are you making?" Aspies, on the other hand, appreciate first and foremost a work environment in which they can be comfortable, which insulates them from undue stress and allows them to thrive and to make use of their special skills and interests. My brother was light-years ahead of me in this. He instinctively realized that he could never be happy outside the music field and that is where he focused his job search. The shadow of the IBM cubicle never darkened his mind.

The truth was that I had little chance of ever landing that corporate-style job. Through her friends, Aunt Rose arranged several interviews for me, and despite my new clothes, my proper haircut and my subdued demeanor, any interviewer worth his salary could look at me and see the not-wanting to inside.

Despairing of finding me a *real* job, Aunt Rose lobbied her neighbors for local part-time gigs: working as an election registrar, answering phones for an uncle, dog-walking, and a recess monitor at the school playground. These temporary jobs were better suited for me. I even tried my hand at babysitting, fulfilling a girlhood dream. This, however, was not without its problems. Like my mother before me, I lacked the ability to deal with children. In theory it should have been easy as, in so many ways, I was still a child myself. Unfortunately, when real children looked at me they saw a grown-up who refused to behave like a grown-up and thought they could put one over on me. That was the road to trouble.

Returning to school seemed the safest course. I took graduate courses in American History and Political Science. At this time, my Dad had, or claimed to have, close ties with several elected officials. He was forever promising to "put in a good word for me," and find me a staff job with a county or New York State politico. I should have learned my lesson as a child when he promised to buy me a new toy. Nevertheless, I believed him and kept waiting for him to come through. It proved to be empty boasting on my father's part. Soon enough, his beloved nursing home project came apart at the seams and not one of his alleged political buddies stretched out a hand to save it.

A local vocational school was offering a career counseling service. Aunt Rose and Uncle Jim drove me there for several nights and I took a battery of aptitude tests. The results showed that I had a strong bent toward the legal profession. That finding was sound. Many aspies are drawn to the legal field and I did show talent for research and analysis and the formation of logical arguments that a career in law demands. In addition, I recalled only too well certain times in my college years when a little legal knowledge would have come in handy. Furthermore, the law was attractive in that it appeared to transcend the arbitrary. There are statutes and there are precedents and these are rules that the court will apply fair and square. (*Like many neophytes, I confused law with justice*). Dad had once confided to me that he himself had planned to attend law school on the GI Bill, but with a wife to support, this goal had become impractical. He agreed that I had the makings of a brilliant legal mind and law school would be an excellent choice.

If a brilliant legal mind was all that was needed for success in law; I would be sitting on the Supreme Court right now rather than scratching out a living from several part-time jobs. Unfortunately, there is also a certain decorum which is expected of lawyers as there is in all professions. One needs the skill to maneuver through the *old-boy's network* that is the legal community and a successful attorney must act the part. After all, it serves one not at all to write the most scintillating well-reasoned brief since Oliver Wendell Holmes, if you alienate judge and jury by acting too eccentric.

On a cold February day, I took the train down to Fordham University in the Bronx and took the LSAT *(the Law School Entrance Exam)*. I passed with flying colors and thank God for that. My college grades had been abysmal. Even with several postgraduate courses to pad my record, admission to law school proved surprisingly difficult to come by. The first eighteen law schools I chose—all located in the South—rejected me out of hand. Then, on the day of my grandmother's funeral, an acceptance arrived from a law school in Boston. It seemed like such an auspicious omen, that I was even prepared to brave the Massachusetts weather. I studied the map, and no matter what angle I looked at, the words *too cold* sprang to mind. Nonetheless, I resolved to bundle up and take the chance. Aunt Rose offered the only dissenting voice. She asked whether I might not be happier if I stayed at home and found what she called "a quirky, offbeat job." Aunt Rose did not know I was an aspie, but she was a keen judge of character. I should have listened to her.

Law school was not the disaster college had been, although, that is not saying much. In Boston I had a minimal social life. My classmates were not unfriendly toward me, although when they broke up into study groups, I was never invited to join them. Yet, Boston was even colder than I had feared, colder than its position on the map would justify, with raw damp winds blowing in from the ocean which seep into the bone. It was cold not only outside, but inside as well. It seems that folks in New England go into debt to heat their homes, and, for that reason, turn their thermostats down to intolerable levels such as 65 degrees. I had to move several times because I could not cope with the chill and wore my winter coat, indoors and out, for nine months of the year.

Still, I felt more comfortable in Boston than I had in Washington D.C. My fascination with revolutionary rhetoric had given way to more acceptable special interests. I found myself strangely enamored of the National Hockey League. Soon I could rattle off scores, rosters and statistics like a lifelong fan. Portraits of hockey players such as Carol Vadnais and Bobby Orr replaced Che and Satan on my apartment walls. I harbored a *tendresse* for rushing defensemen; back in the long ago when the Real Me had played field hockey, that had been her position. I attended many games at Boston Garden, often by myself. Sometimes I was able to drag someone else with me.

Law school was an actual challenge. It was then I realized that school was not just a place to be warehoused when you were too young for the real world or otherwise unfit. You could actually get an education there. Memorizing names, dates, places and facts always came too easy for me, but now a little extra was required of me.

There is a famous radio talk-show host who claims he does his job "with half my brain tied behind my back." Well, you cannot earn a law degree with half your brain tied behind your back. Supreme Court opinions are not written for four-year-olds, not even for four-year old *savants*. It takes quite an effort to reason it all out. Try describing the evolution of due process from enactment of the 14th Amendment to Plessey v. Ferguson. If the police stop you on the highway and your pipe smells of hashish, can they inquire, "What are you smoking?" without having administered your *Miranda* rights? A recent Supreme Court appointee was asked by a senator that, if the federal government could require one to purchase health insurance under the Commerce Clause, could it also force us to buy broccoli? Those sorts of questions are discussed in law school, and some heavy-duty thinking is necessary to come up with a logical answer.

I learned a lot of interesting things at law school, but how to find a job was not one of them. One summer I obtained an internship at a Massachusetts governmental agency. At first I was delighted to be working, and got along well with my colleagues, all of whom were quite young themselves. Two weeks went by and I messed up badly by issuing a press release in my own name rather than in that of my supervisor. The subject of the press release was trivial, but its issuance constituted a serious breach of protocol. Although I repeated, *I'm sorry*, over and over again, with downcast eyes and abject humility, my supervisor threw such a hissy fit that she refused to speak to me ever again. For the rest of the summer I was ignored or given busy work to do. I tried to make the best of it and discover what I could about the inner workings of state government, but in the end the atmosphere was so hostile that I left a week before my grant expired.

In the third year of law school, all my classmates signed up for Bar Preparatory courses which cost hundreds of dollars. I noticed, on a state-by-state chart of attorney qualifications, that the State of Georgia allowed third year law students to sit for its bar exam. Aha! Why pay good money to take a practice bar exam when, for the same price, you could take a real one, and escape Boston in late February? I took a train to Atlanta, where it was already spring, and sat for the Georgia Bar Exam. It was a lark; I never expected to pass, but I did, and the following summer I took the train back down and was sworn in. My mother encouraged me to stay in Georgia. She wanted me as far from Croton and Aunt Rose as possible. To her, my return to my roots was akin to washing our dirty laundry in public. Georgia had its attractions. It was always summer there and the pace of life down South seemed calming and less stressful now that I was no longer a left-wing spitfire. However, I knew absolutely no one in Georgia. I still had no car and hence no mobility and the Wolf of Loneliness was again nipping at my heels, driving me back home.

Nevertheless, I promised my mother I would not settle down in Croton. Freshly armed with a law degree and having lived for a few years on my own without catastrophe, I felt brave enough to try my wings. At first I targeted the State of Connecticut which was familiar enough, and not so far from home as to be overwhelming. I conducted my job search scrupulously by the rulebook, duly composing a resume and sending out a copy to almost every attorney in Connecticut. In those days, one did not apply for work online. No, you took your resume to the copy shop, painstakingly prepared a cover letter and an envelope for each and carried them to the post office. The result was pretty much the same. They disappeared into a black void. Oh, I actually got a few interviews and I believed each and every person who promised to let me know. While I was waiting, I took the bar exam in New Haven. I passed, but the phone never rang.

Six months out of law school, when I was still sitting by the phone and waiting for the job that never came, I read an article about Atlantic City, New Jersey. Atlantic City, the newspaper said, was about to become a gambling mecca, the site of a new gold rush. Opportunities abounded for young people on the way up and jobs were plentiful. As a child I had visited Atlantic City and the article triggered happy memories.

My parents had never taken family vacations like ordinary people do. However, each August, like clockwork, my grandmother in Ossining headed down the shore and stayed three weeks at the Hotel Roma, together with several of her friends and Mom's kid sister, Aunt Bubbles. A few times when the Real Me was very small, before the baby brother was born, she and her mother had joined them in Atlantic City. These were all-girl outings, no husbands or fathers permitted. The Real Me had thoroughly enjoyed herself, and why not? All day long was spent at the beach and the boardwalk. She visited the Steel Pier and saw a show with a diving horse. Each night was a carnival from which she carried off booty of real value, plastic backscratchers, brightly colored beads and cups in the shape of Mr. Peanut.

So, on a whim I hopped a bus for Atlantic City. I took a winter rental at a beachside motel in Ventnor, just across the Atlantic City line, and bought a second-hand bike. For weeks I biked up and down the boardwalk and knocked on the door of every law office in town. I kept my cool, so very politely, I would smile and nod and wait patiently for the attorney to come out of his office and talk to him grown-up to grown-up. That strategy which had appeared so well-conceived, bore no fruit, and after a month, I was about to give up. I decided to place it in the hands of fate.

I would knock on one last door, and, if this lawyer, too, rejected me, I would head back to Aunt Rose's, hat in hand. That final attorney just happened to have a very important paper due to a very impatient judge the next day, and he had not even begun to draft it yet. *Saint Dymphna sent me*, or, more appropriately, *Saint Ives*, the patron saint of lawyers.

The year I spent in Atlantic City was the happiest since junior high and far more joyful than most of the years to come. I loved the scent of the sea—without the harsh Boston weather—and I gloried in trekking up and down the boardwalk. There were new casinos rising every day, and it was all quite exciting. A strange and intriguing culture was being born. Atlantic City had not yet been fully transformed into the Las Vegas of the East. The Hotel Roma and the Steel Pier were gone, but there was still enough left of the quaint old seaside resort to make me feel at home. If you've ever spent time on a rundown beach strand in the off-season, you know the odd, quirky types that gather there. In that milieu, I could almost pass for normal.

I was so proud of myself, having landed a job by the mere strength of my personality. No one had called a friend of a friend and I had not even been answering an ad. My boss was an Atlantic City native who was connected to everyone in town. He could lay claim to fascinating friends who handed out free movie passes and complimentary meals and all manner of treasure. The only other employee was his 23-year-old secretary, a former Marine from Macon, Georgia who found me clever and a bit intimidating. Funny, but she, a southerner, preferred punk to country music. Can you believe that? Still, she did not complain too vehemently when I changed the dial of the office radio to a country station. We worked in a seaside building on Atlantic Avenue that was old and worn-in, our clients were off-beat and intriguing, our cases varied and challenging. So long as I was willing to work late at night, my boss was not too strict about my habit of stumbling in shortly before 10 in the morning. This, in so many ways, was the best of all possible jobs for one such as me.

When my winter rental ran out, I located a basement apartment in an old Victorian house two blocks from the ocean in Ventnor. My landlady was a widow, another old-timer, who treated me well. She would wait up for me at night when work ran late and when the furnace broke down, she had it fixed immediately, knowing that I could not tolerate the cold. She had no children of her own, but possessed a white cat, a bagel-eating dog and a sister and niece who lived nearby. In the afternoon she would sit with the cat and the dog and watch soap operas. Sometimes I would come home for lunch and join them for *Guiding Light*. My landlady filled me in on the current storyline: who was cheating who, who was secretly married to whose long-lost daughter, and who was plotting to kidnap the local mogul, sparking a fascination with the soap that lasted years.

Early that summer, I took the New Jersey Bar Exam and passed on the very first try—this is three, if you are keeping score—but this was the only time the achievement had meaning. My boss and our secretary came with me to the swearing-in and threw a little party that evening. The feeling was sweet. I had found a new home. I would settle down in South Jersey and practice law. Unfortunately, my happily-ever-after did not last too long.

After a year had gone by, I felt so secure in my budding career, that I dug into my savings and bought my first automobile. I had never had a problem making my way around Atlantic City and Ventnor. The island was flat and made for bike-riding. In good weather, I would pedal to work along the boardwalk. At other times I would jump aboard one of the jitneys which came along every few minutes. However, for the long-term, investment in my very own car seemed in order. After all, the county courthouse was on the mainland and so was the township that my boss represented. I was in luck, or so it seemed. One of our clients worked at a Chevy dealership and got me a bargain on a used two-tone red and silver Chevette. How proud I was the day I drove it off the lot! Imagine me, a real grown-up!

As fate would have it—and this is called *irony*—two weeks after I purchased the Chevette, my boss came in on a Friday afternoon and shocked me by solemnly announcing, "Clean out your desk. This isn't working out." My face froze in stunned disbelief. I had thought it was working out just fine! I pleaded, I cajoled, I argued, I begged, but to no avail. His mind was made up to fire me.

In hindsight, I should have seen it coming. Several of my personality traits had frayed the boss's nerves. Now that I had realized it was proper to comb my hair, I did it everywhere, in the office, in his car, even in court. He had asked me not to do it, but I saw no harm in it and continued to brandish the comb at will. My stim also annoyed him as it had Aunt Rose. (*A stim or self-stimulant is a device that many autistic people use to calm themselves down. A stim could be, for instance, a series of repetitive motions like arm-flapping or spinning, or it might entail carrying around an implement and playing with it.*) My stim is nibbling on a pen and I developed the habit in high school when I was deep into regression mode. My boss would ask me, "do you have to do that?" "Yes I had to do that."

One of my boss' fascinating friends was Bob Guccione, the editor of *Penthouse* magazine. As a feminist, the whole concept of *Penthouse* freaked me out. I had no problem accepting his largesse, but whenever Guccione came to visit, I did not have the sense to put on a poker face and hold my tongue like a responsible mature adult would surely have done. Instead I would make catty remarks, never to his face, of course, but well within earshot.

It must have been the *Ducks Unlimited* affair that finally did me in. My boss represented, and was an officer of, the local chapter of a hunting association known as *Ducks Unlimited*. One day a shipment of flannel shirts came into the office destined for the headquarters of *Ducks Unlimited*. They were cool funky shirts, decorated with images of ducks in various poses, and I made known my desire to possess one of these garments. My boss said, no, they had already been ordered and paid for, and he had no authority to give one to me. I was downcast and disappointed, but, so far as I was concerned, this was the end of the matter. Somewhere along the line, however, one of the boxes was broken into and several shirts were stolen. I was accused. Now, I had not taken the shirts, truly not, and I saw no reason to treat the accusation in the serious manner in which it had been leveled. To my boss, this was a *big* deal indeed, and, to this very day, I am probably Suspect No. 1.

On the other hand, the fault could not completely be laid at my feet. My boss was a lone wolf by nature. He really had no desire for a permanent partner or an associate. Now that I had passed the Bar, I was entitled to expect a salary higher than $200 per week, perhaps my name on his letterhead, and the acknowledgment of a permanent status in his office. These were gestures he had no intention of making.

The sensible course would have been to remain in Atlantic City and look for another job. I probably could have gotten one too, for the economy was booming, the city was rising from the ashes. I had a car and a license to practice law in the State of New Jersey, and nowhere near the baggage that I would later accumulate. My boss would certainly have given me a reference, at least *he would have* had I not had a meltdown one weekend and called up all his friends, complaining of my ill treatment at his hands.

Unfortunately, the shock of being fired from my first real job sent me reeling. I fled headlong from New Jersey as Lot had fled from Sodom. Now that I had a car of my own, I heard the call of the open road. I had spent my childhood enthralled by westerns in which the message was always this: No matter what troubles have befallen you, no matter what sorrows clouded your past; a new life waits along the trail of the setting sun. I spent the next year on the road, but, no, I never found what I was searching for. At first I rather enjoyed myself. Owning a car at last made me feel liberated and brave. Avoiding the interstates with all their stress and relentless conformity, I opted for the back roads. With a mild euphoria I sang along with a hundred country stations. I became acquainted with a hundred dots on the map, and ate at a hundred little eateries in small towns with funny sounding names. Soon enough, however, the sense of adventure gave way to an uneasy feeling of dispossession. When you travel aimlessly and alone, every town is a heartless place, and, after a while, each motel room is lonelier than the last.

I drove first to Hershey, Pennsylvania and I settled down for several weeks, drawn there not by the chocolate factory but by the Hershey Bears. I had it in mind to write a novel about a down-at-the-heels minor league hockey team owned by a woman with some serious skeletons in her closet. One night their best defenseman would go down with an injury and all would be in despair. In would walk a former National Hockey League star in disguise and everything would be turned around. It would be a story with a moral. The ringer's arrival would carry the team to victory, sure enough, but murder, mayhem and the laying bare of secrets long-hidden would soon follow. I had it all plotted out in my mind and, although I spent a lot of time doing *research* at the stadium, actually putting the words on paper was just too tedious.

When spring came, I forgot about the Hershey Bears and made my way to Stillwater, Minnesota. I took a tour of the former penitentiary where once the Younger Brothers who rode with Jesse James had been incarcerated after a bank robbery gone wrong. There had been three of them, Jim, Bob and Cole. Bob had died in prison. After twenty-five years, Cole and Jim had been paroled. Jim Younger—and this is a true story—committed suicide soon after his release. One glance at the twentieth century was enough to convince him that he did not belong there, and he flung himself out the window of his hotel room. Cole went on living. He was as intelligent, handsome and personable as an outlaw can be. He hooked up with old friend Frank James and they toured with Bill Hickok's Wild West Show, just two old desperadoes, past their prime, off to see the world. Still, you wonder if, each time they passed a bank or heard a train whistle, a little flame did not flicker forth from the ashes. Cole would wink at Frank who would smile back . . . *nah, not us.*

I followed the trial of Jesse James' assassin out to Colorado. I saw Boulder and Golden and Denver, and what a thrill it was waking up to the sight of those mountains. It is true what they say, the heights do make you giddy. I wound up down in the flats in Greeley where the Broncos conduct training camp, and worked there six months for an 82-year-old attorney whose roots went back to FDR. He sent me to conduct research on an extremely convoluted case involving a lonely widow woman, nine hungry children and a suave but amoral land speculator. I delved into interesting subjects such as *water rights*; a problem that no one in New York or New Jersey bothers their heads about, as water is so abundant. What we here in the East want to know most about water is how to keep it out of our basements. Out West, on the other hand, water is scarce and is often fought over with such passion that you would think it were gold.

My boss in Greeley was fond of me and actually offered me a full time position in his firm, but as winter loomed again, loneliness and homesickness overcame me. I was also becoming incredibly bored with the nine little brats and their foolish mother, having mapped out the case nine ways to Sunday. One day I announced that I was going home for Christmas and headed east.

I never got there. I made it as far as Virginia Beach—yes, I know it is not in a straight line—and I had a major meltdown. To this day, I could not tell you how I got to Virginia Beach, but I remember well what I did there. I lay on my back in an off-season motel room and stared at the ceiling for days on end, listening to the call of the pounding surf outside my window.

I had never come so close to the brink, not even in those terrible first days in the Kingdom of Frost. Here I had wandered from the sea to the mountains and back again, and nowhere had I found a friend or a place I belonged. The spell that bound me was too deep to be broken. Despair overcame me. What point was there in going on? It would only be more of the same, or it would be worse.

At this time I was just past thirty, old for a horse, but not for a human being. Yet, by now I had recognized that something was wrong with me, something deep, something inbred, more than transitory misfortune, but no one had ever been able to give me a clue as to what the problem might be. *Don't fit in on this planet* was not then a cognizable complaint. I might well have been under a witch's spell which no earthly treatment or antidote could break.

A few days after Christmas, I spied a Roman Catholic Church a few blocks away. The Real Me had been an honorable observant Catholic. She had proudly made her First Communion and Confirmation and, before meat was allowed on Fridays, she had eaten popcorn for breakfast, lunch and dinner. Her neighborhood in Harmon contained a small, cozy chapel with beautiful stained-glass windows which gave it the look of a tiny Gothic cathedral. Every Sunday she would dutifully attend Mass, although much of the time she had to go there alone. Her Dad had left his faith in Nagasaki and her Mom was too frightened to enter a church, afraid that the priest could peer into her soul, see that she was using Birth Control and cause the earth to open and swallow her. The Real Me would cast her eyes about for the pew that held Alexis and her mother, Hazel, but they were not always present. Alexis' dad was a Methodist and she was obliged to devote equal time to that persuasion. The Real Me gloried in the ritual and mystery of the Mass, especially the Latin words she did not understand but liked the sound of: *Dominus vobiscum, Spirita sancta.*

On Thursday afternoon, the Catholic students were released early so that they might walk up the street to the parochial school and attend catechism class. The Real Me had looked forward to it. She had a bent toward theology and did not consider it a conflict with modern science. Moreover, ruins of the old Croton aqueduct ran under the Catholic Church, and the kids could happily explore these while waiting for the bell. One day Alexis confronted the nun after class—she was one of those old school nuns with a full habit and a mirthless expression—and posed this question. "The Bible tells us that God created the world in six days. However, in school they teach us the theory of evolution, that it took millions and millions of years. How do you explain that?" She thought she had the nun dead to rights on that one, but the sister did not blink an eye. She calmly looked at Alexis and asked, "How long is a day in heaven?" The Real Me nodded. She understood.

After the move north, my mother located the nearest Catholic Church and dropped me off there for a few Sundays with the baby brother in tow. It was not the same, and I soon apostatized. I was not going to be dumped off at a strange church to assuage my mother's sense of guilt for having fallen into the sin of contraception. Since then I had attended Mass only with Aunt Rose on Christmas Eve and at Grandma's funeral. The sudden appearance of a Catholic church in Virginia Beach after all these years did seem, literally, a godsend.

The following afternoon I marched up the steps to the rectory and knocked on the door. The priest answered the knock with a golf bag slung over his shoulder. That should have given me a clue as to how this intrusion would be accepted. Nevertheless, I persisted. In my despair, I begged, cajoled and pleaded. "*Please, please, please.* This is the end of the line. Can you not see?" The priest stared at me in exasperation. Whatever did I expect of *him*? Stubbornly I held my place in the doorway; my hands folded around my waist, and ranted and raved until he was forced to make some feeble response. Perhaps I should talk to the sisters up on Abbey Road, six traffic lights to the north, and turn right at the Shell station. As if I knew my way around Virginia Beach! No, no, no. I screamed in distress. I did not want to go talk to the sisters on Abbey Road. Was it not his duty to help me, comfort me, and provide me with solace? What kind of priest was he? Hadn't he taken an oath to God at the time of his ordination not to turn away those in need? He just stared blankly and shook his head as if I had been speaking in Sanskrit.

Understand, this was a bad priest, far worse that the priests who molested the little altar boys. God can bestow His grace upon sinners and turn them into saints, but a bucket of lukewarm water goes down the drain. As any true Christian knows, the most deadly sin of all is indifference. It's called *sloth*. *Sloth* means more than laziness; it means failure to act when actions are called for. Had I indeed walked out into the sea, as I was very close to doing, my death would have been upon his head. Had it been within my power to do so, I would have defrocked him then and there, *bell, book and candle*.

I ran right out to my Chevette and gunned it due north. My fury had driven all thoughts of suicide away. With my last tank of gas, I headed straight for the Chesapeake Bay Tunnel and the Garden State. I did not stop at Abbey Road. I was so very angry at this false priest that I even forgot to avoid the highways. All that day and all that night I drove north, composing succinct letters to the Pope in my head. "Your Holiness, there is something you should know. . ." At a rest stop on the Garden State, I parked the Chevette and took a break. Morning saw me in Haverstraw where I stopped to buy Christmas presents—better late, than never. Throwing the gifts on the seat beside me, I tore up the Palisades and stormed across the Bear Mountain Bridge. Soon I was pulling up in front of Aunt Rose's driveway, and what a delightful surprise awaited me there.

In my absence, Toy Garden had taken root. She had never mentioned it, not once, not in all our telephone conversations and letters. It was at its most spectacular, all dressed up for Christmas: a little plastic boy clothed in blue, held a trumpet, surrounded by Christmas ornaments on poles. A miniature castle beckoned me on. Toy Santas and milkmaids were interspersed with the fish, animals and gnomes. My eyes widened in delight. I stepped out of the car and I touched them. A benevolent magic emanated from these salvaged treasures. From that time on, my life began to bloom.

Aunt Rose agreed to take me back, on one condition. This time there would be no moping around. I would have to find a job like any other adult. Later she would claim that she had finally given me *a kick in the pants.*

Kick in the pants or no, my only occupation for months was to help Aunt Rose tend the toy garden. I roamed the streets, like a Viking with an eye to pillage, searching for discarded toys put out for garbage pick-up, and those just thrown carelessly into the street. I would frequent tag sales for hidden treasures. The trophy I reckoned the best? It was a large plastic kangaroo wearing a baseball cap. I found it on the curb, waiting for the trashmen. Tucking my finds under my arm, I would proudly carry my booty home to Aunt Rose and watch mesmerized as has-been playthings were turned into garden ornaments. My Cousin Lou, a housepainter, brought her poles on which to mount the toys. Special soaps were kept above the sink just for these projects. Aunt Rose had assembled various shades of paint and shellacs and various size jars, the rims of which she would heat and press them against the bottom of the toy to burn a circular hole in the plastic. She welded a plastic bat into the outstretched arms of my kangaroo, and we placed him over the driveway gate. He stood there for years like a sentry until some dastardly vandals made off with him.

I was now possessed of a certain cachet. Kids would pause on their walk home from the elementary school around the corner; regard our yard with great admiration, and *ooh* and *aaah.* The media would descend on our door, not only the local press but visitors from New York City. Chauncey Howell of Channel 7, the ABC affiliate, brought a news crew to do a feature on the toy garden. Perfect strangers, upon hearing of my address, would so tenderly remark, "Oh, the house with the toys."

Yet, I was still earning no income to contribute to household expenses. One day, Aunt Rose, exasperated, sent me to see Monsignor at Holy Name of Mary Church. I duly walked down to the rectory, dragging my heels, with the memory of the debacle in Virginia Beach still raw in my memory. However, this pastor was a good shepherd, and he heard me out patiently, perhaps because he knew my family and considered me part of his flock. He advised me to "Get off the dime." When I asked Monsignor to clarify these instructions, he told me to stop lollygagging around and do something constructive that very day.

So I did. I retrieved the new issue of the *Pennysaver* from the mailbox and turned to the *Help Wanted* ads. There was one job listed that caught my eye. It had nothing to do with the law, or anything that would ever have occurred to me. The position advertised was for a photographer's assistant to work on high school proms.

Two decades before I joined the company, a photographer and a salesman had combined forces to create Varsity Studios in Ossining. Varsity did prom photography at many of the high schools in the tri-state area. Every spring they put out the call for two hundred photographers, salespeople and assistants to work from April through June.

Perhaps Varsity had covered my own high school proms. I had skipped them both. Even if I had been invited, I would not have gone. At the time I thought the whole notion of proms terribly *bourgeois* and concerned myself solely with social justice and world peace. Fifteen years on, I as beginning to have regrets.

No one can turn back the clock, but I discovered the pleasures of living vicariously. When I signed on with Varsity, my head was full of visions of high school gyms decorated as moonlight gardens with waterfalls of paper streamers, and stars fashioned of silver foil. At first there were indeed a few of those. By the end of the 1980s, however, most high school proms were held at banqueting houses, country clubs or high-class hotels, places that I would never have had occasion to visit on my own. I worked first as an assistant and later a salesperson, performing every task from passing out silk flowers to posing students for table shots, to taking their orders for prom photos. After each prom, I would bring home a silk rose as a souvenir. (*After Aunt Rose died, my cousins brought a dumpster to the house and tossed in dozens of vases filled with dust-covered silk roses as though they meant nothing at all*). There was music and companionship, and free eats as well. I could cast a surreptitiously covetous look at the boys in tux and tails—well, one can *look*, certainly? Best of all, this was a job that allowed me to work at night when the world is less stressful. For twenty years, I looked forward to each spring and I never had enough of proms. Even so, the concept of *team player* was difficult to grasp, even when the *team* was only a photography crew. Several times I was reprimanded for not following the proper procedures, but my genuine enthusiasm and love of the job touched the hearts of my employers, and I was forgiven. I held on for years after Varsity Studios sold out to a regional studio in Rhode Island and the regional studio then merged with a national school photography corporation. Ultimately, the national company replaced the Varsity part-timers with their own high-tech crews.

This is the lesson I learned from my prom job: Yes, if you are dressed reasonably well and do not behave too weirdly, you could probably hang out in the lobby of the Waldorf Astoria or an equally wonderful place, and no one will bother you. However, nothing opens doors so easily as these three charmed words: *I'm working here.*

I continued to search for work in the legal field as well. For eighteen months I was employed in the collections department of a magazine headquartered in lower Westchester County. Unfortunately, the boss was an ill-tempered harridan and impossible to work for, resulting in an incredible amount of turnover. People would work there for a few days or a few weeks and then disappear. When I first joined the company, the boss would fire employees, left and right, and her unemployment insurance premiums skyrocketed. She then adopted a policy of hounding her workers incessantly until they quit, making them ineligible for benefits. The nature of my job was borderline skuzzy as well, to extract money from the small business owners who advertised in the magazine.

During my stint at the magazine, I met a young attorney my own age who was one of the small advertisers I had been sent out to dun. She had signed up for the court panel which assigns appellate lawyers to represent convicted prisoners. Finding herself overwhelmed, she needed an assistant to draft and research appellate briefs. I jumped at the opportunity. This was work with a high moral purpose. Attempting to free an incarcerated client made me feel ennobled, like a knight on crusade. The attorney and I would travel together to visit our clients in prison. We would have *power lunches* in the North Castle Diner where we would spread the transcripts on our knee and hash over the legal questions presented. I would pick up her mail when she went on vacation, and I took her horseback riding one year on her birthday.

My eyes had been opened through the nurturing magic of the Toy Garden. At long last I had realized that satisfying productive work did not have to include the corporate lifestyle or the windowless cubicle. If these things were not for me, I did not have to dig a hole in the ground and climb into it. I had marketable skills and talents which I could sell on a free-lance basis. In my hometown, and in the little towns surrounding it, there were attorneys who could not afford to hire a full-time associate, but needed someone on a per diem basis, to conduct legal research, to answer calendars and to serve process. There were lawyers who called only once or twice, but with some I forged long-term relationships. Older, more experienced attorneys actually asked me for my opinions and treated them as worthy of respect. They wrote me *checks*. The telephone would ring and it might well be for *me*. I had finally found a way to flourish and be creative in my fashion. I signed up for every part-time and free-lance job that I could find and, from that point on, I was never out of work. No, it was not regular, full-time employment with benefits, and the income I received was rarely commensurate with my education and my skills. Nevertheless, the day I discovered how to carve my own peculiar niche in the workplace was the day I stopped feeling like an absolute, one hundred percent *victim*.

Imaginary Lovers

•

*T*he Greek transgendered prophet Tiresias was once asked to arbitrate a dispute between the gods. Zeus and Hera, the King and Queen of Heaven were having a marital spat. Hera was berating Zeus for his shameless disregard of his marriage vows and his many infidelities. Zeus proffered an ingenious defense. He told Hera that, since women were more capable of sexual pleasure than men, when he did come to her bed, she derived far more delight from the act than he. Therefore, she really ought to cut him some slack! Hera was infuriated. That's nonsense, she roared. What a cop out! Everyone knows that men enjoy sex much more than women do! They decided to put the question to Tiresias, who had seen the issue from both sides.

If sexual pleasure was a pie cut into ten pieces, replied the prophet, one slice of pie would be given to the male partner and nine to the female. You know that Zeus was grinning from ear to ear. Hera, on the contrary, flew into a rage and immediately struck Tiresias blind. That is how the gods deal with impertinent mortals.

The Greeks certainly believed Tiresias. That is why the Athenians kept their wives on such a short leash while they disported themselves with boys. How else could they build a civilization? Give the women the same privileges as men and life would be one long bacchanal.

Times and mores change, of course. Medieval society understood that both genders were naturally lustful, savage, envious and voracious and, left to their own devices, all hell would break loose, literally. It was only the restraining influence of the Church which stood guard between barbarous humankind and utter chaos.

By the Victorian age, sex had become a regrettable necessity. No one really enjoyed it, least of all, women. Whereas the Middle Ages had spoken of a husband "doing his duty" to his wife, now the wife had to submit to the husband. Submit she did, if only in exchange for prizes of real value, such as a comfortable home, children, a respectable place in society. Poor women would sometimes fall into dire straits and sell their bodies for mere money, without marriage. They were objects more of pity than of contempt. Of course, a woman who owned up to *enjoying* sex was considered a medical anomaly. Men, on the other hand, acknowledged their animal natures, but felt obliged to be discreet. Victorian men were not proud of falling prey to such base instincts, nor did they boast of their sexual prowess, the way men do today.

The Real Me did not know much about the Victorians, but Greek mythology was one of her special interests. When she read the story of Tiresias, she was glad that she had not, after all, been born a boy. She understood enough to savor a promise of good things certain to come her way. As a matter of course, she would enjoy a happy and fulfilling sex life in adulthood. She foresaw it with as much certitude as she anticipated fame and fortune and the worldly success befitting to one of her vaunted intellect. Yes, and she expected that her kid brother would be her pal. None of this would ever come to pass.

It is not uncommon for aspies to experience problems in the sexual arena. Many of us are too shy and awkward to succeed at the game. Some of us do not like to be touched. It's a sensory issue. I suspect, as well, that many of us are a bit too androgynous to fit comfortably into pre-assigned gender roles. All three factors would apply to me, but, in addition, with one more ingredient that created a very strange brew.

My own relations with the opposite sex have been so puzzling that I was unable to explain them, even to my therapist. In an attempt to convey my meaning, I was forced to call upon another icon of Greek mythology, the deity Artemis, virgin goddess of the hunt. You could call it the *Artemis Syndrome*.

Have you ever wondered why Artemis the Huntress was worshipped as a Virgin Goddess? It seems incongruous, at first blush, I know. When I was in college, the professors tried to explain it away. "Artemis was not really a *virgin*," they would say, "merely *unattached*."

The Greeks may have been polytheistic, but they were not stupid. They were well acquainted with the difference between a virgin goddess and one who merely had no consort. Since they knew her better than most, we ought to take them at their word. If you have ever run with Artemis, then you might understand. The excitement is all in the thrill of the chase. I disdained the low-hanging fruit and intensely pursued that which was so tantalizingly out of reach. To put it less elegantly, I became a stalker.

As a teenager in the Kingdom of Frost, I was mired in home-sickness and despair, like a child in a storm. Everything of value seemed lost beyond recall or as unattainable as the stars. And so it began—a lifelong yearning for what I could never possess. I was doomed forever to feel like the ghost of a lost little girl, even as my body grew into that of a flesh and blood woman.

When it did, I found that everything that I wanted, all that I had ever dreamed of was embodied in a series of beautiful young men, all extremely desirable and all just out of reach. Most tellingly, each of them possessed that one quality I want-ed most of all. They were loved. They had friends, and lots of them. They were respected and looked up to. They were in the midst of the swirl of life while I watched helplessly from the sidelines.

How did it all begin? A few of my targets had no idea I was even alive, and my pursuit of them was fueled only by my imagi-nation. More often, it began as a passing flirtation whose false promises I had believed. Sometimes a boy would extend me the hand of sympathy, and I would overreach by demanding more.

Yes, you might call it stalking but it was also supplication. Remember that young man on whose account I was thrown out of college? I was supposedly harboring the design to kill his girlfriend Betty. Nothing could have been further from the truth. He could have continued to date Betty. In fact, he could have married Betty and I would have gladly come to their wedding if he had reserved for me a place in his heart, be it ever so small.

I would have so willingly shared any bounty that might have come my way for I no longer had the pride to be possessive. Indeed, I was more like a beggar in the street, thankful for whatever crumbs might fall from Prince Charming's table. At first I was humble and grateful as a beggar should be, head bowed and eyes cast down. It was only when I was kicked aside, rejected, scorned and belittled, that my natural spirit would reassert itself. I would strike back in anger, like a wounded lion. Or a wounded cougar. Then the skies would open and all manner of trouble might befall.

Last fall I attended a conference in Albany, New York where Dr. Tony Attwood, a world-famous expert on Asperger's Syndrome in girls and women was speaking. During the intermission, I approached him and asked if he had any idea why someone such as I might engage in such behavior. Dr. Attwood replied that many aspies become stalkers. He likened stalking to the pursuit of a special interest except that now another person, rather than an object or body of facts, becomes the subject of fascination. I've pondered that and found that his argument has merit. I can recall well the sense of empowerment and exaltation that the Real Me derived in grappling with the intricacies of Olympian theology. When one is on the trail of a special interest, one is seeking to acquire secret knowledge unshared by ordinary folk; the feeling is quite akin to the thrill of the chase.

In pursuing young men I was trying to acquire, not factual knowledge, but knowledge of intangible qualities I needed to make my life complete, and such information could only be obtained by the capture of one who possessed it.

We desire in a lover what we most feel the lack of in ourselves. Plato wrote about it in one of his dialogues, *The Symposium*. He describes how Socrates attended a dinner party with various other Athenian notables. Among them was the exceedingly handsome, athletic young general, Alcibiades, a major celebrity of his time. When the lights were lowered, Alcibiades moved surreptitiously over to the couch where Socrates lay and made a move on the old philosopher.

When the tale became known, it was the source of much merriment. What would Alcibiades, who had youth and beauty and fame, want with an ugly senior citizen like Socrates? Why, he could have had *anyone!* The answer, of course, is that Socrates had that one quality that Alcibiades was missing. Alcibiades had all the gifts the world could bestow, but he did not have *wisdom.* That was why Alcibiades was unaccountably attracted to Socrates, the possessor of wisdom.

That was also why I spent much of my youth in intense, exhilarating, but ultimately fruitless pursuits of handsome, charismatic, popular young men.

One or two of my quarries were actual celebrities, but most were celebrities only within whatever community I was knocking on the door of at the moment. That student body president in college who brought me so much grief was a prime example. Because they were all surpassingly beautiful and highly popular, other women desired them as much as I did. Even if temporarily unattached, they had no use for the likes of me. The moth is drawn to the flame, and not vice versa. Prince Charming searching high and low for Cinderella makes a fine fairytale, but in real life he would have married an eligible princess without a second glance at the girl with small feet sweeping the palace walk.

But there was another side to the equation as well. If the young men I chased all scorned my advances and ran the other way, I need not have spent a lifetime of celibacy on that account alone. There were plenty of others who did ask me out, and occasionally I did go out on a date, if only because I felt that it was the healthy thing to do. They were not all losers, either. Many of the males who approached me were good-looking, intelligent and personable. Nevertheless, these relationships were doomed from the start.

Right off the bat, any man who asked me out devalued himself in my eyes. What was it that Groucho Marx said about any country club that would have him for a member? Why would any rational man prefer an outcast like myself to someone like Betty, the svelte sophisticated sorority girl, who had all the attributes treasured by the world? Was it just pity? Or did he have some hidden defect, readily apparent to all the Bettys of the world, who were far more savvy than I?

Secondly, I was ill-suited for dating in the traditional sense. I do not drink or mix well at parties. I could not make small talk and I lacked the social graces to sit around and disguise my sheer boredom. I can passably perform the dances the Real Me did at the junior high sock hops, where you twist and spin and wave your arms in the air. Slow dancing? No, sorry. *Two left feet* is the traditional phrase, and that does not even begin to describe my total ineptitude at dancing close together.

Watching a movie is pleasant when you can put your feet up, scarf down popcorn and stim as needed. However, sitting in a crowded theatre for three hours with some guy's arm around your shoulders, mindful of the duty to be on your best behavior is altogether another thing.

Then there were my food aversions, so terribly hard to explain. If we went out to eat in a diner or a pub, I would be just fine. If, however, a man thought to impress me with a meal at a fancy upscale restaurant, his gallantry would fall flat on its face. Worst of all, he might take me home to dine with his parents and disaster would inevitably ensue.

This actually happened to me one New Year's Eve. A cousin had set me up with a friend of his, slightly younger than myself, handsome, bright, considerate and willing to carry the conversation, possibly the very best of those I threw away. His mother had slaved over a hot stove for hours and prepared a gourmet meal for us and, of course, I could eat none of it. The biscuits were tasty and I downed several of them, but the rest I just stared at and fiddled with and tried to hide under the plate. I knew this was going to be our last date, but there was not a thing I could do. This *picky-eater syndrome* arises from autism, but at the time I had no words to explain it.

Often it all came down to sex and my reluctance to engage in it. There was a fellow in Boston who managed one of the boarding houses I passed through seeking a warm place to live. He was a hockey fan like myself. We went together to Bruins and Ranger games, and had spirited discussions about the merits of one team or the other. We might have become pals. He *did* take me to a pub where I could feast on a burger and fries and that problem was avoided, but sex was the crux of the matter. He had not been looking for a pal. What for me was a fun friendship was to him mere foreplay. What he really wanted was for me to take off my clothes and go to bed with him. I strung him along as far as I could, but when he finally put it to me point blank, I had to refuse. That was the last I saw of *him*.

As excited as I might be when stalking a young man, I had little or no interest in sharing an intimate relationship with any of those who actually asked me out on dates. As starved for sexual satisfaction as my body might be, their embraces were unwelcome. If they kissed me with their tongues, I would gag. The missionary position was not for me. I would feel as though I were suffocating and gasp for breath. If we rolled over and I was on top, I was more comfortable, but still derived only mild pleasure. It's not that my partners were all boorish or brutish, not at all. It was me. Only the thrill of the hunt could arouse me. Without the exhilaration of the chase to excite me, I was as bored and unresponsive as an ice sculpture. The wild-eyed huntress turned into a frigid Victorian spinster.

Several winters ago, I happened upon a novel, set in Vienna in the early twentieth century. The hero, a young disciple of Dr. Freud, found himself with a patient, a *petit-bourgeois* accountant who was under the sway of a rather unusual delusion. The accountant fancied that a certain *(married)* Grand Duchess was secretly in love with him, and that she would eventually throw caution to the winds and run to his arms. In expectation of that day, the accountant spent a lot of time hanging around the palace gates, hoping for a glimpse of her carriage. Eventually he became too much of a nuisance for the palace guards to tolerate. They took him into custody and put an abrupt end to his hanging about. It fell to the lot of our hero-psychiatrist to bring the poor accountant to his senses and spare him a long stretch in the loony bin. Rising to the occasion, the hero—in rather short order, I might add—persuaded his patient to turn his attentions from the Grand Duchess to a pretty young widow who worked in his office. Happy ending? Perhaps, but, not in my eyes. No pretty young secretary in the world could have turned my eyes away from the Grand Duchess, not so long as I harbored the faintest flicker of hope that she would one day bestow her grace on me. No, I would have been back down at the palace gates the very next day, come hell or high water. I might never win her, but I would damn well try, and the sheer exhilaration of the attempt would make me feel alive in a way that no everyday secretary ever could though she gave me her whole heart and soul.

Unable to capture my chosen prey, I chose to go hungry. I had once believed that the very act of sex—like the ownership of a car—was a necessary rite of passage and, without physical intimacy, one could never be fully adult. I had a bit of sex, simply because I felt I should, but soon enough grew resigned to its absence. I had no talent or inclination, nor indeed patience, for *faking it* with men who I did not really desire. I let them go their way and turned instead to the lovers there in my mind.

There was a song that I remember from my youth, recorded by the Atlanta Rhythm Section: *Imaginary Lovers Never Turn You Down*. Nor, I may add, do they require lengthy explanations of why you will only eat certain foods or why you feel the need to nibble on a pen. While my parents were still alive and I had numerous relatives around, I felt no pressing need for a husband and family of my own. It was easy enough then to wrap myself in fantasy. Today, I regret the ones I rashly let slip through my fingers. If I had only learned to stifle my discomfort and pretend! When I was young and beautiful, I could have traded my body, as those frigid Victorian women did, in exchange for things of real value, a home and kids and someone with whom to celebrate Christmas.

As the years went by, Aunt Rose would look at me quizzically. My female cousins, all younger than I, would duly show up on family occasions with boyfriends in tow, highlighting the fact that I was always alone. You might think my solitary state would have evoked sympathy, but it was met only by curious stares. Had I been unattractive, physically deformed or mentally retarded, I might have gotten a pass. Instead, I was a sitting duck for the question: what's wrong with *you*?

For a time, I claimed to be gay. There was some basis for this self-identification. The years of longing for the sight of Alexis and that dangerous craving for my mother's love that bordered on the incestuous had persuaded me that, I might indeed, be gay. Moreover, I could fob off a lot of annoying questions that way.

"Will you go out with me?"
"Sorry, I'm a lesbian."
"Why don't you have a husband like your cousins do?"
"Lesbian."
"Why did you lose that job?
"Homophobia."

As far as alibis go, *Because I'm gay*, consistently trumps *Because I'm weird*. Eventually, however, I had to admit the truth to myself. As much as the memory of Alexis might tempt me, I had no real desire for a physical relationship with her or with any other woman. All my imaginary lovers were male. Furthermore, as time wore on, and I failed to produce a girlfriend, the lesbian defense fell flat on its face. It was not until fairly recently that I heard the term *asexual* used to denote a legitimate sexual orientation. For most of my lifetime, asexuals were too cowed to speak up lest they, too, be considered weird. Lately, they have come out of the closet and even have their own website, *Asexuality.org* or *AVEN*. An asexual is defined as someone who has little or no libido and does not experience sexual attraction.

Asexuality is distinguished from *celibacy,* the latter being considered a product of choice.

Had I known about asexuality in my youth, I would without doubt have glommed onto that label as I did to that of gay, and for much the same reason—to ward off embarrassing questions and to place myself within decipherable parameters. Nevertheless, I do have a libido. I am no more a true asexual than I am a lesbian.

The goddess Artemis has another avatar, and that is Selene, the Goddess of the Moon. The moon was treasured by many primitive peoples far beyond the sun—its light pierces the darkness when it is most needed. Were it not for the moon, the night would hang over the earth unbroken like the very shroud of death. Now the moon is beautiful and welcome, but cold, remote and untouchable as well, and faithfully follows her own prescribed path, as the people of Aspergia do. Yet once, even the moon fell in love.

It is said that, as the Goddess Selene passed over the darkened earth, she noticed a beautiful young shepherd boy named Endymion. Selene caused him to fall into a deep enchanted slumber. Thereafter, the moon would pause each night and shed its light on that hillside where Selene made love to the sleeping Endymion. I could well relate to such a tale.

Of course, you cannot take an imaginary lover to a cousin's wedding, and there are times when the glaring absence of a flesh-and-blood companion cannot be disguised.

My cousin Karen was scheduled to be married on my thirty-fourth birthday. When I received my invitation, I was prepared to tender my regrets. By this time, I had had enough experience of life to realize that a wedding is no place for the fatally unattached. Send a gift, send a card, but spare yourself unnecessary pain and *stay home.*

Unfortunately, I had not reckoned with Aunt Rose who was very scrupulous when it came to family obligations. "If you want to live in my house," she thundered. "You live by *my* rules!" You know the drill. As I did want to live in her house, there was no way out but to R.S.V.P. "Yes, I'll be there. No, I won't be bringing a guest."

I took some solace in the expectation that my Aunt Carmela, usually so conscientious about such matters, would surely find me an escort for the evening. I had been to another cousin's wedding some years before, and it had not been so unbearable. Dinner had been a buffet, and there were no assigned tables, and I simply immersed myself in the crowd of relations. Grandma Mariangela had been with us, and I could pass myself off as her caregiver. Now, however, my grandmother was gone, and there was no way around it. Only a date could legitimize me.

When I arrived at Karen's reception, I was shocked to discover that it was a sit-down dinner. Not only that, but I had been *sat down* at a table on a dais with the flower girls and ring bearer. True, a handsome young gentleman was seated there, as well, but he was not meant for me. He was the fiancé of one of the bridesmaids. He announced that, right away, dispelling any illusions that I might have momentarily entertained. That news imparted, he hardly spoke another word all evening. I might as well have been wearing a scarlet *W* on my gown for *Weirdo*.

I tried to make the best of it, but there was no getting past the damage that had been done. When the dancing began, at least I could move around and I danced a few rounds, trying my best not to be clumsy, with another cousin, with Uncle Spence and the DJ who had taken pity on me. I also went out to the terrace for air, a lot of air. Out on the terrace I seethed, I stimmed, I beat my hand against the stone ledge, and I took a solemn vow.

If I live to be 106, I will never, ever again attend another wedding, under any circumstances whatsoever. Better to be hanged, drawn and quartered or broken on the wheel, than to put myself through this kind of anguish again. The earth will open and the Last Judgment will arrive before you'll see my face at anyone's connubial fest.

I have scrupulously kept that vow. Once when I was working a prom I did wander by mistake into a wedding held downstairs at the beach club, and yes, I did linger awhile to partake of the barbecued lamb chops that were peeking out of the buffet. "I'm an old friend of the groom. Indeed, it's a lovely gathering." That does not count. Crashing a wedding is quite permissible.

It was soon after Karen's wedding that I met Julio.

Julio

•

Of all my lovers, there was one who was not entirely imaginary, or, to put it more precisely: *Not imaginary enough.* That was Julio. We met under the sexiest of circumstances. He was brought to me in chains.

After I returned to Croton from my *nearly ending-it-all* in Virginia Beach, I gradually began to put together a patchwork quilt of part-time jobs which might earn me a respectable, if modest income. Much of my work was definitely quirky and a bit off-beat, like the proms, a stint as a night clerk in a motel and another part-time job taking phone orders for *The Federal Jobs Digest.* More often, though, I was given *per diem* assignments by local attorneys that involved legal research and writing, the field in which I had been trained and had substantial skill. These lawyers just assumed that I was studying for the New York Bar and seeking an apprenticeship until then.

In truth, I had no real inclination to take the New York Bar Exam. I already had three bar certificates and little to show for any of them. I had begun to suspect that I might be, as Aunt Rose might say, *barking up the wrong tree.* I strung these attorneys along for some time, but eventually, in order to keep my credibility with my new employers, I had to file an application to take the New York Bar.

While I was waiting to take the bar exam, I volunteered to counsel inmates at Sing-Sing Prison down in Ossining, where my grandfather Charlie had predicted that I would one day wind up. Ever since high school, I had identified with the downtrodden, but by this time I had come to realize that I had little in common with Vietnamese peasants, or migrant farm workers in California, or teenage moms in Harlem. Ah, but the wrongly *(or rightly)* incarcerated? That was a different tale. Did not the Eagles have me in mind in *Desperado* when they sang 'your prison is walking through this world all alone?' What then was more natural than I should gravitate toward criminal law?

I signed on with a volunteer organization whose founder, an attorney from Long Island was himself a former resident of Sing-Sing, having embezzled or commingled clients' funds, the sort of white-collar crimes that lawyers commit when they go bad. When we reported to the prison, we were assigned to work with a cadre of inmate law clerks or, as most people refer to them, *jailhouse lawyers*.

There are not many ways that one can become a big wheel when one is sent to prison. If you are built like a defensive lineman and handy with a shiv, you might try throwing your weight around. If you have a lot of money, you might try throwing *that* around. However, if you have neither brawn nor riches, your best bet might be a job in the facility's law library. There are many places on earth where legal knowledge proves useful, but penitentiaries might well top the list. Become a jailhouse lawyer, and you will have a ready made clientele. They will be most appreciative as well. Many inmate law clerks are, in fact more knowledgeable and trustworthy than real lawyers and enjoy well-deserved respect and status among their fellow prisoners.

Most convicted felons claim to be innocent of their crime, and when I first started working in Sing-Sing, I believed them all and wondered how the world had come to such a sorry state, that so many should be wrongfully imprisoned. Gradually, it dawned on me that most were really guilty although, of course, some were guiltier than others.

One of the inmate law clerks in Sing-Sing was a young man named Leo who had drawn a bid of twenty to life under the Rockefeller drug laws for the sale of two ounces of cocaine to an undercover officer. Chances are, if you grew up in New York State, you are all too familiar with the Rockefeller Drug Laws, the bane of several generations of young people in New York, including my own. Enacted under Governor Nelson Rockefeller and on the books for forty years, they imposed draconian penalties for what we would today consider minor drug crimes.

In New York State, twenty to life means exactly that. There is no chance of parole for twenty years. You would walk the streets sooner with a manslaughter rap than if you ran afoul of the Rockefeller Drug Laws.

Thus, Leo was clearly a law-breaker, but not necessarily a rogue. He had many good points, first and foremost being a genuine fondness and respect for me. He held me in such regard that one day he asked me if I might try to help a friend of his who was in deep trouble, and without hesitation I agreed.

Sometime before, there had been a celebrated incident when three prisoners went over the wall at Sing-Sing, apparently using ropes constructed of shoelaces that had been purchased at the prison commissary. My mother, who had grown up near the prison, remarked on how clever and daring these inmates must be. Sing-Sing has a well deserved reputation as impregnable. She could not remember a single escape.

The prison was still abuzz with the recent escape. However, although daring, the attempt had been doomed from the get-go. The breakout took place in December. No one was dressed for the weather. Nor did anyone, apparently have a map. To head toward New York City and mingle with the crowds seemed like a good plan, but in reality, it is much too far to walk, even in the summertime. There was no getaway car waiting for them at the gate and, even if they had had the money for train fare, they could hardly have hopped aboard in prison garb. Two of the escapees were promptly captured without much ado. Julio, youngest of the three made it as far south as Sleepy Hollow, the next village downriver from Ossining. He was discovered a few days later, curled up and shivering inside someone's Lincoln Continental, ironically, only a few driveways down from the home of my present landlord, and a few blocks from the historic site where I work today. It really *is* a small world.

I recall well the day I met him. I was seated behind an ancient desk in some musty out-of-the-way room in the bowels of Sing-Sing, trying to look professional.

Leo was there with me, as well as the coordinator from the volunteer program. Then two prison guards brought Julio in, and my blood ran hot and cold at the same time. Like a wounded bird, my heart plummeted through my innards and down my legs. He was the most beautiful creature I have ever seen on this earth, either before or at any time thereafter. His fair skin, deep brown eyes and dark hair cut long in a mop-headed style reminded me of the boys and young men I had chased all through my youth, but he surpassed them all as the moon did a two dollar nightlight.

Julio was twenty-four, but with his slender form and boyish good looks, you might have taken him for a college freshman. That was the day it all caught up to me, the bitter years of scorn and solitude, the dearth of social development since the age of thirteen, the built-up torment, rejection and mockery that had seethed inside me for so long. One look at Julio awakened the sleeping beast inside. Yes, I was a thirty-four-year old adult but I might as well have been a child agog at the sight of a new toy. *I just had to have him,* despite the fact that the circumstances were not, to say the least, auspicious.

His parents had emigrated from Uruguay to Queens when Julio was a baby. Uruguay is a country which few have ever heard of, located high up in the mountains of South America, vaguely near Argentina, and comparatively affluent. Julio's parents were white and middle-class and, like myself, part Italian. Julio was adored from the day he was born. It was not a feeling of disenfranchisement or oppression or lack of other avenues that made him choose a life of crime, as is often said of inner-city youth. No, if anything, it was the sense of entitlement that seems to accrue to many young people possessed of astonishing beauty and gifts, who seem the darlings of fortune. He recognized the world as his for the taking, and he saw no reason not to take it all.

Julio was bright, brighter than anyone I have ever met. Take it from me, however, a high I.Q., even when combined with surpassing good looks, is rarely enough to succeed, not if your chosen line of work is thievery. To really achieve the heights, you need a special talent, one that no Aspergians and few neurotypicals have. That is, the ability to peer into the hearts of others and read the dreams, fears and desires written there. If you can do that, you can manipulate people with a wave of the hand, and the stars will fall out of the sky for you. Julio had that talent, although not as much of it as he suspected. He thought he would be a master thief, a thief of thieves, but life taught him differently.

His first rap was as a teenager, a year and a half for burglary. You might have thought he would have learned his lesson there and then, but no. He simply determined to aim higher and try harder.

At the age of twenty, the prosecution alleged, Julio conceived a plan to rob the home of a rich family in Long Island. The daughter was a friend of his. They had dated, in fact, and her parents were conveniently off on vacation. Because Julio is not built like a defensive lineman (more like a field goal kicker), he thought it advisable to bring along some muscle. The muscle he chose was someone he had met during his stint at the juvenile facility, someone who was big, black and of evil visage, someone whose very appearance might cow the girl into allowing them to pillage her house without a fuss. Or so he supposed.

One beautiful summer's day, Julio and his accomplice, or *crimee,* as the folks at Sing-Sing say, pulled their van into her driveway and knocked on the door. Blissfully ignorant of their true intentions, the girl opened the door and let the duo in, and they began to chat in a friendly manner. However, when the girl realized what was afoot, her cooperation abruptly ceased, and she put up a storm. That is when things began to go downhill. Julio told the muscle to take the girl into the bathroom and tie her up while he went about the business of looting the house. After a while the accomplice joined him, they carried away all that was of value, placed it in their van and drove back to town. The two divvied up the loot, shook hands and parted.

The next day Julio read in the *New York Post* that the girl had been found dead. When her brother returned home from work, he had discovered her body in the bathroom, an electrical cord around her neck. Many wealthy homes and fancy hotels have hair dyers built right into the ceiling. Press a button and the cord stretches down. Apparently, the crimee had used that cord to tie a ligature around the girl's neck a little too tightly. An accident? Accidentally on purpose? Who can really know? What was certain is that the girl was dead, and Julio felt it wise to skedaddle.

Unfortunately, before skedaddling, he had pawned the stolen television set. Eventually it was traced to him. Worst of all, the muscle was arrested and made a statement, implicating Julio.

Julio enjoyed three months of freedom in Nevada, scheming his way into employment at a casino, and surreptitiously casing the joint. Then one day a homicide detective from Nassau County shows up, and the game is over. On the plane back to Long Island, Julio is seated, in handcuffs, next to the detective. To pass the time, they engage in conversation, except, however, the detective does not talk about the weather or the annoying babies seated in the next row. Instead he remarks, "Oh, by the way, your accomplice says that you did the murder." Indignantly, Julio replies," That's a lie! I never harmed her. I never *meant* for her to be harmed." He made it clear to the detective that he was a thief, not a *murderer,* and he imparted that information without benefit of *Miranda* warnings.

When the plane landed in Mineola, Julio was taken to the police station, properly Mirandized and made a full voluntary videotaped confession, to the robbery, not to the homicide. The twenty-year-old desperado did not know, but would soon learn, that under the law it mattered not whether he had actually strangled the girl or even knew that she had been killed. He was guilty of felony murder. This is how it goes: If you willingly participate in a robbery and someone innocent dies, you are a murderer, *no ifs, and or buts.* To make matters worse, the victim's family was not only wealthy, but politically connected. The judge showed no mercy.

There is a rule in law called the *cat-out-of-bag doctrine.* If you make two confessions to a crime, and the first is inadmissible as being coerced or in violation of your *Miranda* rights, a second statement that flows from the tainted one should be thrown out as well. Therefore, Julio had what we in the legal profession refer to as *an appealable issue.*

That was not all, however. While awaiting trial in Mineola, Julio decided to make a dash for freedom. At a preliminary hearing, Julio and his accomplice grabbed the police officer's guns and tried to shoot their way out of the Nassau County Courthouse. A cop was injured in the ensuing fracas, and now Julio was in deeper trouble. Add to this the escape from Sing-Sing, and by the time I first met him, Julio was facing a combined sentence of 56 to life. In New York, this means *at least* 56 years in prison and, even to a person in their twenties, that is equivalent to a life sentence.

I counseled Julio as his legal advisor on all his cases, but I labored extra hard on the appeal of the underlying felony-murder. Hours upon hours were devoted to law library research, composing airtight legal arguments and drafting appellate briefs. Julio maintained that he had never intended that the girl come to harm, and I believed him utterly. I still tend to believe him today. He had the heart of a thief, not a murderer. Yes, he had concededly come to the house with robbery on his mind, but I was willing to accept that as a minor character flaw. After all, I was an outlaw myself, of sorts.

There was no financial remuneration, of course, for all the days, weeks and years that I slaved away on his appeals, and I never sent him a bill. Julio gave me a treasure worth his weight in gold. For once in my life, I knew what it was to love and be loved in return.

You might be skeptical here. How could I be certain that my feelings for Julio were reciprocated? Was he not *just using me?*

I had my suspicions. I am not that much of a fool. However, I am fairly comfortable in asserting that Julio did share my feelings, at least to some extent. You see, I had something that Julio desired as much as I desired him.

When I was young, women used to laugh and say they wanted a man who would love them for their minds. I actually had one. Julio loved me for my mind.

Remember that when I met him, I had just aced three bar exams and was about to pass a fourth. My head was chock full of legal knowledge, court decisions, doctrines, constitutional theories, statutes, rules and regulations. Julio realized that if he were ever to see daylight again, he needed some of that. Would you not love the one who held the key that might literally unlock your prison door?

Shortly before we met, Julio's father had been to see a fortune-teller and have his Tarot cards read. It had been foretold that a woman would appear who would win his son's freedom. The image appealed to me. It gave me a sense of purpose. I was a knight on a quest to rescue my beloved from durance vile.

The Fifth Amendment to the United States Constitution protects a criminal defendant from being forced to be a witness against himself, and I believed the whole scenario of the Long Island detective on the plane wheedling a confession out of Julio to be a clear violation of his rights. I essentially promised him a reversal, and that was the kind of rash promise only a naïve, inexperienced attorney would make. I did not know then what I soon learned. You have to move heaven and earth in the State of New York before a criminal conviction is overturned on appeal. Take it from me, I know whereof I speak. I worked for ten years for a criminal appellate attorney and we perfected a hundred or more appeals. There were cases where I uncovered a high court case so dead on point, a precedent so compelling that I could not imagine how the judges could avoid it, but somehow they twisted the facts and managed to do so. Relief was granted in only a handful of cases, usually where a technicality was so black and white that the courts simply could not ignore it.

I never did win a reversal of Julio's underlying conviction, but I had it modified. The intentional murder count was dismissed. That had little practical effect as the felony murder count was upheld, but it was nonetheless a moral victory. Julio had always maintained that he had never meant for the girl to be harmed, and the quashing of that count may stand him in good stead when he faces the parole board in December 2016. Yes, I had the sentence lopped off as well. Like Cole Younger, Julio should walk free in his early fifties with quality years ahead, rather than die in prison or stumble out the gate as a doddering old man. You think he might have been thankful, but in law, as in politics, it is a game of expectations.

Until he could gain his freedom, Julio wanted to be an inmate law clerk, and I was glad to endow him with my sizeable knowledge of the law. For seven years he had essentially a private tutor. Julio was quite possibly the brightest person I ever met, the quickness and scope of his comprehension surpassing my own. After all, I had had years and years of book-learning, courses and degrees to inculcate facts and theories into my mind. With no formal education to speak of, Julio appeared to pick it up almost by instinct. His ability to grasp ideas which befuddled the most astute law-school student never ceased to amaze me. At the end of the seven years, the pupil far outshone the teacher. Last I heard, Julio was one of the most high-profile jailhouse lawyers in the State of New York, and I was the one who made it so.

During the time I was seeing Julio, I also reconciled with my parents. It happened like this:

As set forth hereinbefore, my life as I knew it had come to an end at the age of thirteen. My parents had sold our house in Croton-on-Hudson and moved us all upstate to a crumbling estate overlooking the river in the middle of nowhere. All this was done in pursuit of a federally financed nursing home project that my parents wished to sponsor. For the following ten years my parents were entirely consumed with putting this project together. They painstakingly dealt with bankers, investors, architects, contractors, suppliers, federal and state officials, all while their two children spiraled downward into the whirlpool of autistic regression.

Now, my mother had a high school diploma and my Dad not even that. While I am hardly one to tout the merits of higher education as the be all and end all of things, it is helpful to know the rules of the road when you are navigating the world of high finance. Still, my parents nearly pulled it off. The project was ever so close to consummation when the owner of a bank took my Dad out to lunch in a restaurant called The Ship's Lantern.

To make a surpassingly long, convoluted and agonizingly tedious story, short, a conversation took place that went something like this:

Banker: "If you want us to invest in your nursing home project, you must secure the loan with a mortgage on *all* your property."

Dad:" I will gladly give you a mortgage on most of the property, but there is one tiny parcel that, according to federal regulations, must be kept free and clear. It is where the sewage plant for the nursing home will be built."

Banker: "Not a problem! Just sign this here mortgage over to us, and when the time comes to close on your project, we will give you a document releasing this tiny parcel from the mortgage lien."

Dad: "That sounds fair enough."

Banker: "Shall we shake on that?"

Now if you envision a banker as a gentleman or lady in a grey flannel suit, a cog in the wheel of a giant financial corporation like J.P. Morgan, Chase or Citibank, you do not have the picture here. This was still the 1970s. Upstate New York had its share of privately owned and operated banks—Ma and Pa banks, if you will. This particular banker viewed his institution as a private satrapy to be used to reward his friends and relatives and to punish his enemies. Unbeknownst to my Dad, he was seething inside because my parents had also taken in a rival bank as an investor as well. Therefore, when the day set for the closing of the nursing home project arrived, and a multitude of lawyers and feds and financiers were gathered around, a certain document was missing.

To amuse the Real Me, Dad had often spent Sunday afternoon building troop formations out of playing cards. Like paper soldiers, they marched from his bedroom down the hall into hers, looped around and stood in formation at the top of the stairs. Then the Real Me would squeal with delight as, with one flick of a fingertip, an entire army melted away in a perfect chain reaction. Just so, the Far North Nursing Home project came tumbling down.

The required document was eventually provided, and my parents spent another decade trying to salvage the project, but they might as well have been dealing with Humpty Dumpty. The general contractor suddenly fell ill and died. The state withdrew its approvals because construction had not been timely started. The suppliers raised their prices. The architect demanded his money, and, sooner or later, everyone else did as well. The banker who had caused all the trouble sold out to a modern banking corporation which knew nothing of my family's travail, only that they held a mortgage which had not been satisfied. My parents' dreams collapsed in a torrent of litigation.

Rather than retain a large experienced firm which might have made heads or tails out of this imbroglio, Mom and Dad threw it into the lap of one small-town practitioner after another. Imagine, for a moment, that you have a solo law office in Nowheresville, USA. You eke out a modest living helping people buy a home or pleading out traffic tickets. Then, one day, my Dad walks through your door with this tale of woe and a carton of papers sufficient to fill a small library. Yes, they were in way above their heads, but the small town lawyers actually did a pretty good job. They held the bad guys at bay until I was ready to be drafted.

I received that first phone entreaty while I was doing collection work for the magazine in Mamaroneck. "Won't you please come home and help us out?" They offered me a cottage of my own for an office *cum* crash pad, to prepare my meals and do my laundry. They would pay me a salary like a real employee, more than I was earning at the magazine. Nevertheless, I turned them down cold. In all honesty, I could not have cared less about the fate of the nursing home. "Serves them right," I thought with grim satisfaction. I had also conducted a bit of preliminary legal research and discovered that in the State of New York, it was virtually impossible to beat a bank in court. It may well be different today, now that the concept of *predatory banking* has entered the lexicon, but, as of 1989, there was not one recorded case I could uncover where a family prevailed against a bank.

While I was seeing Julio at Sing Sing and dwelling with Aunt Rose in the Toy Garden, I was relatively happy, and turned my ears away when my parents begged me to come north. After Julio was transferred from Sing Sing to a prison closer to my parents' home, I began to waver. Aunt Rose finally made the decision for me. She and Uncle Jim left for vacation and changed the locks. Aunt Rose believed very strongly in *family obligations*, and mine lay upstate with my parents.

I spent over three years working for my parents and attempting to unravel the tornado of litigation which had descended on their heads. Like the small town lawyers before me, I was quite overwhelmed and unequal to the task, but I did my best. Although I was not licensed to practice law in New York State, the judge gave me special admission, *pro haec vice*, as it is called, to represent my parents.

A lawyer representing family members is the stuff of TV movies, I know. Dad, unjustly accused of a crime, happens to have a son with a law degree who rides to the rescue. Niece represents nephew, and wet-behind-the-ears cub attorney extricates grandma from the clutches of a corrupt retirement home. Your ex-wife, for whom you still nurture a *tendresse*, accused of murdering her abusive second husband? You'll be right there. That's engrossing TV. In real life, it is not such a good idea.

The very last thing an attorney wants are clients clustered around his dinner table, clients chatting about their cases while he tries to watch a soap opera, clients pulling him out of bed at eight o'clock in the morning and yelling, "Remember that those papers have to be in court *today!*"

There is also the very tangible danger that you will lose perspective. When you are emotionally bonding with a client as I was bonding with my Dad, you begin to think like a client, rather than like a lawyer. You might turn down a perfectly reasonable settlement offer or unconsciously begin to sabotage your own case. Think about it. Does the ex-husband who still loves his wife really want the litigation to come to an end? She'll be off to start a new life in California while he will forever be stuck here with his dreary solo practice. In my parents' case, I grew most unwilling to compromise. I wanted to impress my Dad by wiping up the floor with the other side. Ha!

Of course, the Bank was not represented by anyone's daughter or nephew or jilted lover. They had retained the largest, most powerful law firm in the county, as banks will do, and if anyone was mopped off the floor, it would not be them. Strangely enough, my Dad never seemed to mind it. It was as if bonding with me and telling his story from the stand was more important than the actual money involved, and that was a sizeable sum.

Returning to my parents' home upriver caused me much unease, as a slew of unpleasant memories came rushing back. Nevertheless, living on that haunted northern estate as an adult with a car and a full tank of gas was much less frightful than it had been to a lonely stranded teenager. Nor was it still the middle of nowhere, not after twenty years of urban sprawl. I kept my car keys close at hand and continued to commute to Croton three days each week for a part-time job. The knowledge that escape was an option helped me survive another sojourn in the Kingdom of Frost where scary happenings were still the rule. I survived the Plague of '92 when a mysterious illness ravaged our barn cat population and left the landscape littered with dead and dying felines. Two thirds of the adults and all but one of the kittens born that year succumbed, leaving the handful of survivors dazed and on the dole. When the hammer of foreclosure had finally fallen and my parents had moved to Rhode Island, I went from house counsel to adoption agent for two dozen dispossessed felines, the remnant having repopulated itself the following spring. If you have ever tried to find homes for displaced cats, you can appreciate the Herculean nature of the task.

Nevertheless, it was during this period that I forgave my parents. Now that I was an adult, I saw them in a new light and while we were working together on the litigation, I tried my best to understand them. *Tout comprender est tout pardonner* as a wise Frenchwoman once said. To understand everything is to forgive everything. The dark cloud of rage, resentment and recrimination which had hung over our relationship since the move north receded. I realized that they had not let me founder out of malevolence, but because they had really never known me. What more could you expect of fully grown adults who had entrusted their entire fortune to a handshake deal with a Bank President? Of course, in those days I was in love and love softened my heart. That is one of the gifts that Julio gave me.

If you suppose that lack of contact with the opposite sex is one of the drawbacks of a prisoner's life, you might be surprised. Prisoners have pen pals and they have dates. Back in the day, there were newspapers and magazines in which an inmate could advertise for a friend to correspond with and even come visit him. Today, they probably have their own websites.

One enters a fascinating subculture when one takes to visiting a prisoner. What kind of woman would fall in love with an inmate? A woman like me, obviously, but more generally, a female who wants a man in her life, but does not want him always around. A woman who wants to exercise a certain level of control and keep a certain distance. A woman who believes her love can redeem a bad boy and who finds that love all the sweeter when tinged with the forbidden. *Ladies love outlaws* as Waylon Jennings sang, and it is true, so true.

There is always the risk that a woman from out of his past might suddenly re-emerge in your inmate's life and elbow you into the cold. During the years I spent with Julio, a childhood sweetheart appeared from out of the blue and temporarily snatched his heart away. She was to him what Alexis was to me. Indeed, she even looked like Alexis—same pixie figure, same dark blond hair, same glint of mischief in her eyes. She was young, of course, as young as Julio and, at the time, unhappily married to a third party. Julio must have seemed like the one who got away, *really, really, got away*. I was torn between happiness for Julio who had found his lost love, as I wished I could do, and grievous envy of the unbreakable bond that shared memories had forged between them. It would have been a good time for me to walk away, but did I take the hint? *No, of course not*. I sat on a lakeside bench and wept bitter tears of rage and jealousy. Then I shrugged and decided to wait her out. After all, I could provide Julio with a gift that no other woman had to offer, a free legal education, a gift more valuable than gold when you are serving hard time.

It was not only the sentence of a zillion years to life which haunted Julio, but the treatment he received within the prison system. Correction officials considered him to be a troublemaker and he spent long stretches of time in the Special Housing Unit, both in protective custody and in administrative segregation. The Special Housing Unit or S.H.U. is better known among inmates as *the box*, and it entails being locked in one's cell 23 hours per day. For one hour per day the inmate is taken out in the yard and allowed to exercise by himself. Even during that one hour of relative freedom, he is not allowed to interact with other prisoners. Although never called by that name, S.H.U. is solitary confinement and, take it from me, aside from those medieval implements of torture, it is one of the most exquisite punishments devised by man. Julio survived two years of S.H.U. for which he thereupon sued the Commissioner of Corrections in federal court and was awarded over $19,000 in damages. *Good for him*.

If you are a woman who prefers a slow-burning romance to immediate sexual gratification, that, too, might cause you to consider a relationship with an inmate. Your prisoner is not going to turn to you after a second date and demand you take off your clothes and hop into his bed. In fact, most penitentiaries distinctly frown on any significant physical contact between an inmate and a visitor.

Compared to the strictures placed on visitation by most prisons, Sing Sing is virtually a resort. The visiting room at Sing Sing is large, open and sunny with a beautiful view of the Hudson River. The back wall is lined with vending machines which dispense soda and popcorn and other snacks quite inexpensively. You and your inmate can sit down at a table and dine together as you would in the lunchroom cafeteria. There is a photographer's station, and you can have your picture taken together. Or you could engage in some discrete hanky-panky. When I was there visiting Julio, I actually observed people kissing and visitors sitting on inmate's laps. Again, the key word is *discrete*. Even in Sing Sing, there are boundaries as to what is permissible. Exceed them, and you will be summarily tossed out, and your inmate transferred to someplace near the Canadian border.

Most penal institutions, however, do not permit you to do much more than hold hands. There will be a sinuous S-shaped table, looking a bit like the counter at your neighborhood bar, running through the visiting room. You will be seated on one side, and your prisoner on the other. There will be a wooden panel between you, and any contact beneath the waist will be impossible. You can lean over and run your hands through his hair or give him a peck on the cheek, but that is about the sum of it. Of course, if your relationship is official and your inmate is well-behaved, there is another option. Good time might earn him the right to a conjugal visit now and again. Of course, honeymooning in a trailer in the prison courtyard is not every outside woman's view of connubial bliss.

Julio and I did not have to resort to such stratagems. As his legal advisor, I was entitled to the use of a small room off to the side of the visitors' hall. I was careful not to abuse the privilege. At least, not at first. For a long time, we would just sit and talk. I would purchase cokes and popcorn from the vending machines, and we would engage in spirited discussions of all sorts of things, his cases, the New York Bar Exam I would be sitting for, the GED he was going to earn, the many variations on the *Miranda* Rule discussed in Supreme Court opinions. Throughout the time Julio remained at Sing Sing, I held myself in check. After all, my Grandpa's spirit was peering over my shoulder; I might be willing to throw caution to the wind, but not in my ancestral town.

After Julio was transferred upstate, we grew careless. There was no question of going all the way, of course. Back in the day when full-scale sexual intercourse was still considered off-limits for high school students, archaic terms such as *petting* and *necking* were commonly employed to describe a pleasant in-between activity. You get the drift here. *Inappropriate behavior* was the phrase employed by the corrections officers who caught us in a compromising position one day.

Not only was this incident extremely embarrassing. It came at the worst possible time—after I had successfully passed the New York Bar Exam but before I had been vetted by the Character Committee.

If you are an attorney you are familiar with the two-step process of gaining admission to the bar. You must pass your state's bar examination, naturally, but before you can actually practice law you must also gain the approval of the Ethics and Character Committee. In most jurisdictions, this is a simple enough matter of submitting references from respectable citizens who will attest that you are a good and honest soul. In New York, however, the Character Committee takes its job very seriously, perhaps because so many New York lawyers go bad. They do not usually go bad in the way that I did, of course.

A few days after the episode at the prison, I received a letter in the mail. *It has come to our attention. . .*

Confessing to my parents was not easy at all, because, for once, I could not blame them, not in any way, shape or form. This was one miscue I had made completely on my own. All in all, they took it better than I expected. Here, finally, was proof that I was not gay.

This time, at least, I was well aware of my due process rights. This was not the same as college where I could be disappeared by the simple expedient of changing the locks of my dorm room. I had the right to confront my accusers and the right to an evidentiary hearing. I immediately demanded one.

For once my father was supportive. "Listen," Dad urged. "Don't let them get away with this. You don't have a criminal record. You didn't kill anyone. You did not rob, cheat or steal. You passed four bar exams, all on the first try. Can half the members of the Supreme Court say *that*? Are they going to ban such a brilliant legal mind because of one error of judgment? Hardly! All they want is for you to get down on your hands and knees and apologize."

Dad's advice made perfect sense. I was duly prepared to abase myself, to be contrite, to beg, cajole and plead. After all, I had been on the defensive all my life, had I not, apologizing to family, to school officials, to employers? Once more I would hang my head and say I was sorry.

However, between the day I filed my application for the hearing and the time it was scheduled, the Character Committee must have conducted some opposition research. On several occasions, a document entitled *Supplemental Notice of Charges* arrived in the mailbox. Now it was not just Julio. Now my infractions included unpaid parking tickets and unpaid student loans and unauthorized practice of law. They even went back and dredged up the stalking allegations from college, which I was directed to address. There was more. "Oh, by the way, can you tell us why you were fired from your job in New Jersey? Can you explain that *Ducks Unlimited* shirt we found in the trash bin behind your house?" And so forth and so on. As the date of the hearing approached, the case mushroomed and I found myself buried beneath ten or more accusations. I spooked.

That is the way they do it in New York. Arrested for a simple burglary? At first, you might suppose you can handle it. It is your first offense; no one was hurt, no fingerprints, no witnesses, and no big deal. The next thing you know, you are staring down the barrel of a thirty-count indictment, alleging every conceivable charge from criminal trespass and malicious mischief to burglary in the first, second and third degrees, three counts of attempted robbery, petit and grand larceny, reckless endangerment and whatever else the prosecutor can dream up. Not only that, but a half dozen other folks will come out of the woodwork to swear that you broke into their homes as well. It will not be long before you are crying for mercy and copping a plea, Henry the Eighth might have put you on the rack. Here in New York State they crush your spirit by piling on.

Even with all this, I probably could have appeased the Character Committee if I had only bowed my head. Arrangements could have been made to pay the traffic tickets and student loans. Most of the other charges were window dressing, inserted to impress upon me that admission to the bar was not a gift to be granted lightly. This was the rub. Now that I realized the Character Committee meant business, I was well aware, that at the very least, they would extract from me a pledge never to see Julio again. This was the one condition I could not agree to, though it meant my career. Three days before the hearing, I called up the head of the Character Committee and withdrew my application.

Did I feel shame in doing this foolish thing? No, I felt like a dime-store Duke of Windsor, defiantly abdicating my throne for the sake of the one I loved. Rather proud of myself I was, standing with my back upright and refusing to submit to their bullcrap as I jettisoned my once-promising future.

I told my father not to worry, that I would return to New Jersey and practice law. I made that promise in good-faith, for indeed I had every intention of doing so. In my spare time, I drafted an update resume, took it to the copy store, and sent it out to hundreds of lawyers in Jersey. Like the resumes I had previously dispatched to attorneys in Connecticut, these, too, were swallowed up by the void. I announced that when my parents' case was over, I would relocate to New Jersey and look for a job in person. In the meantime, there was Julio, and he led me on quite a merry chase.

If you have a relationship with a prison inmate in the State of New York, odds are that, sooner or later, you will do some traveling. New York is a big state, many criminals live therein, and numerous correctional facilities have been constructed to service that population. Most housing is for men, a few, like Bedford Hills, are for women. Some prisons are maximum security, some are medium and others, almost liveable, are classified as minimum. I became familiar with the inside of many, for besides Julio, I worked legitimately for a criminal appellate attorney and often visited her incarcerated clients.

Even a prisoner who is well-behaved is likely to be transferred around, seemingly at random, so that he or she does not get too comfortable in one facility. If the inmate has an *incident*, he is likely to be shipped out on the next transport to a prison far away. Within days of our episode, Julio was headed to Attica where he lived on a tier with Mark David Chapman, the assassin of John Lennon. Julio said that Chapman was not a bad sort, although as someone who grew up listening to the Beatles, I might beg to differ.

Attica has a reputation as a forbidding place, a reputation that a visit there will bear out. Not that the people are unfriendly, it is simply a grey, gloomy, overpowering, hulk of a prison with the look of a medieval fortress. And bitterly cold, I might add. Up in that neck of the woods, it snows each day from November to April. *Lake Effect Snow*, they call it. I know. I was there in December, and you could not even walk down the street without danger of being blown away.

There are buses from New York City that regularly take family members and friends up to various correctional facilities. Julio's mother would take these buses. I could never put myself through that ordeal, cheek to jowl with screaming children and teenage mothers. On my first visit to Attica, I took the train and rented a car. The second time, in better weather, I drove up very slowly, taking the back roads all the way, and stayed in a village near Attica called Batavia where they have good chicken wings.

There were no more legal visits for us, of course, and no more little rooms. We had to put up with the S-shaped tables. In truth, I did not mind so very much. It felt more open and honest. I have no talent or comfort level for deceit, and it had been quite burdensome for me to pretend that my relationship with Julio was only professional. Our physical contact now was restricted, of course, but I could dream of marriage and the trailer visits that certainly waited down the road. Yes, I was an idiot. Not even an *idiot savant*, but just an idiot. Idiot in love.

On that second, springtime visit to Attica, I drove to Niagara and looked at the falls. All by my lonesome, of course, like Princess Diana at the Taj Mahal, but I really did not mind. The falls were awesome, and, so long as I had Julio in my life, I was legitimized. *Yes, I do have a boyfriend, but he's been unfortunately detained. . .* There was a method, even to my idiocy.

The end finally came at Dannemora which is a prison about 300 miles due north from Croton, on the way to Montreal. The nearest city is Plattsburgh, which, you may remember was the hometown of Ms Livingston, the best fifth-grade teacher that ever was. (*Yes, I finally made it there.*) Julio met another celebrity while he was housed at Dannemora, Robert Chambers, better known to us New Yorkers as the Preppie Killer. Chambers was a little too sleazy, even for my desperado, especially when he began casting his eyes at Julio's younger sister.

Plattsburgh is a small, self-contained city on Lake Champlain. It has the feel of a world in itself, like a soap opera town. The air is crisp and clear, the nights are full of stars, the traffic sparse and the scenery, sweeping. Of course, few can actually live there, as it is extraordinarily cold and snowy. Its very charm is owing to its location. Were it in a more temperate clime, it would have long since turned into Poughkeepsie.

My first visit to Dannemora was at Thanksgiving, and I left Plattsburgh in a hurry, a blizzard close on tiny heels. The following year I planned my visit for late September, and reserved a weekly rental at a Plattsburgh hotel, complete with a kitchenette. I took an animal companion with me on the journey, one of the survivors of the Great Cat Plague, and I was looking forward to an enjoyable interlude.

The first day I visited Julio was the day his final appeal had been rejected by the federal courts. He was sullen and uncommunicative. His face was darkly overcast and he glared at me for two hours with the eyes of Medusa. I had sabotaged his case, he claimed, deliberately misinterpreted the *Miranda* rule, persuaded him of the merits of fallacious arguments so that he might remain in prison. I had never really tried to free him, had I? Did not trust him, did I? Afraid that he would run away with another woman, now wasn't I?

Moi? The one who had slaved for hours upon hours upon tedious hours at the typewriter and in the law library, without ever asking for financial compensation? The one who had gladly devoted the bulk of her time to his case when she should have been more assiduously helping her parents save their home and business? The one who had knocked off his intentional murder count so as to give credibility to his claims of moral innocence? The one who had sliced his sentence by twenty years and more? How dare he accuse me of sabotaging his case! Was it my fault that he had chosen a life of crime in his reckless youth?

That is one more reason why, in real life, it is not wise for an attorney to represent her family or friends. When things go wrong, as they often do, who is the first to be blamed for it all? The attorney, of course.

When I went to the prison the second day, Julio refused to see me.

After crying my heart out, I took it better than you might have supposed. As I was trapped for another six days in the North Country where the leaves had already began to turn, why not see the sights? One day I drove past the Canadian border where the traffic signs were all in French, and visited a quaint river town with a strange sounding name, *St. Jean sur Richelieu.* On Sunday I took the ferry to Grand Isle, Vermont where you might well believe yourself lost in the midst of an enchanted forest.

Plattsburgh was not so bad at all, not in early autumn. I was still a fervent hockey fan, and it was a kick to be able to pull in Hockey Night in Canada on the motel TV. Of course, as a history buff, I had to visit Clinton County museum. Plattsburgh can lay claim to quite a colorful past. Looking out into Lake Champlain, you can make out the distant outline of Valcour Island, the site of America's first naval battle. During the War of Independence, the Colonists, with a few patchwork watercraft, fought the redcoats to a draw, delaying the Brits' march southward until the American forces could rally at Saratoga.

Who was the hero of Valcour Island? Benedict Arnold. Honest to God, and on the American side, too. You see, things are not always as they seem, and despite what you might have been taught, Benedict Arnold was not a bad sort through and through. He was brave, feisty and a master of military strategy, and one of the first leaders of the American Revolution. Arnold helped Ethan Allen capture Fort Ticonderoga. He almost captured Quebec, and, of course, he was one of the heroes of Saratoga where his leg was buried with full military honors. The rest of him lies somewhere unknown and forgotten. You see, Benedict Arnold fell in love with the wrong woman, a beautiful Tory spy. She flipped him. It happens.

Even after we had broken up, Julio and I still corresponded sporadically. He would send me copies of briefs he had written on his own behalf or for other inmates.

Several years after Dannemora, he actually wrote to me and proposed that we marry. I would like to say that I had come to my senses by then and no longer found the prospect of trailer visits with Julio enticing in the least. That would not be the full truth. Had Julio been in Sing Sing, I would have had my hair done and been there the following day. However, by then he had been transferred to another facility in another cold place, up in the Finger Lakes region. My mother had just passed away, and, for you who luckily have not yet learned this, grief is a tiring occupation. It saps your energy like a five-mile sprint through Hell. I turned him down.

I have not completely let go. I keep tabs on Julio through a helpful service provided by the New York State Department of Corrections. It is called the *Inmate Locator*. I call it *ClientFind*. You can call a toll-free number or pay a visit to their website, plug in your inmate's number and *voila,* you will learn his present location, race, and age and parole eligibility date. The purpose of *ClientFind,* is to provide notice to victims, crime victims that is, not victims of broken hearts, but it is there for our use as well.

I've harbored in my heart a measure of pride in Julio, when all is said and done. On the day we met, he was a diamond in the rough, an outlaw of twenty-four facing a life behind bars with scant hope of parole. Under my tutelage, he became an effective advocate for prisoners' rights and has gone on to win several suits seeking due process and fair treatment behind bars, in both state and federal courts. Far better to *play the hand you were dealt*, as Aunt Rose would have put it, than spend your life chasing mirages and thirsting for nothing but the fruit of the forbidden tree.

World of Strangers

●

ngraved on my tombstone should be the image of a small child with her nose pressed to a windowpane and her eyes wide with wonder. I would like that. It would be the perfect illustration of the way my life has been, always on the outside, peering inquisitively through the windows of this world, knocking on the doors and begging, to no avail, to be allowed in.

Or perhaps I could put it another way. Recall the tale of Lord Tennyson's *Lady of Shalott*. A character drawn from Arthurian legend, she lived alone in a tower, weaving beautiful tapestries, and saw the world outside only as reflected in a mirror. Then one day she glanced out her window and saw Sir Lancelot riding down to Camelot. That did it. The mirror cracked from side to side and the Lady left her tower and drowned herself in the river flowing down to Camelot. Perhaps Lord Tennyson had a foreshadowing of what it meant to live with Asperger's Syndrome. The Lady of Shalott was happy, productive and content so long as she accepted her fate to be solitary and apart. It was the desire for the things of this world, *(ie. Sir Lancelot)*, that brought doom upon her.

In 1911, a Swiss psychiatrist named Eugen Bleuler coined the word *autism*. Bleuler had previously coined the term *schizophrenia,* and he referred to the tendency of his schizophrenic patients to screen themselves off and withdraw from reality as *autistic.*

Today we would label the people Bleuler described as *catatonic schizophrenics* rather than autistic.

Autism stems from the Greek word *autos* meaning *self alone,* and to be born on the autistic spectrum is to inhabit, to one degree or another, a world apart.

That is the very definition of autism, but when people speak of autism today, they are generally talking about individuals who display behaviors seen as characteristic of those on the autism spectrum: an inability to pick up on social cues, an undue attachment to routine and to familiar people, place and things, deep but narrow interests, sensory problems, unwillingness to look one in the eye, resistance to change, difficulty in expressing one's emotions or poor control over one's emotions and so forth. The fruits are well-known, but the tree remains a mystery. Many persons today live with a diagnosis of autism spectrum disorder, or self-identify as autistic, because they exhibit, or once did exhibit, certain of these behaviors and not necessarily because they are living in *a universe of one* as the term was meant to imply.

The modern conception of autism arises from studies conducted by Dr. Leo Kanner, a child psychiatrist working at John Hopkins University in Baltimore. In 1938, Dr. Kanner began treating a group of 11 children with unusual behaviors, not arising from a mental illness like schizophrenia, but from innate neurological characteristics. In a report presented in 1943, Dr. Kanner described these children as *autistic* and attributed to them certain common traits which included impairment in social interactions, good rote memory, great difficulty in coping with change, undue attachment to routine and ritual, a fascination for objects over people, food problems and oversensitivity to certain stimuli such as loud sounds or bright lights. Three members of Dr. Kanner's group were completely non-verbal, and the communication ability of the others was severely restricted. Many exhibited *echolalia* whereby a child repeats verbatim what he has heard, rather than speaking in his own words. My baby brother practiced *echolalia*, driving us crazy with his repetition of jingles he had heard on television.

Dr. Kanner lived until 1986, and by then, the concept of childhood autism had spread far and wide. However, a new element had inserted itself into the equation: *mental retardation.* Kanner himself had believed that high intelligence actually lurked within the autistic brain, but that finding was largely ignored. If you cannot communicate with them, they cannot be intelligent, or so the rationale implied.

Back in the fifties, sixties and seventies the Kanner model was what people had in mind when they referred to someone as *autistic*. It was often used as a synonym for the word *retard*. A child who was bright, verbal and articulate, who had an above average intellect and no language delays, would never have been diagnosed as autistic even if she displayed many of the classic behaviors associated with autism. While the Real Me resembled Dr. Kanner's children in many ways, her verbal skills and high intelligence served to mask her autistic nature.

Yet back in the early 1940s, at the same time that Dr. Kanner was conducting his studies in Baltimore, a Viennese psychiatrist, Dr. Hans Asperger, was also performing autism research. The children treated by Dr. Asperger—he referred to them as autistic psychopaths—were similar in many ways to Dr. Kanner's patients, but manifested significant differences as well. There were no language delays or echolalia. Instead, the Asperger children exhibited high intelligence, talked like grown-ups or little professors and had special interests about which they might be quite obsessive and knowledgeable. Dr. Asperger also noted that the children in his study were clumsy and had more motor skills problems than normal children. In other words, they were a lot like the Real Me.

Kanner was an American. His work was quickly adopted by the American psychiatric establishment. Dr. Asperger, on the other hand, worked in Nazi-occupied Austria. Any medical discoveries coming out of Nazi-held lands were suspect as though tainted by association with evil scientists such as Dr. Mengele. Dr. Asperger's findings went largely unnoticed in the English-speaking world until the 1980s when they were translated into English by Dr. Lorna Wing, a British psychiatrist and mother of an autistic daughter. It was not until 1994 that Asperger's Syndrome was recognized in the United States as part of the spectrum of autistic disorders.

But what of Asperger-type autistics who were born and grew to adulthood before the diagnosis of Asperger's Syndrome was known? We lived on the periphery of life, in a world of shadows like the Lady of Shalott, or spent our lives in vain pursuit of that which we could never attain, a place in this world of strangers.

It was not until 2007 that autism expert Simon Baron-Cohen and his colleagues at Cambridge University coined the term *lost generation* to describe adults with Asperger's who came of age without knowing their own natures. All through their school years, he noted, they had had trouble making friends or fitting in. Many had been the targets of bullies. By young adulthood, many suffered from depression and had thoughts of suicide. Some were able to maintain high grades and go to college. Some simply gave up and immersed themselves in their special interests. There were those who formed relationships, only to see them break down while some landed jobs and lost them due to a lack of team skills. Dr. Baron-Cohen, and following his lead, other diagnosticians opened their doors to adults on the autism spectrum.

For decades, autism was a diagnosis given almost exclusively to children and, of those children, the majority were male. Society demanding more of boys, it was easier to spot one who was shy, introverted and kept to himself, while a girl who displayed the same behaviors—or, conversely, was tomboyish and aggressive as many females on the spectrum are—went unnoticed. However, in recent years, Asperger's Syndrome has been diagnosed in adults, at various stages of the lifespan, from their twenties to their seventies. Quite a few of the late-diagnosed have been middle-aged women who, like myself, breathed a sigh of relief and achieved a new sense of empowerment when they were finally given the key. For, as the *Toronto Star* wrote of the lost generation (see "The Autism Project 11/20/12):

> "It's a sad way to spend a life, by living in the unknown, always unable to connect, incapable of organizing their lives or being on the fringe, never quite accepted."

Because of my own struggles, I have been attuned to stories of others who have undergone a similar travail. A few years ago a tragedy occurred here in the Hudson River towns. In a village just south of Tarrytown, there lived a bright young scientist of twenty-six. He had just graduated from a prestigious university with an advanced degree in chemistry and, to all appearances, was on the threshold of a brilliant career. Yet one morning he drove his Dad to the train station, parked his car by the side of he road and took his own life by ingesting a mixture of toxic chemicals. This young man did not have Asperger's, but he suffered from a severe case of Obsessive-Compulsive Disorder which has autistic-like components. As a result of his condition, he was shunned. He had no friends and no social life. His grief-stricken father told the local media that his son, "only wanted to be like other people."

To be like other people. That was the Real Me's goal as well. My mother, like many of her contemporaries, believed that this should be an easy task for one with such a high intellect as I. Had I really, truly desired, I could have been just like other people. The fact that this never came about was further evidence of my recalcitrance, selfishness, and willful failure to launch. She would tell me, time and again, that parable of the hatchling leaving the nest, and time and again, to please her, I would try to fly strong and true. With each attempt, my wings would fail me and I would show up on Aunt Rose's doorstep, for it was only there that I might find succor.

When my parents' torrent of litigation was finally over, they retired to Rhode Island and the Bank foreclosed on the Kingdom of Frost. I duly stuffed my belongings into a few suitcases and headed back to New Jersey. When I had left Atlantic City, nearly a decade earlier, before my landlady had hugged me and sobbed and said, that if I ever changed my mind, the apartment would be waiting. I drove right to her home, and, yes, she was still there, and her, by now, ancient-bagel-eating dog as well, but, of course, the basement apartment had long since been rented to another. She could not wait to show me the door. How could I have supposed that an apartment two blocks from the ocean would be held open for nine years on the chance I might wander back in? It made no sense at all, yet I had been convinced of it, and my belief had been so strong that I had no back-up plan. The rents in Atlantic City had skyrocketed. There was no other housing I could afford, not even in the off-season. I meandered up and down the Jersey shore, from Asbury Park to Cape May, crashing in winter rentals, spending the days wandering deserted beaches or making cursory inquiries about jobs. No one was eager to hire a forty-year-old attorney with gaping holes in her resume and skeletons in her closet. I skirted large cities like Trenton and Newark where I might actually have *found* work. Such places were too stressful, stark and anonymous. All their motels were out on highways where the Wolf of Loneliness roamed free.

The pattern was repeating itself once more. I sank into depression and edged closer to the whirlpool. Each night the sound of traffic on the road beyond my window filled me with terror. It was the sense of rootlessness that posed the gravest danger, a constant reminder that there was no sanctuary on earth for someone such as I. Before the economy tanked, you would see bright-shiny signs up and down the highway, heralding the construction of new condominiums: *If you lived here, you'd be home by now.* All it took was the sight of one of these signs, and I would burst into tears.

Even then, I had no clue that I was autistic. Yet it was there, in a winter rental, on the deserted strand, that I was finally forced to acknowledge certain traits in myself, traits that I now know to be signs of autism. Chief among them is the utter inability to cope with change. This is neither feigned nor chosen as my mother had supposed. My need for the safe and familiar is particularly strong, even for someone on the spectrum. The cycle was broken. Packing my bags, I headed home to Aunt Rose for the third and final time. Soon I had resumed my free-lance work for local attorneys, identifying myself as a paralegal with no more pretensions of being a *real* lawyer. I resumed my work at the proms and at other quirky part-time jobs to supplement my income. When people asked why I did not return to New Jersey where I was an actual Member of the Bar or seek a high-paying job in the City, I replied that I was needed here to take care of an elderly aunt. In reality, of course, it was the other way around. The elderly aunt was taking care of me.

Coming home again kept the wolf at bay and banished the inner chaos which so often threatened to swallow me alive. Nevertheless, the brave, confident days of my childhood never returned. As an adult, I did not reside in Croton so much as haunt it. Day and night, I prowled the streets, peering into every window, following every trail, walking down by the river, swimming at Silver Lake, riding my bike in the moonlight, playing the booths at the Firemen's Bazaar, hanging out in every deli, diner and park in town. *There was buried treasure here, if only I could remember where I hid the map.* I could find *my gang.* But I never did.

Aunt Rose bought me a book, Dale Carnegie's *How to Win Friends and Influence People.* I read it from cover to cover, and, while I may have influenced a few people, I won no friends. I joined clubs, I took courses, and I dragged myself to local events. In an attempt to overcome my social awkwardness, I initiated conversations with total strangers, and listened sympathetically to their tedious little problems. Aunt Rose would invariably meet me at the door upon my return from one of these excursions with this one question: "Did you meet anyone you liked more than yourself?"

Several years ago a movie came out entitled *The Lovely Bones.* It spun the tale of a murdered 14-year-old girl who haunts her hometown for years thereafter. She refuses to move on to the afterlife, until she finds a way to communicate with her family and see the neighbor responsible for her murder brought to justice. It is a modern retelling of an ancient fable, the oft-told story of one who perishes untimely and, unable to accept her own death, becomes trapped between two worlds. So it was with me. I was not so much alive as a revenant, the ghost of the Real Me. I felt more like a shade, one of the shadowy inhabitants of Persephone's realm, than a breathing human being of flesh and blood. Suffer that treatment long enough, and the feeling will gradually take hold. *You are not really here at all.*

There was only one way I could become a real person again. I must find and rejoin *my gang*. Although I searched hard and long, there was one time, and one time only, that I almost made it happen.

When I first returned to Croton after college, there was an active women's softball league in town. My Cousin Jan was a player, and I wanted to be one, too. The Real Me had loved softball, and had, in fact, been quite good at it, despite problems with motor skills coordination. Although I had not played organized sports since junior high, I still fancied myself a tomboyish, athletic kind of person. The lack of a car until the age of thirty made me feel less than an adult, but it also kept me in good physical shape and built stamina. Walking and biking remained my primary modes of transportation while my contemporaries moved from block to block, seated in comfort behind the wheel of a two-ton machine. Of course, to play softball, you have to be part of a *team* and that presented a problem. I left my name everywhere, at the recreation department, on posters, on fliers, on telephone poles. *Anyone need a sub? Empty spot on the roster? Contact me at. . .* For several years, my heart would ache relentlessly each time I passed the ball field at the sight of the happy young women playing there. No one ever called me, and in hindsight, it was probably just as well. In an actual tryout, I would almost certainly have fallen flat on my face, resulting in more tears and a new reason to curse the world.

It was in the days of the Toy Garden that word reached me of an open volleyball program held at the elementary school gym every Friday night. The idea of playing volleyball attracted me. *Right up my alley*, as Aunt Rose said. Best of all, you could just drop in. You did not have to be part of a *team*, at least not in theory.

Unlike many recreation department programs, the level of skill displayed by the Croton volleyball players was excellent. Moreover, they were a cohesive, tight-knit group with a certain small-town allure. Parents and kids, husbands and wives played together. Afterward, they went out to a local pub. In the summer, when school was closed, they attended barbecues at each other's homes, and I heard tell of volleyball matches down by the river. Shortly before I arrived on the scene, one of the male players had stolen the wife of a teammate, and for years the scandal was bruited about. The star player happened to be the son-in-law of the folks who now lived in the Real Me's house, a fact that alone would have endowed him with certain glamour. Several members of the group had gone to school with my Cousin Jan who joined us from time to time, stealing the show whenever she walked in the door. Cousin Jan possesses just about every quality I ever desired in myself, including the inborn athletic ability I would have died for.

My eyes were opened the first time I tried to play volleyball. Surprise, surprise, the ball would drop right through my arms, more often than not. When I did manage to get my hands under it, my shot would fall short, carom right into the net or take on a life of its own and fly unbidden off the court. My own incompetence astonished me. How could I be disgracing myself like this? Perhaps volleyball was not *right up my alley*, after all.

The other players had no patience with such ineptitude and refused to pass the ball to me. I became invisible once again, a ghostly presence on the court watching as the ball flew back and forth over my head. After several such sessions, I became so frustrated that I began to jump out of position and grab passes meant for other players. Such improper volleyball etiquette provoked annoyance and anger and endeared me even less to my teammates.

But this time I did not slink away with head down and my tail between my legs. After searching for many years in vain, I had finally found them—*my gang*, the playmates I had lost so many years before and would do anything to recapture. With the sole exception of Jan, I had never laid eyes on any of them before that Friday evening I first turned up at the grade school gym. Yet I could not shake the inexplicable sensation of having known each and every one of them in the long ago. A determination took hold in my heart. Whatsoever it took to reclaim my place in their magic circle, I would do—much the way my mother felt about reclaiming her birthright in the landed gentry. So I set out on a mission to learn to play volleyball.

For years I honed my skills in rec department programs in Ossining and other nearby towns where the level of play was not so demanding. I took part in pick-up volleyball games. I practiced by hitting a ball against the side wall of the house for hours on end. I watched instructional videos.

All the while, I kept showing up at the grade school gym. Let me make believe, if you will be so kind. Refuse to pass the ball to me, no problem. I will hang back until the ball *just happens* to come my way, and then I will astonish you with my newly acquired skill. When I moved back in with my parents for three and a half years, I often drove down to Croton on Friday nights specially to play volleyball.

After I returned to Aunt Rose's for the third time, I became a regular once again, and eventually my persistence paid off, sort of. The other players accepted me as a teammate. They would engage in friendly conversations with me. They would occasionally send the ball my way. From time to time I joined them late in the evening after the game, usually when Cousin Jan was present to give me cover. Even so, I was never invited to barbecues or parties and, if the others played volleyball down by the river in the summer, I could never find them although I often hiked the trail that runs along the water.

One of my fellow volleyball players inadvertently showed me the way to forgive my parents. His name was Paul, and he was an accountant from my mother's hometown of Ossining. Paul was about as white bread and middle class as you could be. He had a teenage son named Damian, a cute auburn-haired boy that occasionally accompanied him to volleyball. There came a time when Damian got into some trouble at Ossining High School. It may have concerned drugs or bullying or misbehavior; I no longer recall. In those days a rather rough inner-city type element had taken over the student body at Ossining High, and things may very well have grown problematical for a shy skinny white kid. Paul and his wife sent Damian north to Hudson to live with his aunt and uncle. Bravo! Paul became a hero in my eyes. I recalled how my parents had selfishly refused to allow me to spend my final year in high school with Aunt Rose, when something of the Real Me might still have been salvaged. Paul, on the other hand, so loved his son that he was willing to relinquish the reins.

Yet even when parents do the right thing, events can go hopelessly wrong. That is why they say that the Road to Hell is paved with good intentions. In the upstate city of Hudson, Damian made a new best friend, a geek whose name was Wylie. Wylie was not a good geek, but a geek with evil designs. Wylie disliked his parents, disliked them so much that he did not just yell at them and talk back, nor did he simply pilfer cash from their wallets and make off with the car keys. Wylie planned their murder, and to that end he wove a conspiracy into which Damian and a third boy were drawn.

Was Damian a willing accomplice, as the prosecution alleged, or an unwitting dupe as his father maintained? Who can know the truth? To listen to Paul tell the tale, and he spoke of little else, the jury had been fatally biased against his son because he came from downstate. It also occurred to me—although I sensibly kept the thought to myself—that it does not help the defense when the defendant bears the name of *Rosemary's Baby*. Damian was convicted and sentenced to twenty to life. In New York, *twenty to life* means no parole for at least twenty years, and even then, as you can imagine, the stigma will follow him wherever he goes.

Aware that I had a legal background, Paul would corral me each Friday night before the match began, and talk incessantly about Damian's latest appeal. The stress began to take a toll. Years later, I ran into Paul; he was working as a cashier in a self-service gas station in Ossining and looked much older than he possibly could be. I asked about his son. Damian, he said, was still in jail and another appeal was being prepared.

There came an autumn when many of the regular players no longer showed up on Friday nights. I kept playing a while longer. Less demanding and less skilled newcomers had taken the place of the original group. With them, I could dominate the game, but I was not happy. Without the core players, it was never the same. Eventually the volleyball program itself folded.

Every now and then I'll bump into one of them on the street or in the store and it will be, "hi there, how's the world treating you these days?" "Holding my own, thank you. And yourself?" Like old acquaintances that just happen to meet. None of them have the slightest idea of the heartaches they caused me, the sleepless nights I racked my brains for the elusive key to their enchanted world, the years I devoted to practice in the hope of winning an entrée, my bittersweet agony at the ambivalent pay-off that ensued. *Just someone I used to know.* They will nod and go on their way, without a backward glance, leaving me to wrestle with the memory of yet another treasure that slipped right through my fingertips.

In the mid-nineties, soon after my third and final homecoming, Uncle Jim suffered a fatal stroke. Aunt Rose did not take to widowhood well. She turned increasingly curmudgeonly. Bit by bit, she began to dismantle the Toy Garden. Unable to understand how devastating grief could be, I came up short in the empathy department. In fact, all of her weeping and wailing befuddled me. She had not married until she was forty-one; why should she find it so distressing to be single again? After all, I was single and getting by. Besides, Uncle Jim had been seventy-three, which seemed to me a great age, even then, and he had been frail and sickly for some time. Certainly it was nowhere near as shocking as when Uncle Spence left for work one morning, a robust and energetic sixty-year-old, all full of vim and vigor and been slain by a wrathful tree.

Still, she was inconsolable and not just for a little while. Uncle Jim had died in early March, and when mid-December rolled around, I was wondering where our Christmas tree might be. Uncle Jim and Aunt Rose had always had the biggest, truest, greenest Christmas trees erected in our front room. That was one of the best parts of life on Grand Street. As December wore on, Aunt Rose made no mention of a Christmas tree or any attempt to buy one. I finally asked her point blank, "What about our Christmas tree this year?" "We won't be having any more Christmas trees," she replied. I stared at her incredulously. "No Christmas trees?"

In the mistaken belief that her reluctance was due to financial hardship, I drove down to the lot by the Croton Shoprite on December 23rd and spent $20.00 of my own money for a Christmas tree. The tree-seller was so very kind; he even strapped it to the top of my little red Suzuki. However, when I proudly drove up to the front door, Aunt Rose started screaming. "Don't bring that tree in here! I won't have a Christmas tree in this house! Get rid of that tree!"

In the hope that she would calm down, I left the tree atop the car overnight. However, she remained adamant the next morning, and I found myself on Christmas Eve, driving all over Westchester County with a Christmas tree tied on top of my Suzuki. You might suppose it would be easy to give away a free Christmas tree, but, take it from me, that is not the case. Everyone that wanted a tree had one by then, and many, strangely enough, expressed a preference for artificial trees. A guard at Pace University Law School finally took it off my hands.

A few years after Uncle Jim passed away, Aunt Rose began to have medical problems herself and, as she aged, she grew increasingly cranky and short-tempered. She watched her siblings die, one by one, and the nieces and nephews whose photos she so proudly displayed on her wall, drifted away. Now, I had made a promise, when she first rescued me after college, that I would help her in her old age. There are those who would tell you that I did not do a very good job in taking care of Aunt Rose, and perhaps they are right. I made a poor caregiver, needing one myself. Still, I was *there*. I ran errands for her, provided companionship and walked the dogs—and *that* was more than any one in the clan could say. Now and then, Cousin Jan or another in that rogue's gallery of relations would swoop down and make a fine show of affection and concern, but almost always, it was just the two of us, ignored and forgotten.

I was stranded on the sidelines of life, but I had learned to eke out a little happiness. Although I had no social life, I did have my special interests—obsessions which would take hold of me and which I pursued with a single minded passion for years. They were not all as erudite as foreign policy or ancient theology, When Prince Charles married Lady Di, I had paid scant attention. It was billed as a Cinderella story to which I could not relate. Nonetheless, when the discord began, I sat up and took notice. Something in the saga caught my fancy when events began to spin out of control. I was puzzled that Diana complained so vociferously that there had been "three people in my marriage." Was that so terrible? *Far better than a marriage of one.* I found a kindred spirit in Prince Charles, although his mother was a real queen and mine only a fairy-tale one. Perhaps it was his shy awkwardness, his quirky fascination with modern architecture and organic farming, his insistence on the old ways and his resistance to change. Perhaps it was because I sensed that, despite all the sycophants, servants and bootlickers who had surrounded him since the day he was born, he was lonely. He truly loved only one woman and held onto her for dear life. A man, not previously renowned for his moral courage, he clung tenaciously to Camilla through Hell and High water, much as I had tried to cling to Julio. That won my admiration.

As the convoluted tale unfolded with its scandals and secret audiotapes and the tragedy of Diana's death, I became seized with the need to know every detail. I combed the TV Guide for shows that had any relation whatsoever to the British monarchy, I raided the library for books on the House of Windsor. Once a week I drove to Greenwich and picked up several copies of the British tabloids. I studied maps of England, so I could understand precisely where each incident had occurred. In the process, I became very much the expert, not only on the royals, but on the intricacies of British politics. I followed the infighting among factions. Had anyone but asked, I could have explained why Tony Blair was known as *Tony Blur* and described the difference between the old Labor Party and the new one.

On occasion, my father would visit us in Croton to take care of business and check up on old friends. Dad would take me to lunch in the local diner that the Real Me had once frequented. It was no longer the battered greasy spoon that it had been back in the day. The jukebox was gone and the waitresses were more modestly attired. A makeover and new management had turned it into a modern eatery with state-of-the-art diner décor and a pricey menu. Still. It was good to have lunch with my Dad.

Two or three times a year, i would visit my parents in Rhode Island. There were no more arguments or blame. When we met up at the motel or their condo, I was greeted with a hug. They took me out shopping, to dinner or to hear a local band. We even went to the zoo. Once we visited a western-style club where Mom laughed at my clumsy attempts to line dance. Even so, there remained a fragile, tentative quality to our relationship. It was as if a glistening, smooth but paper thin sheet of ice had formed over a reservoir of hurt. My parents had too many unspoken questions, and I could never forget the disappointment which was written in their hearts.

No, they never pulled the *Where are the grandkids?* routine. They dared not, for that is how I came to be born. Not that my mother had any real hankering for a grandchild—just someone else to push out of the nest. Dad, on the other hand, would have made an excellent grandpa and I regret that neither I nor the baby brother were able to provide him with one.

It was more in the nature of: *You did one better than the miller's daughter. You spun gold into straw. All that money wasted on your education and you threw your career away for no conceivable reason.*

At times, the pain would break through unbidden. Once we were all invited to spend Thanksgiving with my parents' new neighbor. I had my hair done, put on my best clothes, tried to be pleasant and even forced myself to make small talk. The evening was almost over when my Dad asked the neighbor's thirty-year-old nephew why he looked so glum and somber. The nephew replied that he had the blues because his girlfriend had left him. We all felt compelled, as people do at such gatherings, to offer him words of comfort and advice. When I put in my suggestion, my mother tossed back her head and remarked, not maliciously, merely in a matter-of-fact way, "How would you know? You never were much for dating, were you?"

The dam broke like the Lady of Shallott's mirror. I drew back like a wounded animal and spouted: "Well, thanks to you! *You* took me away from the real world! *You* made me come of age in the middle of nowhere! *You* taught me none of the things a woman needs to know! I could have been someone. I could have been *normal,*" and the tears began to flow. I soon recovered, wiped my eyes and tendered my sincere apologies, but the evening had been spoiled beyond repair. Once again I had made a spectacle of myself.

It was about the turn of the century that I first heard of Asperger's Syndrome, and then only by chance. The attorney I worked for represented a couple whose 18-year-old son had been diagnosed with Asperger's. The legal question before us was whether the boy was competent to handle his own affairs or needed a guardian. I was sent to the law library to research the issue. Before I left, I asked my boss what in the world Asperger's Syndrome meant. He described it as *a little bit autistic.*

That was the day I took the first step on the long winding road to self-discovery. I can still see myself, sitting in the library cubicle, staring in stunned fascination at the open pages before me and exclaiming out loud, "Golly, they have a name for it now!" A veil lifted from my eyes. Autism was not only a condition of the intellectually impaired as I had always been led to believe. I nodded and said to myself: "How could I not have known?"

From that day forward, I was certain I was an aspie, although another decade was to pass until the diagnosis would be confirmed by a professional. For years, I told no one, nor did I investigate further. I just filed the information away in the back of my mind. The articles I read that day in the law library focused almost exclusively on the negative side of Asperger's Syndrome. There were, in those days, no in-person support groups or on-line communities for adults on the autism spectrum. Scholars had yet to conclude that notables such as Albert Einstein, Mozart, Emily Dickinson or Hans Christian Andersen were probable aspies. The only concrete example I had before me was the exceptionally bright, but otherwise clueless young man who had occasioned my research—someone every bit as dysfunctional as I had been at 18 when I could well have used a guardian of my own.

Still, I now had a key to unravel one of the biggest mysteries of my life, the riddle of my long regression.

"Other Kids Move." That was my mother's mantra. "Some parents work for large companies. They can be transferred from one city to another at their employer's whim. Some parents are in the military and are sent to the ends of the earth. Kids are uprooted all the time. Their parents move to strange towns, buy new homes, they enroll in different schools. *Other kids cope.* They adjust; they make friends, *but not you.*"

Baffled by this enigma, my mother believed that I had the answer and was stubbornly refusing to disclose it. Over the years, she persistently confronted me with that single question: "Why only you?" Once, when I lived in Atlantic City, she surprised me with a visit and stayed several nights in one of the just-opened casinos along the Boardwalk. It was the kind of treat that seldom came my way—my Mom all to myself for several days. All in all, we had a splendid time, taking in shows, dining out and strolling along the Boardwalk. She even had a roll-away bed brought to her hotel room so that we could have a sleepover. We watched *Dallas* together. Mom was deeply confounded by the behavior of Sue Ellen Ewing. For the life of her, she could not understand how Sue Ellen could hate J.R. so fervently one minute and tenderly invite him into her bed the next. With less experience in such matters, but a more vivid imagination, I perceived nothing contradictory in Sue Ellen's behavior, and rose to her defense.

It was after we shut out the lights that she lit into me as she so often had before. By then, I was thirty years of age. My mother was in her fifties. We were both grown-ups, but as they said about the Bourbon royal family in France, she had learned nothing and forgotten nothing. "Why did you give us such trouble when we were trying to build a new business? It was all for *you,* you and your brother! I wanted you to taste the finer things of life. When we lived in Croton, your father worked in construction. Construction is a back-breaking job. Suppose he were laid up? How should we have supported ourselves? How could you have been so selfish—ranting and raving and putting on acts and banging your head on the floor! Why, one night I had to call the police! You were acting so bizarre! *Other kids move. They* don't drag their parents through hell. *Only you.*"

It was like a sword twisting in my gut. I knew no words to satisfy my mother. Sure, I had been able to decipher Sue Ellen, but my own behavior remained a puzzle. Finally, I piped up: "I missed Alexis very much. She was the only best friend I ever had. I hurt so badly, and you did not give a damn. *It was not all my fault.*" That shut her up. She never mentioned it again, but it was always on the tip of her tongue.

Other kids move, and they adjust. Yeah, they do. I've seen it with my own eyes. There had been a new boy in the Real Me's fifth grade class. His name was Eddie, and he had relocated from Georgia, a fabulous land never touched by ice or snow. Eddie arrived in Croton extremely sad and homesick, that was plain to see. All he spoke of that first semester was Georgia. He brought photos to show and tell of his hometown, his former school, and the friends he had left behind. Nevertheless, by spring, Eddie was running around the playground with the rest of the boys, whooping it up and having fun. Georgia figured less and less in his conversation, and by the following year he hardly mentioned it at all.

In high school, I was one of the new kids in town, but there were plenty of others. In due course, like Eddie, my fellow transferees came around. One by one, they assimilated, and were treated as classmates not as strangers. They ceased to carry a torch for their lost childhood friends. Their souls did not freeze within them and they did not seek the solace of sleep twenty-four hours a day. *Children with Asperger's Syndrome, I read, like those with other forms of autism, have great difficulty coping with change.* Perhaps it was not, after all, *only me.*

Fire Bicycle

•

*I*t was during the 1990s that I had a Great Adventure. I spent three weeks in Baghdad back in the days when it was still the capital of a sovereign nation, and they were pretty much the most delightful three weeks I had known since junior high.

This was an anomaly in my life. I am rather a homebody. Other aspies tout the benefits of travel abroad, and rave about how other cultures are more tolerant of those of us on the autism spectrum. This is not, I think, due to the fact that people in other countries are more inherently accepting of neurodiversity, but due to their lack of preconceived notions of how we should behave. This is an entirely logical construct. Imagine, for example, that an aspie from Lapland or Zambia or the Fiji Islands moved into your neighborhood. Having no expectations of how a typical person from his culture should behave, you would likely ascribe any eccentricity he displays to the fact that he is a Laplander or Zambian or Fiji Islander rather than the chance that he is simply weird.

Some American aspies have even married foreign spouses or, given the opportunity, pulled up stakes and moved to distant lands. I am not likely to join them. My year on the road following the loss of my job in Atlantic City did much to cure me of the wanderlust. If one is doomed to be a stranger wherever one goes, one might as well stick close to home where a comfortable sofa is waiting, where you can adjust the thermostat to your liking and the chef at the local diner knows how to cook your burgers just right.

This is how my pilgrimage to Iraq came about: During the drumbeat leading up to the Gulf War, it began to disturb me greatly that I could not comprehend what seemed so clearly evident to everyone else, the political and moral necessity of war with Iraq. True, Saddam Hussein had invaded Kuwait-an action whose soundness one might reasonably question—but Saddam had taken care to run it by the American ambassador first. Ambassador April Gillespie had given him the green light and then everyone squawked when the deed was done. Well, I have learned not to take saber-rattling at face value. I did a little reading and I discovered that Iraq had a long-simmering historic claim to Kuwait which prior Iraqi leaders had tried to assert. This had not come out of thin air. I did a bit more reading and I realized that half the population of Kuwait—that is, women, were treated badly there. and would fare much better as citizens of Iraq, a secular state where women had equal rights under the law, attended college and entered the professions. Neither country was a democracy, but, for the life of me I could not understand why Saddam Hussein should be considered a greater villain than the Emir of Kuwait. The latter—and this was made known to all the world by Ross Perot—had a minister whose only assignment was to procure a fresh virgin for his master each Thursday night. In fact, the Emir did not even live *in* Kuwait, but on the French Riviera where such behavior was more acceptable and the weather was fine. Yes, certainly Saddam may have used poison gas against the Kurds, but such lethal tactics are employed by dictators against insurgents the world over—did not the Chinese mow down protesters in Tiananmen Square?—and no one in the U.S. Government ever said "boo." I delved a bit further, and I uncovered Saddam Hussein's real crime. He had thrown out the foreign oil companies and nationalized Iraq's vast oil wealth. He built himself palaces, yes, but he also built highways, airports, hospitals and universities for his people. They all bore his name, too: Saddam International Airport, Saddam University, and the Saddam Museum—but they were just as useful as if they had been called Iraqi Central.

As a teenager, I had fiercely opposed the Vietnam War, but, looking back, I could see that our initial presence there had a moral underpinning. Vietnam had no oil. We had not gone there for plunder, but to prevent the spread of Maoist style communism. It was the wrong way to go about it, of course, and it backfired into a swamp of sorrow and savage brutality. Nor had I been alone in opposing Vietnam. My high school teachers had also believed the war was wrong, and had viewed me as sage and precocious for speaking out against it despite my tender years. The Gulf War, on the other hand, entirely incomprehensible to me, was cheered on by all. Each time I turned on the TV, my sensibilities were assaulted with lavish and loving praise for the latest military aircraft, munitions, bombs big and small. I cringed inside. What were we about? Spilling blood for the sake of Big Oil and a dissolute Emir and to restore Kuwaiti women to bondage? Even Aunt Rose had been caught up in the war fever. The girl who had cursed FDR for sending her kid brother to Okinawa was now perfectly willing to rain death and destruction down on people who had done her no injury. Indisputable evidence that my brain was wired differently from those of my countrymen was finally staring me in the face.

It was the photos of the Highway of Death that really did it for me. If you were not around in '91 or have forgotten, the Highway of Death was the main road from Kuwait City to Baghdad along which the retreating Iraqi troops and thousands of fleeing civilians were trapped in an enormous traffic jam as American warplanes blithely strafed them from above. Like *shooting fish in a barrel*, the commentators on CNN declared. Or like one of those canned hunts they used to hold back in the Gilded Age, the sort that Teddy Roosevelt viewed with such disdain. The gamekeeper would drive the animals into a pen so that the wealthy amateur could bring home a trophy without actually having to chase around the forest where his carefully pressed safari suit might get all smudged and dirty. Not very sporting, is it? And not in accordance with the civilized rules of war, either—*Thou shalt not fire upon a retreating army.*

One newsman had angled his camera so that you could see inside the open door of one bombed-out automobile. The body of a young man sprawled across the front seat, half in and half out of the wreck, his legs dangling into the desert sands. In the passenger seat beside him, was an overturned cat carrier. That image engendered within me the same surge of instant identification that I had experienced with the tale of the young Viet Cong woman so long ago. *I'm on the way home with the cat.* The sensation was so strong that I set my heart on a venture I would otherwise never have chosen. I would journey to Iraq to see for myself whether these people were deserving of the carnage and desolation we had lately wreaked upon them.

The logistics of putting this trip together in the early 1990s were far from simple. Diplomatic relations between the United States and Iraq had been broken off, and I had to go through channels until I found the Iraqi Interests Section which had taken shelter in the Hungarian or Uruguayan Embassy. My quest led me to the United Nations and to the Union Square office of Ramsey Clark, the former U.S. Attorney General who had ties with the international peace movement. I had originally planned to bring a cat with me to replace the one who would never return, but, by the time my plans came to fruition, that had proved unworkable. When I learned that Iraq did not issue tourist visas, but welcomed foreign journalists, I wheedled a press card out of a local newspaper in return for a promise of a free article recounting my adventures.

A lot of people assured me of their assistance, but the months turned into years, and I had almost given up on the idea, when I received a telephone call from an Iraqi diplomat. Saddam Hussein's government had invited a 95-year-old lady from Cleveland to visit the annual festival for the restoration of Babylon, and would I like to be her companion?

Babylon? You don't say? Fabled Babylon, home to the goddess Ishtar whose chariot was pulled by lions and to the god Marduk, slayer of the dragon of the primordial waters? Babylon, cursed by the prophets, where Hammurabi wrote the earliest extant code of laws and Nebuchadnezzar built the Hanging Gardens? Well, wasn't that *right up my alley? Why, yes!* I accepted without a moment's hesitation.

I met my traveling companion at JFK airport. We all called her Miz Mary, and, she was indeed ninety-five and from an old family in Cleveland. Born at the dawn of the twentieth century, Miz Mary reminded me of the heroine from the movie, *The Unsinkable Molly Brown*. She belonged to a travel club that awarded some sort of prize to each member who had visited 100 countries. Miz Mary had been to 98. Iraq would be Country No. 99. The political precariousness of the situation did not perturb her one bit. Miz Mary was a citizen of the world. She told me how, while living in the Philippines during World War II, she had been arrested as a spy and imprisoned—I forget by which side—in a tone that suggested the experience was a minor *contretemps*. She had seen everything and was totally unflappable.

She held my hand during takeoff on Royal Jordan Airlines and recited calmly, "The Lord lifts us up on Wings of Eagles." All I could think of were those astronauts who had "slipped the surly bonds of earth to touch the face of God," and I was not quite sure I was ready to join them.

Some people view air travel as romantic. I am not one of them. If I never board another plane, it will be too soon. These were the days before full body scanners and invasive pat downs. Still, I found the check-in protocol rather confusing and an annoyance. After that, I was trapped for fourteen hours between two crying babies and the foreign-looking gentleman behind me who grimaced each time I tried to adjust the seat back.

Train travel is romantic. Before I purchased my first automobile at the age of thirty, I took the railroad everywhere. Even today, I take the commuter trains whenever I go to Manhattan. I sit on the side by the river, throw my bag on the seat next to me, stretch out and peer out the window at the ducks on the water and the impregnable cliffs of the Palisades. I can study the timetable and count off the stations—Ossining, Tarrytown, Irvington, and Dobbs Ferry. Aah, that. Whenever the Real Me misbehaved, Mom always threatened to send her to Dobbs Ferry. If her wrongdoing continued, it would elicit a thunderous reply, "Now, it's off to Dobbs Ferry with you!" Years later, I discovered the message my mother was trying to impart. That riverside village was once home to a famous reformatory. To the Real Me, it was her spiritual destination—a kind of Never-Never land, full of lost boys and girls, where she might one day be transported.

As a teenager, I took the train alone down to the City for the first time. When the conductor called out, "Station Stop! *Dobbs Ferry!*" I looked up startled. In haste, I peered through my hands out the window, expecting to see a tribe of wayward children racing up and down the platform, menacing travelers with toy guns and fierce war whoops. Instead, my eyes were greeted with the prosaic sight of suburban men in grey flannel suits and women in tailored suits with briefcases. Nevertheless, whenever the train stops at Dobbs Ferry, even to this very day, my heart will go thump and my eyes will hurriedly scan the platform for the Lost Boys I had hoped to see there.

On the plane, there was nothing to see even in daylight, although I sat by the window. I was greeted only by an unrelenting expanse of blue. If I looked down, I only saw the steel wing. There were no station stops, either. We did land at one airport, and they told me it was Amsterdam. However, when I walked to the door of the plane and peered out, all I saw was a foggy runway that could have been anywhere in this world, or, for that matter, in some other world.

Moreover, I could not forget, not for one second, that here I was, in a huge metal tube somewhere in the sky, and that my life was entirely outside my control. Despite all Miz Mary's assurances, I could never be certain, could I, that the pilot was not someone like me, who might fall asleep at the wheel, who might not see that stop sign, or who might have a sudden meltdown and decide that life was not worth living after all. When the pilot took his microphone and declared, "Turbulence," I was convinced it was all over. I began to make my peace with my Creator. Miz Mary did not so much as bat an eye.

Due to the United Nations sanctions on Iraq, it was necessary to land at Amman and journey overland. While Miz Mary made the arrangements for a driver, I hailed a cab and visited the Amman Safeway where I stocked up on provisions I could not live without—two cases of Coca-Cola and two more of Diet Pepsi. Aunt Rose had kindly baked my favorite Italian cookies, and sent me off with a container full. These, carefully husbanded, would last me until Baghdad where, despite the sanctions, treats could still be found. Indeed, I would survive three weeks on Jordanian soda, sugar wafers from Turkey and rotisserie chicken from the Arab bazaar.

It had been a fourteen-hour flight from New York to Amman. It was another fourteen hours' drive through the desert sands. At least, now I could open the window and feel the wind blowing on my arm, a hot dry wind. It was like traveling along an endless beach. I kept expecting to hit water, but none was in sight.

There were a few interesting moments when we arrived at the Iraqi border. I duly presented my passport to be stamped but the Iraqi customs official thoughtfully declined it, advising me that I would have some explaining to do if I arrived home with *Iraq* stamped in my passport. Tell the folks at JFK that you were visiting friends in Jordan. What they don't know won't hurt them, ha, ha, ha!

The route out of Amman had been a two-lane highway, rather like my favorite back roads, except with a steady stream of oil tankers headed the other way. Once we crossed over into Iraq, we might as well have been driving on an interstate. The highways were modern, broad and expansive with no signposts to keep you oriented, just more desert sand. It was dusk by then, and I was growing sleepy but struggled to keep my eyes open. I was gripped by an illogical fear that I might fall asleep and wake up in Kansas.

Two hours north of Baghdad, we all agreed that it was time to make a pit stop. The driver pulled over to the side of the road. I said, "Well?" The driver pointed to somewhere over the dunes. There was nothing to be seen but a vast tract of sand. He suggested I walk out there and do what had to be done. I stared at him blankly and said, "You have got to be kidding me!"

The driver and Miz Mary shrugged their shoulders and went out into the sand and did their business. I could not do it. I absolutely *could not*, although, by now, my need had also grown great. When the driver returned to the car, I insisted he take me to a rest room. We argued the point. The driver contended that I was being unreasonable—after all, I had the *entire desert*—but, in the end, I got my way and we left the highway at Ramadi. He took me to the house of someone he knew, a friend or a relative, and I was allowed to use the bathroom. It was only a hole in the floor, not a proper bathroom at all, but it beat venturing forth in the trackless nighttime desert with your pants down.

Upon our arrival at the Palestine Hotel, we were given a sheet of paper, inscribed in both Arabic and English: "Dear Guest," it read. "Welcome to Baghdad. The Ministry of Information, your host, has advised us that they will bear the charges of your accommodation, three soft drinks and three meals only, at the coffee shop and laundry. All other charges incurred in restaurants, bars and room service will be paid for in foreign currency at the time of check-out. We hope your stay at the Palestine will be unforgettable."

My balcony, on the thirteenth floor, overlooked that titanic statue of Saddam Hussein, the one that was later pulled from its pedestal by the U.S. Marines during the invasion to the cheers of some scruffy street urchins. The statue did not bother me. After all, even a brutal dictator might sport a good-looking physique, and perhaps the sculptor had been kind. I would sit outside on the balcony when the day's activities were done, basking in the balmy night breezes from the Tigris, and listen to the music from the Ishtar Sheraton across the road where weddings seemed to take place with alarming regularity. Sometimes I would tinker with my portable radio, turning it this way and that, until I pulled in the BBC World News.

At the Palestine I soon fell in with a handful of western female journalists who were also staying at the hotel, one was a professor from West Germany, one was a reporter from Jordan, and a third was Italian. We were all in our thirties and early forties and shared an instant sense of camaraderie which perhaps arose from banding together on a faintly forbidden venture. Add to the mix, Anwar, the Kurdish waiter, Ema, a Libyan-Iraqi trinket and jewelry merchant, Allia, a young Baghdadi antiques dealer who proudly sported a CNN T-shirt, Nadira, our beautiful Iraqi guide, Thanar, a student at Saddam University, and the varied and sundry travelers who crossed our path. One never knew whom one would run into at the Hotel Palestine. A Palestinian Christian exile from Bethlehem was staying there; she regaled us with stories of life under Israeli occupation. A blockade runner from Turkey, who even looked like Rhett Butler, brought us assorted boxes of cookies which sustained me through my stay. One evening I encountered another Palestinian wayfarer, a young man from Tunis, who, by his own account, served as an aide to Chairman Arafat. Oh, oh, I immediately thought, something nefarious is afoot. Not to worry. He was no terrorist, but a folksinger, come to perform at the Babylon Festival.

Something miraculous had occurred. I, who had had difficulty making friends all my life, who had never belonged anywhere at anytime, who was treated like a ghost in my own hometown, suddenly fit right in. Yes, perhaps it was curiosity, perhaps they thought me as quirky and odd as all the rest, but were just too polite to say so and perhaps the government was paying them to keep me company. It did not matter. I only knew that suddenly I was sought out. My opinions were solicited and, when offered, treated with respect. That circumstance in itself transformed Baghdad from another outpost on a lonely planet into a city of magic and mystery.

Surprisingly, I found that Americans were not held in disfavor, as Iraqis would have been here, but rather viewed in high regard. Not so the American government. A favorite child's rhyme, recited whenever a plane flew overhead, started with the invocation, "Bush, Bush." If you were not *Bush,* you were treated as a friend. During my stay in Baghdad not one person—*not one*—walked right through me as if I were not there.

Each evening our little group piled into a car to be driven down to the restoration of Babylon, ninety kilometers away. Our driver was a handsome young man named Sa'id, a member of the Republican Guard who had been wounded in battle and decorated by Saddam himself. He proudly displayed his commendation to us, and taught us a few words of Arabic of which I remember only one—*Inshallah,* if God wills it. Sa'id might be a hardened warrior, but he was also a modern sensitive nineties kind of guy, as well. On every third night, it was his turn to mind his adorable three-year-old son who would accompany us on our ride.

At Babylon we were ushered into a large Greek amphitheatre which had been built at the time of Alexander the Great who died in Babylon in 332 B.C. We were greeted by 10,000 excited Iraqis loudly chanting (*as translated by Nadira*):

"Bush, Bush, listen well,
We all love Saddam Hussein."

I glanced over at Miz Mary, who had already declared herself an unwavering Republican, whose grandparents had been personal friends of William McKinley. She was completely unperturbed. "You cannot blame them for standing by their guy," she explained, "as much as I stand by mine."

The program was all in Arabic, of course, but I was enthralled by the haunting music, the exuberant dances and the exotic costumes. There was one skit that even an outlander could understand. A tall handsome dark-haired gentleman in a silver caftan delivered a rousing speech to the assembly, met by wild applause, while a pint-sized actor dressed up as George Bush, Sr. ran in circles about him, ineptly wielding a paper sword.

Afterwards, we walked through the replica of the Ishtar Gate and down the Street of Processions in the moonlight, just drinking in the wonder of five thousand years. As we approached the parking lot, we took in the nightly fireworks display which was greatly enjoyed by all. Now, if I had recently been on the receiving end of an air war, I doubt I would have been able to appreciate fireworks. However, the Iraqis clapped and cheered as if it were all great fun.

One night, as we pulled away, Margrete, the German professor, pointed at a group of young men who were laughing and smoking and engaging in horseplay. Except for their guns and the lack of booze, they might have been college boys at a frat party. "The feared Republican Guard," she said.

During the day, we toured museums, schools, hospitals, the Iraqi Women's Federation, mosques and churches. Yes, there were Christian churches in Baghdad and quite a few of them. Our guide, Nadira was herself a Catholic and Tariq Aziz, Saddam's right hand man, was a Chaldean Christian. There was also a smaller Jewish community in Baghdad which had been granted freedom of worship, although, to be honest, the Jews were not accepted as well as the Christians.

A doctor from the Saddam Hospital explained to me why the Iraqis disliked the Jews: It seems that, along about 587 B.C. Nebuchadnezzar, the great King of Babylon, conquered Jerusalem and carried the Hebrews off into captivity in Babylon. However, instead of throwing them into dungeons or relegating them to slavery, Nebuchadnezzar treated the Hebrews as honored guests. During their sojourn in Babylon, the Israelis received free education, free healthcare, and high-paying jobs. Jews were invited to come to court and dine at the King's own table. Did those rascally Hebrews appreciate this Babylonian largesse? No! When Cyrus the Persian laid siege to Babylon, they turned upon their kindly hosts and opened the gates of the city to the invaders.

I was fascinated by this story because the Iraqi doctor spoke as if these events had occurred only the past summer, rather than two thousand years before. In America, matters which took place twenty years ago are gone and forgotten, but here was an educated Iraqi recounting ancient history as though he had been an eyewitness.

One day we went to the zoo. While in Jordan, I had read in an English-language newspaper the tale of Hani, the Lonely Lion of Baghdad and I just had to see for myself. Hani's distress was caused by his status as the only male lion in Iraq. The obvious solution was to import a mate for him. This had indeed been in the works. A mail-order lioness was on her way when the U.N. slapped sanctions on Iraq and no further traffic in lions was allowed. For the foreseeable future, Hani was doomed to a life of celibacy and social isolation—sort of, like myself. Sadly pacing up and down in his solitary enclosure, he just exuded loneliness. Of all those whom I met in Baghdad, my heart went out to Hani most of all.

I had it in mind that a trek to Tikrit, Saddam Hussein's hometown, would be in order. After all, Tikrit on the Tigris was to Saddam what Croton-on-Hudson was to me, and certainly no one could sit in judgment over me without a trip to Croton. Thus, on the Thursday morning of our second week in Iraq, after obtaining permission from the powers-that-be, Sa'id drove us up to Tikrit. This was all my idea, met with a marked lack of enthusiasm from Margrete and the others. Miz Mary had remained back at the hotel, declining to accompany us in the desert heat. Nevertheless, I was high as a kite. It was the thrill of the chase all over again. At that time, few, if any, westerners had ever seen Tikrit, and once again I experienced the lure of forbidden pleasures. Not that there was much to see there—or that we were allowed to see—just a small oasis in the midst of the Mesopotamian sands. It was the *idea* of it that had seized me with delight. *Here I am, the first American that you have ever seen.*

I purchased a papier-mâché lion from an old man at a shop in Tikrit and asked him for his views on the American government. "George Bush eats little children," he replied with great alacrity.

Sa'id brought us to a modest-looking house where we met a widowed mother, her two daughters and teenage son. Unlike the women I had seen in Baghdad who wore either Western garb or bold colorful dresses, this family were dressed in a more traditional Muslim fashion, with long black skirts and head scarves, reminding me of the nuns I had known in childhood. The mother, who looked to be about Saddam's age, described to me how Saddam had to do his schoolwork under the light of the streetlamp. His family had been too poor to afford electricity. I said that my Aunt Rose had told me quite the same story about her own upbringing in the Great Depression. While I was lapping all this up and my companions were looking on skeptically, the elder daughter offered her complaint as to the lack of access to Pepsi-Cola now that the U.N. embargo was in place. I recalled my own stash back at the hotel and nodded in sympathy. The mother then went into the kitchen and came back with a basketful of warm, whole wheat pita bread. This was, without a doubt, the best pita bread I have ever in my life tasted, far superior to anything you could buy at the supermarket. It was so delicious that one did not feel the need for butter or to make a sandwich. You could just pull it apart and savor it. She gave us several pieces to take back and, even the following day, the bread was tasty and fresh. It was a welcome change from my usual fare of Diet Pepsi, rotisserie chicken and sugar wafers which had been smuggled across the border from Turkey.

I often wandered the streets of Baghdad, all by myself, visiting shops, hotels, and bazaars. A lot of people spoke English and, once I identified myself as an American, most were eager to chat. I never had the sense of being alone in a foreign land. Baghdad seemed strangely familiar to me. It reminded me of New York City set down in the world of the *Arabian Nights*. Now, looking back, I realize that I was so comfortable in Baghdad because it was like going back in time, closer to the era of the Real Me. It was not just the old cars and the black and white TV's or the small-hole-in-the-wall emporiums which had not yet been replaced with big box stores; it was an attitude that, by then, seemed delightfully primitive.

One morning we were taken to the Saddam Children's Museum I gaped in fascination at the antiwar posters that lined the walls, replete with white doves and peace signs. One poster depicted President Bush as a vampire, his voracious mouth chewing away at the wriggling bodies of Iraqi babies. A popular theme, it appeared. Yes, it was propaganda, but these looked eerily similar to the posters I had had on my walls in high school and college. In fact, the style was *so exactly* like that adopted by the anti-Vietnam movement that I was gripped by a certainty that some exiled American counter culturist was hiding down there in the basement and churning out this artwork.

It was not all like the sixties, however. One day I was invited to speak before a class at Saddam University. I boldly advised the students that, when I had gone to college, we had questioned everything our professors taught us, and expressed regret that they lived in a country without freedom of speech. My guide piped up and said that this was not true. Iraqis enjoyed freedom of speech. Why, right down the hallway there was a bulletin board on which the students could express their opinions with no fear of reprisal. I ran down the hallway, demanding to see this bulletin board. It was there, all right—and completely blank. I looked at my guide quizzically. "Well, as you see," he said, "Iraqi students are so happy that they have no complaints."

A few days later we were taken to see the editor of the *Baghdad Observer*, the English-language daily. I asked him why Iraqi journalists did not band together and demand freedom of the press. He assured me that they had such freedom, and that this was due to the powerful Iraqi Journalists' Association. And who was the head of the Journalists' Association? None other than Udai Hussein, elder son of Saddam. Come again? I raised my brows. Well, explained the editor, did you want us to choose someone *with no influence?*

At night there would often be barbecues in the courtyard to the rear of the hotel.

The days were often very hot, even though it was autumn, but the nights would be perfect, with the breezes blowing in from the Tigris. I would hastily scribble everything I had seen that day in a notebook, thinking that perhaps I would write a book about my journey to Iraq, a guide for political pilgrims. I even had a title: *Still Standing.* While we dined in the open air, entertainment was provided by a rock band that *looked* American and *sounded* American, without a trace of any accent. The musicians sang the haunting lyrics of *The Signs of Love,* a song which I had never heard before and never would again.

Of course, it was not all lightness and joy. Early on, we were conducted to the *Al-Amariya* Bomb Shelter, a must-see, I suppose, for all Westerner visitors. If you have forgotten the story of *Al-Amarya*—and you doubtlessly have—it was a shelter located in a working-class neighborhood in north Baghdad which American intelligence erroneously reported to be a command and control headquarters. One night, early in the Gulf War, a laser-guided cruise missile slammed into the shelter, incinerating over a thousand civilians, most of them, women and children. Our guide for the visit was an Iraqi teenager who had, at his parents' insistence, taken his sister to the shelter that night where they would presumably be safe. The sister had died and the boy himself had been badly burned, requiring six months' treatment in a German hospital. Candles were burning along the darkened ruined corridors, below photographs of the lost children, their names also scrolled on the walls, in a universal expression of grief. A few years later, when 9/11 happened right here in New York, I immediately recalled *Al-Amariya*. If you went down to Ground Zero in the days following the attack, you might as well have been standing in the ruins of *Al-Amarya*.

At the time, the American government was so shamefaced at bombing civilians, that they tried to deny it had ever happened. Of course, it happened and, what is more, it happens all the time, everywhere, on all sides. Did Dresden happen? My Dad was at Nagasaki. That happened, too.

At the historical site where I work now, there is displayed a tapestry that was made of Picasso's famous painting *Guernica*. Guernica was a small village in the Basque area of northern Spain, not a military target at all, just a village full of innocent civilians. One day in April, 1937, German warplanes, in support of Francisco Franco, one of the combatants in the Spanish Civil War, flew above Guernica and bombed the village to smithereens, killing thousands. This was the first recorded instance of modern military airpower being used indiscriminately against civilians, and people were *outraged*. Picasso, who *(luckily for his own longevity*) was already living in Paris, was *outraged*. He thereupon began work on a painting which he exhibited in Paris eight months after the assault. *Guernica*—still considered the strongest antiwar statement in all of art history—was greeted by worldwide acclaim and made Picasso a legend. I wonder if Picasso would have been capable of such outrage, or such art, if he were living today. Perhaps he would simply have reacted the way so many of us do, "*Well, ho, hum.*"

My original visa expired after two weeks, but I protested that there was so much I still needed to see, that an extension was granted. I watched Miz Mary leave for home, and the others departed as well, but I lingered on. During my last week in Baghdad, Iraqis celebrated an event in their history that fascinated me. The radio programs and the movies were all in Arabic, but I asked the hotel staff what they were commemorating, and I was filled in.

Back in 1959, Iraq was ruled by a brutal dictator called Abdul Kissim. He had started off as a great hero, having fought to free his nation from the British yoke, but he turned into an evil despot, oppressing his people and even invading Kuwait. At this time there was a small band of handsome and fearless college students in Baghdad, one of whom was Saddam Hussein. They vowed to liberate Iraq from the tyrant, even if it meant their lives. One day, as Kissim's motorcade traversed the streets of the capital, a daring but unsuccessful assassination attempt took place. In the cross fire, the young Saddam Hussein was wounded. Being the brave soul that he was, he grabbed the penknife he carried in his pocket and dug the bullet out of his leg. Where do you go when you find yourself in a heap of trouble? Where did I always wind up? *Home.* Saddam swam across the Tigris and fled to Tikrit, where he borrowed a motorcycle and made his way to Egypt. He spent two years in exile and then he returned to Iraq, to marry his cousin to whom he had been promised since childhood, and to fight for freedom in his native land. One of the managers at the Palestine told me that there was a museum in Baghdad where the actual motorcycle could be seen. I insisted on seeing it. The very next day, my new driver, Jerwahl, took me to the Ba'ath Party Museum.

While Sa'id had been a member of the elite Republican Guard, Jerwahl's whole demeanor said "foot soldier." He was very young and rather soft and rotund. Unlike Sa'id who had been fiercely loyal to Saddam, I suspect Jerwahl harbored rebellion in his heart. He kept a stack of cassettes in his car. Whenever we were alone, he would slip in a tape of the Village People. His favorite track? *Liberation*. If he has survived the bombing, Jerwahl was probably happy to see Iraq become an American protectorate. I liked Jerwahl a lot. He took me to places that Sa'id never would have, bazaars and tiny shops in working-class neighborhoods, and just laid-back cruising around Baghdad.

There it was, standing proudly on the steps of the Ba'ath Party Museum—a rusted old motorcycle, 1950s vintage. A placard that hung around the handlebars proclaimed, in English and Arabic:

FIRE BICYCLE
Upon which Brave Leader
Fled to Egypt After Attempt
On Devil Kissim.

After that, I wandered in fascination through the halls of the Ba'ath Party Museum, absorbing many dates, names and places of Iraqi history.

Of course, the supreme irony is that Saddam—the name means *he who confronts*—turned into exactly what he once tried to destroy. The fearless young freedom-fighter became a ruthless dictator, every bit as tyrannical as the Devil Kissim. The man of the people—who read his schoolbooks under the street lamps and wanted to use Iraq's oil wealth to help the poor, who himself wielded a shovel to begin the rebuilding of Iraq after its war with Iran—had turned into a tin-horn despot, surrounded by yes men, who walled himself off from his constituents and lived in luxury while they suffered. I guess this is a fable as old as the human condition. The scariest monster of all is the one that lurks within our soul.

My sojourn in Baghdad had come to an end. I flirted with the notion of applying for permanent residency and becoming like those white folk in the Old West who had forsaken their own kind to live among the Indians. Even if asylum were granted, could I have supported myself in Bagdad? I thought of the Chicago refugee dwelling deep in the bowels of the Saddam Children's Museum, grinding out posters of Bush chomping down on Iraqi babies. Could I have done likewise? I spoke no Arabic, but many residents of Baghdad spoke English. Could I have helped Allia sell antiques? Written for the English-language newspaper? In the end, however, I looked at my return ticket from Amman to JFK dated October 24th, and regarded with alarm my dwindling supply of Coke and Diet Pepsi. I could not live in a land where my favorite drinks were under a UN embargo. Besides, I suspected that, sooner or later, the American government would find an excuse to begin bombing Baghdad again, and I had no wish to become target practice. *Like shooting fish in a barrel.*

On October 23rd, I paid two of Allia's cousins to drive me to Jordan. I was naïve enough to believe, that because I had a return ticket for October 24th, I could merely show up at Amman International on that date and be seated on the next airplane bound for New York City. As a neophyte traveler, I was totally ignorant of the custom of *bumping*.

Imagine my surprise when I was told that there would be no seats available on a flight to New York for another three days! I argued, I begged, I cajoled, all to no avail. They were not going to put me on a plane that day no matter what.

When my pleas fell on deaf ears, I took a cab to downtown Amman and spent my last few American dollars on a room at a good hotel. During my stay in Baghdad, I had encountered another American woman about my age and with a similar college-educated, middle-class background. She was in Iraq on a free-lance assignment from *Penthouse* magazine. *(Yes, Bob Guccione resurfaces).* Like me, she was held over in Amman while waiting for a flight home. I ran into her there, and we shared a repast at the Jordan branch of Kentucky Fried Chicken. While we dined, I went on and on about what a magical fairy-tale place Baghdad had seemed to me, full of wonder and delight. She grimaced, looked me straight in the eye, and said, with utter conviction, "I saw it as a giant prison camp run by the thugs of Saddam Hussein." *Oh.*

When I returned to New York, true to my word, I submitted an article to the local newspaper describing my experiences. It was well received in town. Croton has an artsy and left-wing tradition to uphold, and for a while, my adventure provided me with a certain cachet. People would stop me in the streets and commend me on my insightful tale. My hope was to return to Iraq someday and continue my research, but it did not work out, and I never wrote the book I had envisioned.

On the third Saturday in February of 2003, when George Bush the Second was preparing his invasion of Iraq, I took the *peace train* down to the City with other antiwar protesters from the Hudson River towns. It was an exceedingly cold weekend, but I gamely joined the gigantic peace march that wound its way up Third Avenue, looped around Second, and headed down First. We had planned to demonstrate before the United Nations, but the police would not let us anywhere near the U.N. The right to protest, I learned to my dismay, had been significantly curtailed since my college days. Back then demonstrators had regularly marched right in front of the White House and the Pentagon, waving Vietcong flags, wooden poles and placards and yelling out all sorts of epithets. No one had dared object. It was democracy in action, after all. In the modern era, new ground rules apply, I discovered it was forbidden to carry a pole made of anything more durable than cardboard. You might hurt someone with it, for God's sake! Yes, you could still hold up a sign, but you had to be mighty careful of the writing on it. Back in the day, your sign might boldly proclaim: *Nixon is the Devil Incarnate* and your right of free speech would be respected. It is best not to venture a similar sentiment in reference to the current occupant of the White House. My placard read *I stand with the Pope,* a reference to the now beatified John Paul's staunch opposition to the invasion. Who could object to that? Antiwar marches were held throughout the world on that day. I wondered if Margrete was marching in Germany. In New York City it was so bitterly and unusually cold with a high temperature in the low twenties, that, despite my honorable intentions, I had to leave the march before it was done and nurse my frostbite in a Food Emporium near the Queensboro Bridge. When I finally made it back to Grand Central, I was shivering uncontrollably.

Four weeks later, on the very eve of military action, there was another peace march. This time, it was close to 60 degrees, a balmy afternoon in early spring. I had dug out a tambourine that a member of a disbanding rock group had given me long ago, and I kept the beat with the chanting of the crowd as we strode down Broadway to Washington Square. There was an almost festive atmosphere due to the break in the weather, and many parents had brought their little kids along. One toddler held up a sign declaring:

"BUSH, DON'T BE LIKE YOUR BAGH DAD"

This advice was greeted with stamping feet and whoops of approval from the crowd. I myself was in a more somber mood. For a long time it had been clear that George Bush the Second was bound and determined to invade and take Iraq, even should the very heavens sound a protest against it. Like my mother with the crumbling country estate, *He just had to have it.*

By that time, too, the earth had begun to slip away beneath me. I had lost my Mom the summer before. Within another few years, I would lose, first my Dad, and then Aunt Rose. I would become adrift on a dark sea with no anchor. To make it all worse, as soon as Aunt Rose lay dying, the schoolyard bullies of my youth would reappear in the form of my evil paternal cousins who would pile on and banish me from the clan. Seven years in the throes of hell lie in wait, and I had already stepped through the portal.

The Sorcerer's Apprentice

•

*I*f my evil paternal cousins have a leader, it is my cousin Jan who had held me in thrall for virtually my entire life. To her, I was both bound by chords of astonished admiration and riven with envy. Not too long ago, she nearly drove me to suicide. With my diagnosis, the spell was broken and Jan no longer has any power over me. Still, I will never forget that, like a thief in the night, Jan pilfered the life that should have been mine. Whenever I looked in the mirror, I saw her image. She is the person I might have been had I not been born autistic.

The saga began to unfold when the Real Me was in second grade. She hopped on her bike and coasted down to Penfield Avenue, to the home of her favorite uncle, Uncle Spence, his wife, Aunt Liz, and their newborn daughter, Jan. Aunt Liz not only introduced the Real Me to her infant cousin, wrapped up in a fuzzy pink blanket but actually let her hold little Jan, a privilege that her mother had never allowed her with the baby brother. The Real Me was very proud to have been granted such responsibility. Unfortunately, in her eagerness, she dropped both baby and blanket on the rug. The baby's head came within an inch of striking the wooden arm of the sofa. The Real Me expected to find herself in deep trouble, but Aunt Liz did not yell at her or call her parents. She just picked up the squalling infant and rocked her to sleep.

The Real Me thought she had escaped retribution for that particular act of negligence, but the angels were watching, and they righted the score. All the good things in life—friends, dates, natural athletic ability, laughter, social graces, four years in Croton High, beachside barbeques, Superbowl parties, a brother who was a real pal and not a little stranger, glamorous jobs, gorgeous lovers, children, Christmas trees—were taken away from the Real Me and given to Jan. How else to explain why fortune bestowed all its treasures upon my cousin and left as my portion only loneliness, rejection and despair?

Jan was the target of my jealousy right from the start. She had had the luck to be born the daughter of the mischievous, risk-taking, fun-loving, brimming-with-self-confidence, Uncle Spence, the possessor of all the qualities the Real Me valued in a grown-up. That was a treasure so great, that, even though her mother was a mere mortal, and mine, the Snow Queen, the points added up in her favor. The scales tipped decisively when Jan was awarded a kid brother who was everything a kid brother should be, a buddy to tagalong when they were young, a shoulder to lean on when the world is dark—not that Jan's world is ever dark—an accomplice when nefarious doings are afoot, the friend that will never desert you, and someone who, in adulthood, will give you nieces and nephews and invite you to his house for Thanksgiving.

Uncle Spence was my Dad's favorite sibling. Of Grandpa's ten children, they were the closest in age. Spence was the ninth to be born, Dad's junior by only a year and a half. In their twenties and thirties, they worked together in construction, but, like my parents, Uncle Spence and Aunt Liz thirsted for finer things. In midlife Uncle Spence bought a cluster of low-rent apartments in Beacon, New York that could only be called *tenements,* located midway between Croton and the Kingdom of Frost. From his perch in Beacon he often drove up to visit us, and Uncle Spence was one of the few relatives I did not lose touch with during my exile. However, Spence had the common sense my father lacked. He knew enough not to uproot his children and bring them up to live in Beacon. Instead he left their lives undisturbed and commuted to work as good parents do. Perhaps he had seen the way I had collapsed and wished to spare his own kids that fate. Ironically, his own kids could have weathered the storm much better than either Brett or I. Not only do they have each other, but Jan and John are neurotypical to the bone. My cousin John is a good-natured hunk that gets along with both women and men, and Jan attracts friends like flypaper draws flies, any place and any time.

Jan, of course, is not only clever she is exceedingly beautiful. In fact, she looks like a slightly younger version of myself.

Ah, that's the rub, the undecipherable riddle that would have stumped the Sphinx. All my life, I have watched in amazement, as one handsome male after another fell prostrate at Jan's feet while the ones I pursued scurried away. Jan was lucky in love and lucky at cards, and lucky in life as well. As for me, *I did the miller's daughter one better. I spun gold into straw and did not even require the aid of Rumpelstiltskin.*

This was a mystery more baffling than my mother's constant litany of *other kids adjust.* The enigma was so unfathomable because its answer seemed to depend not, on my own behavior, but on that of others. Why did people flock to Jan's side, while they fled from me? We were first cousins; we looked much alike; we shared many of the same interests. Both of us were intelligent and articulate. Why then was she the popular, de-sired one and I the outcast?

Dr. Dichter could probably have given me a clue. Dr. Ernest Dichter (1907-1991), who is called the *father of motivational re-search,* was an Austrian psychologist, born and raised in Vienna. (*Yes, the same city where Dr. Asperger practiced; perhaps they ran into each other at one time or another*). Dr. Dichter, a follower of Sigmund Freud, graduated from the University of Vienna, and, in 1937, immigrated to America with his wife Hedy. They set-tled here, in Croton-on-Hudson. In 1946 the Dichters founded the Institute for Motivational Research, and became famous by wedding Freudian theories to marketing techniques. Dr. Dich-ter is credited with coining the phase *focus group*, and inventing the slogan *Put a Tiger in Your Tank* for Exxon Gasoline. In his old age, he took on my cousin Jan as his acolyte, fosterling and protégé. At the feet of the master, she imbibed the wizardry of manipulation, and she learned her lessons well.

Many years ago Aunt Rose tried to apprentice me to the Dich-ters as well. She convinced Jan to take me on as her assistant.

I was eager to find the key and unlock *the science of behavioral motivation*. Who, more than I, needed to acquire that hidden knowledge?

For two weeks, I faithfully followed Jan each morning, over the hill and through the winding back roads to the woodlands where the Dichters kept their studio. However, when she introduced me to the material, I was puzzled and dismayed. It was a mountain of statistical analysis, piles and piles of indecipherable data, documents with no discernible rhyme or reason. It baffled even me—one who read train schedules for amusement and who had always loved to study graphs, charts and maps. Now I was quite young at this time, but Jan was younger yet, perhaps still in her teens. Yet, despite her tender years, she was as fluent with the incomprehensible gobbledygook as if it had been her native tongue. I, on the other hand, was utterly stumped.

At the end of two weeks when the Dichters called me in, gave me my paycheck and told me that my services would no longer be required, I just nodded and slunk away in silence. I did not beg, plead, protest or tantrum as is my usual practice. I knew when I was beaten. Since that time, I have lost many other jobs, but typically for reasons like tardiness, insubordination, failure to cooperate with others or inappropriate behavior. This was, the first and only time I was fired due to a lack of intellectual ability to grasp the nature of the work.

Jan went on to master the art of manipulation, to fame and fortune and a glamorous career jetting all over the country to set up focus groups for high-profile clients, to high wages, to friends and lovers and parties galore while I was again relegated to the sidelines of life.

Nevertheless, in a strange, relentless way, her life seemed to mirror mine. While I attended law school in Boston, I became fascinated with the National Hockey League. I knew the names of all the teams, and all their rosters. I had posters of NHL stars on my walls, I read books on the history of the game and the strategies involved. I could name the fallen stars of the

Montreal Canadiens or dissect the curse a disgruntled coach had placed long ago on the Chicago Blackhawks. Hockey players skated through my daydreams. One year I came home for Christmas and found that Jan was actually *dating* a pro hockey player, a minor-league goalie, who she proudly showed off to friends and relatives. How better to remind me how silly and pathetic I was, relegated to the realm of posters and fantasies while she possessed the real thing.

Her image haunted me during my years-long struggle to find acceptance and companionship within the Rec. Department's volleyball program. While I carefully attended each Friday night and considered the evening a success if they would pass me the ball or even allow me to touch it, Jan would strut through the gym doors every now and then and steal the show. There was no reluctance on anyone's part to pass *her* the ball; she was greeted like a long-lost hero, the star quarterback, come out of retirement, still at the top of his game. There was no gainsaying it. She was a natural who outshone them all without breaking a sweat.

In the 1990s I was devoted to a certain political candidate. I went to work in his campaign, gladly performing all the lowly tasks that volunteers do, stuffing envelopes, rousing myself in the cold grey dawn to hand out leaflets at the train station, putting up signs and attending rallies. In the midst of all this I came home one evening, and there is Jan sitting at the kitchen table and regaling Aunt Rose with tales of her exciting new job. She had been hired to conduct focus groups by no less than the Democratic National Committee. She was on a first name basis with everyone from Bill Clinton to the very politician who had inspired me to work like a slave without pay or recognition. That was the night I finally freaked out. I ran screaming out the door and through the neighborhood, turning on my heels, and storming back to the house to confront my tormentor. "How can I ever forgive you," I yelled at Jan, "for stealing the life that was meant for me?"

This is not to say that I hated my cousin Jan. Nothing could be more untrue. I was crazy about her. She was the kid sister that I had always wanted. I adored being in her company, and why not? She was fun to be with, invariably bouncy and in high spirits as one ought to be when the world is at one's feet. Perhaps I cherished the hope that, with Jan in my life, some of her magic might rub off on me.

Of all the myriad nieces and nephews that Aunt Rose possessed, four were particularly close to her. Two of these had moved out of state as soon as they reached adulthood. That left Jan and I. Like me, Jan had had a rocky relationship with her own parents when she was young and had turned for guidance to Aunt Rose. As a result, I saw a lot more of Jan through the years than I saw of my other cousins, and certainly more than I ever saw of my baby brother. Her affection for Aunt Rose appeared genuine; she accompanied her to many medical appointments, even at five in the morning, while I was taking refuge in the Land of Nod, Jan sat with her in the hospital when Uncle Jim died. Being skillful with data and documents, she prepared Aunt Rose's taxes each year. Once I believed Jan cared for me as well. When my beautiful tragic mother died of smoking-related lung cancer at the age of seventy-four, and I was immobilized by grief, Jan drove me to the funeral. A few years later, it was Jan who took me back to Rhode Island to see my Dad when he was dying. Had we not fallen out as we did, Jan would have been the one to keep a watch over me once the older generation was gone. She has a strong sense of family responsibility and nurtures her blood ties. After Aunt Rose died, I found her letters, describing visits to relatives I hardly knew existed. Had things not gone so horribly wrong, I would today have Jan to throw me a lifeline. I might not be condemned to spend the rest of my Christmases alone and in tears.

One early summer day in the late 1980s, Uncle Spence went to work at his tenements in Beacon and never came home. He had gone up in a cherry-picker to prune certain trees on his property, and being the brash, daring, reckless person that he was, he had neglected to wear a protective hardhat. Therefore, when a branch struck him in the head it caused him to fall to the ground mortally injured. He was rushed to St. Francis Hospital in Poughkeepsie where he lapsed into unconsciousness and was soon put on life support. When my father and I went to visit, Spence did not appear to be brain damaged or in an irreversible coma. He looked as if he were sleeping peacefully and might open his eyes and greet us at any moment. In truth, however, he was in so deep an enchanted sleep that not even the kiss of a fairly princess could have awakened him. The respirator caused his chest to rise and fall, but he was not really breathing. His body was there, but his soul had already flown away.

Several weeks went by and the family was confronted with the inevitable question: How long should the life support be continued? Under the law, the sole authority to make that decision was vested in his wife, my Aunt Liz. One day Aunt Liz announced that she had decided to turn off the respirator. This did not sit well with our big, blue-collar, Catholic family, and was the source of much internecine strife. Many of the relatives, including Aunt Rose, raised their voices in opposition, not always couching their protests in diplomatic language. My father was not one of the more vociferous, but I knew he felt the same way. He did not want the plug pulled.

This all transpired at the time when I was beginning to reconcile with my parents, and sharing this experience with my Dad may have broken the ice between us. I had a rare moment of empathy when my heart suddenly opened and I was able to see through my father's eyes. We both loved Uncle Spence, but my father's love was deeper. They had been together all of their lives. My Dad was losing not only a brother, but a best friend; all that Alexis had been to me and more.

On the evening before the respirator was to be disconnected, there was a large family gathering at Aunt Liz' home. This was not the place on Penfield, but the large three-storey house that Uncle Spence had built near the Duck Pond while I was in exile. My father would not go, but he sent me to speak for him. It was a hot, sultry night, right before the Fourth of July, and tempers were fraying. We were all clustered in a semi-circle on the veranda, Aunt Liz at the head. Jan was seated on her right hand and I was on her left. "Can you not wait a while?" I argued. "Think what this is doing to my Dad. Sure, maybe Uncle Spence is not really there, maybe he is brain-dead, but it gives my father some comfort just to be able to visit him, to see his brother lying there, looking like the old Uncle Spence we all remember. What harm could there be in delaying this for a couple of weeks? Just give my Dad time to get over the shock."

All the while I was pleading my case, Jan had her arms around her mother's shoulders and was urging her not to listen to me. "You've made up your mind. You have to go through with it, Mom. Pull the plug. Pull the plug."

I begged, I cajoled, and I pleaded. I was as persuasive as I knew how to be, but the decision was upheld. Aunt Liz made what sounded like a very strange comment that night. "I thought you were incapable of love," she said to me." Now I can see that I was wrong, and you love your father very much." She explained that she had consulted with the doctors, and that my uncle's brain stem was gone. Therefore, she saw no reason to put off what had to be done.

Neither Jan nor I were present at the hospital the next morning when the respirator was turned off. Aunt Liz was there and so were my parents. I found out later that they sat at opposite sides of the bed and did not speak to each other.

Twenty years later, that same drama with Jan and I, playing the same parts, was to be repeated before Aunt Rose died. The difference was that Aunt Rose was not in a coma and she was not brain-dead. She knew when she was being put down.

When Aunt Rose first took me into her home and rescued me from the abyss of utter dysfunction into which I had fallen, I made a promise that I would care for her when she was old and ill. At that time Aunt Rose was a strong energetic barracuda of a woman in her mid fifties, and I could not imagine her as old and debilitated. However, twenty, twenty-five and thirty years went by and I was called upon to fulfill my promise. I tried. I really did, but my attempt to be a caregiver began and ended in disaster.

At the age of seventy-five, ten years before her death, Aunt Rose was diagnosed with an aortic aneurism, a life-threatening condition. She needed to have an operation and she was compelled to give up smoking. She relinquished her three pack a day habit when the cigarettes on hand were gone, and then scheduled the surgery. Jan and I brought her to the Westchester Medical Center in Valhalla. Aunt Rose was eight hours in the operating room. One of her doctors said later that it was the largest aortic aneurism he had ever seen.

After the surgery, her health was never the same. She tired easily. Her limbs were always swollen because her blood did not circulate properly, and she developed mobility problems. She struggled with hypertension, failing eyesight and acid reflux as well.

Despite her great heart and all her goodness, Aunt Rose had always exhibited other qualities which could only be described as wicked. As the new century began, and her physical health deteriorated, her wicked qualities became dominant. She grew progressively more cranky, curmudgeonly and demanding. We quarreled over money. Aunt Rose hated to spend it, even to buy what she needed. Many people hate to spend money, but Aunt Rose took it to the extreme. You could fairly call her a miser. Aunt Rose attributed her penny-pinching ways to her experiences growing up in the Depression, but my parents, only slightly younger than she, had never displayed such stinginess.

When her eyesight faded and she could no longer drive, she sent me to the supermarket to shop for her. I was glad to do so, in the belief that this was one service I was competent to provide. Soon enough each shopping trip resulted in a battle. If I brought home the wrong brand or the wrong size, she would insist I return it. If she asked me to bring home bread from the bakery, it would be either too stale or undercooked. If the item on sale was sold out and I purchased another for a slightly higher price, she would go berserk, and it did not matter if I offered to pay the difference, or, indeed, to pay the entire bill. I took the blame even when she misread the circular. Once, the local A & P advertised, *Russet Potatoes, $0.59.* Aunt Rose interpreted this as offering the potatoes for 59 cents a pound. When I got to the store I found that the Russet Potatoes were, in fact, 59 cents *per potato.* I had no cell phone at the time. My only options were returning home without the potatoes Aunt Rose had requested or paying the 59 cents *per potato.* After due deliberation on my part, I opted to purchase three potatoes. Aunt Rose had a meltdown. "I have never in my life paid 59 cents per potato!" She insisted that I immediately drive back to the A & P and return the three potatoes. I told her never mind, it was on me, but that did not slake her anger. It was the principle of the matter. She proceeded to pelt me with the offending potatoes. Incidents of this sort happened nearly every day. There was worse to come.

Aunt Rose had always been known for her loose tongue and her aptitude for stirring up trouble within the family. At one time or another, she fought with most members of the family due to her unguarded remarks. As she grew older, she resorted more and more to this tactic. Perhaps she developed a bit of dementia, or, more likely, pretended to, in order to get away with saying outlandish things. For example, one of my uncles had left a will bequeathing his entire estate to his widow, and, in the event that she had predeceased him, to his two children in equal shares. This is a typical sort of arrangement. My parents themselves had similar wills. However, Aunt Rose insisted that my uncle had bequeathed his estate to his daughter, and no one could convince her otherwise. I even went down to the Surrogate's Court in White Plains, and brought home a copy of the will. We went over it line by line, but she insisted on misinterpreting the legal gobbledygook. She would call up that cousin and inform her that her mother had robbed her blind. She would then phone her sister-in-law and ask her why she was stealing her daughter's money.

She accused me of many things, some of which are not printable. She was convinced that I was having an affair with Jan's ex-husband. Yes, Jan had finally married a member of the brigade of hunks that had trailed in her wake since high school. After a decade or so, the marriage had gone sour. At one point Jan had thrown her husband out of the house and, having no where else to go, he had moved in with us for a little while. Loyalty to Jan did not prevent Aunt Rose from offering him a room. After all, here was someone to mow the lawn and shovel snow. Alan was extremely handsome like all Jan's men, and I was lonely, so yes, I did make a play for him. However, like most of my pursuits, it amounted to little beyond harmless flirtation. Aunt Rose suspected much more. At first I protested and set her straight, "No, Aunt Rose, of course not." Eventually, I shrugged and let her believe what she wanted to believe. After all, I *had* lusted in my heart after Alan. Satisfied that she now had something to hold over my head, Aunt Rose threatened to tell Jan each time I stepped out of line.

Even as she entered her eighties, Aunt Rose stubbornly refused to slow down or take better care of herself. As long as I could remember, she had cut the grass with two huge, unwieldy gas-powered lawn mowers. These were difficult to maneuver, even for a younger woman. I tried it a few times and then gave up. Jan was more persistent, but eventually she also gave up. Aunt Rose refused to replace the ancient mowers with lighter, more modern models or to hire someone to mow the lawn. At that time, there was a handyman in town who took care of this task for the local seniors in exchange for a very modest fee. I suggested, quite logically, that she hire him. Instead, she chose to wait until a male relative or friend showed up and prevail upon his sympathies for free lawn service. Each autumn, moreover, the heavy mowers had to be lugged down into the cellar and carried upstairs in the spring. When Aunt Rose was eighty-two, no male friend or relative came to retrieve the mowers in a timely fashion. I was at work one afternoon in May when I received a phone call. An ambulance was at the house. Aunt Rose had climbed down into the cellar and tried to drag one of the mowers up the stone steps. She had just reached the top when the mower collapsed upon her, crushing her sternum, causing her excruciating pain and a fracture which never fully healed.

That might have taught her a lesson, but no. One Sunday the following March we had a heavy rainstorm. That evening the ceiling began to leak, as the roof was in a state of disrepair. Now, Aunt Rose had taken very good care of the house since acquiring it from Aunt Car as a wedding gift, and through the years she had made many renovations and additions to the property. However, now that the roof was falling apart, she put off having the repair work done. On her behalf I had spoken to several of the roofers in town, and she found fault with each one: whose price was too high, who did not return her calls, which roofer had a reputation for shoddy work. On the night in question, I was busying myself with the microwave or the television and scarcely paying attention when Aunt Rose climbed onto a step stool with a putty knife and attempted to patch the leak. As soon as I turned and saw where she was, I yelled, "Aunt Rose! Get down!" That very instant, the stool slipped out from under her and she crashed to the floor, banging her head upon the edge of a closet door. Blood streamed from her skull and I was frightened out of my wits, certain that she was mortally wounded. Somehow I had summoned the presence of mind to call 911 and the paramedics soon arrived. They drove us down to the Emergency Room where I called Jan. We waited in the hospital until the wee hours of the morning when a doctor stapled the crack in Aunt Rose's skull together. By then, she was in good enough spirits to joke with the ER nurses, and we all heaved a big sigh of relief.

As this was unfolding, I was dealing with other turmoil in my life. In the spring of 2002, I landed my present employment as a tour guide at Kykuit, the Rockefeller mansion, in Sleepy Hollow, New York. That job was my lifeline, when I quickly lost both my parents, four years apart. I had no friends to comfort me in my grief, but there were people at work who offered me shoulders to cry on. I threw myself into my work at Kykuit and my other gigs in an effort to stay busy and on the go. It was the only way I could deal with my bereavement. It never occurred to me, as perhaps it should have, that I might do better to stay home and watch over Aunt Rose instead.

Several months after sustaining her head injury, Aunt Rose lost her balance while hanging curtains over the sink, and bruised her ribs. Another time she fell after taking a walk down to the corner, and a neighbor helped her home. One night she tripped while searching for the dog in the front yard where he had gone to do his business. Her fall was broken by one of the remaining pieces of the Toy Garden, a statue of the Virgin Mary.

Yes, Aunt Rose should have had a home health care aide, and one could easily have been obtained. There are many fine agencies in our area that provide services for seniors ranging from housework to light medical care. Right down the road in Ossining, the Dominican Sisters run a non-profit health care service, and for a brief time she consented to employ an aide for a few hours a day. The fee was modest, only $18.00 per hour, but, even so, when the bill arrived she took umbrage and canceled the contract. Aunt Rose had money. She had scrimped and saved all her life, and she could well afford to make herself comfortable in her old age, but there was no reasoning with her. In the end, she left her fortune to my cousins' attorney who has probably put it to better use that she did.

Aunt Rose had a primary care physician whom she persistently complained about but, illogically, refused to abandon. I accompanied her from time to time on her regular check-ups and did indeed find him brusque and abrasive. I compiled a list of the other doctors in town, including several who were highly recommended. Aunt Rose obstinately refused to see any of them, or to follow her own physician's advice.

A test determined that she had an enlarged kidney and she was prescribed a medication called Procrit. It appeared highly effective and gave Aunt Rose renewed energy. Nevertheless, she complained about how costly the drug was, although she had Medicare and other insurance besides. Two days before my Dad passed away, she was strong enough to accompany Jan and myself to the hospice in Providence to which my father had been admitted. I thought that Dad might like to see his only surviving sibling, and I was aware that Aunt Rose would never agree to drive that distance with me behind the wheel even in the best of times. I had asked Jan to drive us.

That was the day I had my first serious fight with Jan. My cousin wanted to leave me behind in Providence so that I might stay with my father until he drew his least breath. She was right, of course. That was what I should have done, but I was incapable of it. Dad was so heavily medicated that he was virtually in a coma. In addition, he had wasted away so much that he no longer looked like the father I knew. I had not been prepared for any of that, and I walked about the hospice shaking and trembling, in stunned disbelief.

There was not one single soul in Rhode Island who might have put me up. After my mother died, my Dad had begun courting a local widow. I never begrudged him that. Being alone was difficult for me, and I knew it would have been impossible for my father. I actually welcomed my Dad's new girlfriend into the family and considered her my stepmother. She liked to play the casinos and two or three times a year the three of us would meet at Mohegan Sun in Connecticut. She promised me, in front of my father, that if anything happened to him, she would be there for me. I believed her, and felt comforted. However, when my father was sent to the hospice, she refused pointblank to let me stay with her and stopped taking my phone calls. This unexpected betrayal upset me beyond reason.

My brother would have been around, but he was no better than a stranger. I asked the receptionist at the hospice if there was somewhere nearby where I might find a room, and she handed me the Providence Yellow Pages. I could not read them through my tears. I felt scared and helpless like the orphan I was about to become and I cravenly demanded that Jan drive me home. For four hours I huddled in shame in the rear seat of her car while she sang to herself and made aimless small talk with Aunt Rose.

Shortly after my Dad died, Aunt Rose discontinued use of the Procrit, and her medical condition rapidly deteriorated, just at the time when I needed her most. My own despair and sorrow were so overwhelming that I thought of nothing else. I could not be a caregiver. I needed one myself. She repeatedly asked me, point-blank, whether I believed that my grief for my parents trumped her own failing health and physical pain. I always gave her the reply she expected, which was "No," but it was always a lie.

The crisis began when Aunt Rose's primary care doctor prescribed a medicine called Aranesp, a drug used to treat anemia related to kidney failure. She was to purchase the Aranesp in liquid form, and bring it to the doctor's office so that he might give her injections. Aunt Rose flat-out refused to order the Aranesp. She did not know what the drug was for or why she needed it. I drove down to the local pharmacy and requested a print-out on the medication. We even called up the pharmaceutical company. Finally, her doctor threw up his hands and told her to see a kidney specialist. For weeks, she delayed making the appointment, although the office of the kidney specialist was right down the street. As she procrastinated, Aunt Rose grew progressively sicker and was beset by constant pain, for which she was reluctant to take even over the counter painkillers, derisively referring to such benign medications as Advil and Aleve as *dope*.

During the last telephone conversation I had with my Dad, he had said to me "Take care of Rose." Unaware that he had less than a week to live, I replied, offhandedly, "Sure, Dad," and thus bound myself further to my promise of so many years before.

I became angry and frustrated, frightened that Aunt Rose was about to kill herself—not as I would have done, by throwing myself off a bridge, but by foregoing the care she needed. My parents had just died, and now I was going to lose her as well. The prospect was terrifying. How was I supposed to cope? I took it personally, as if she were doing an injury to *me*. We began to bicker and fight over every little thing. Things flew through the air. At times she shouted at me to leave and, on a few occasions I did, although I never stayed away long.

Over St. Patrick's Day weekend when Aunt Rose was eighty-four, her kidneys gave out and she was wracked with unbearable pain. On Monday morning, as soon as his office reopened, I drove her down to see the kidney doctor. By then, her condition had grown so grave that her only option was to undergo dialysis.

It was then that Jan swooped down and took control of Aunt Rose's healthcare. At first I was relieved, because Aunt Rose had to be talked into the dialysis as well, even while she stood on death's very doorstep. My aunt turned a deaf ear to all my entreaties, but Jan, she listened to—and why not? My cousin was cool and confident and her manner was professional, while I was well, a middle-aged autistic who acted more and more inept as things headed downhill. The two of us took her down to the hospital to be fitted with a dialysis tube, and when the first procedure failed, we drove her down again in April. Jan roped a couple other cousins into service and we took turns driving Aunt Rose to the Dialysis Center in Peekskill until her application for Para Transit was approved.

During the year that Aunt Rose was on dialysis, the clouds slowly receded. The treatment was not easy for her. The tubes that were inserted in her arms never fit properly, not even after the second operation. Several times she bled out and had to be taken to the hospital. Yet, she regained much of her fighting spirit, vowing that she would "beat this thing," and live to be one hundred. She made jokes and tried to lift the spirits of the other dialysis patients. The sharp anguish that had taken hold of me with the death of my father gradually abated and I became more attentive to Aunt Rose. I grew into the responsibility. I felt proud to go pick up her medications at the drug store, see her off on the Para Transit bus or take her shopping at the grocery. I even planned to throw her a bash on her eighty-fifth birthday, but all the cousins begged off, and in the end we celebrated quietly at home.

That year we had kittens. Following my Dad's death, I had adopted the habit of taking long rambling walks around town to sort out my thoughts. A semi feral calico cat followed me home one night and took up residence in our backyard. In due course, she took up with a neighborhood tom, an incredibly huge tuxedo cat that I dubbed *The Big Meow*. The calico cat made a nest under Aunt Rose's all-but-inoperable 1988 Volvo and, one day, when she came to eat the food I insisted on placing at the corner of the porch, she was trailed by three offspring. One was all orange, one was all black, and the third was Boots. Cats never appealed to Aunt Rose. These three kittens, however, won her heart. Each afternoon that final summer, after she returned from dialysis and on her days off, she would fix herself a sandwich and sit out on the porch to watch their antics. She shared her meal with them, dialysis having robbed her of her once healthy appetite. As long as the weather remained warm, the front door was left open. The kittens would wander inside, eat from the dog's dish and scamper away.

As Thanksgiving approached, another problem loomed, but this one had a happy resolution. Aunt Rose had always prepared the biggest, plumpest turkeys on the market, always toms; never hens which she maintained were tough and scrawny. It had become obvious that she no longer had the strength to handle a large tom turkey, and not trusting me to do the job, she decided to forego Thanksgiving dinner entirely. At the last moment, she changed her mind. The bachelor who lived next door had lost his parents several years before and now lived alone with his dogs. Each Thanksgiving, Aunt Rose would send him over a large turkey dinner with heaping side dishes. For his sake, she sent me up to the store on the very eve of Thanksgiving, even agreeing to waive her long-standing prejudice against hen turkeys. When I returned with a 14-pounder there were no recriminations, no second-guessing, and no aspersions of my turkey-buying abilities.

We cooked it together. There was plenty for us, the neighbor and all the animals.

Our last Thanksgiving together was a bright one. On Wednesday Aunt Rose had won a raffle up at the dialysis center and was awarded a *basket of cheer*—vegan crackers and such. Although she complained about the paltry gift, she was secretly pleased. Then, while the turkey roasted in the oven, we were visited by a cousin with whom Aunt Rose had long been estranged due to her big mouth. He is a man who likes traveling, and he had recently been to the very village in Italy where our grandparents lived as children. He brought us ancient family records from the local constabulary there and displayed photos of villagers who might well have been long-lost relatives.

One evening, a week before Christmas, I went shopping for holiday decorations. Aunt Rose had never consented to have a Christmas tree after Uncle Jim died, but I had come up with a compromise. For several years, I purchased table-top treelets, the kind they sell in Shoprite, and adorned them with tinsel and small ornaments as if they were full-size trees. I had forgone even this now. With all my grieving over my parents and my aunt's failing health, there had been little holiday spirit in recent years. However, a voice inside told me that I should celebrate Christmas this year, as there might never be another.

I purchased a treelet, two packages of napkins decorated with Christmas designs, some cookies and a jar shaped in the image of a snowman. Aunt Rose had had one like that years before and used it as a container for her coffee creamer. The jar had shattered long ago, and each season since I had looked in vain for a replacement. I felt a certain exuberance to have finally come upon another snowman jar, and I rushed through the door, eager to show Aunt Rose my find. This was at 9 pm. But for our old dog slumbering obliviously in the hallway, the house was empty.

The lights were turned on, the television was playing and Aunt Rose's half-filled coffee cup was on the table, but *she* was nowhere to be seen. Panic took hold of me. I raced frantically from room to room, calling her name. I was about to dial 911 when the telephone rang. It was the neighbor next door. Aunt Rose had fallen, bending over to retrieve a Christmas card which had dropped behind the table and felt a biting pain in her sternum. The neighbor had called the ambulance and Aunt Rose had been taken to the Emergency Room. I immediately phoned the E.R. Aunt Rose was there and Jan was with her. Apparently, she had given Jan's name as *next of kin*. Now, in similar circumstances, I had always notified Jan, but she had not thought to contact me, leaving me to freak out when I discovered that Aunt Rose was missing.

Jan had assured me that it was only a minor incident, and that they would soon be home. When they had not returned by midnight, I got into my Toyota Echo and drove down to the hospital. That is when the nightmare began. Aunt Rose had reinjured the bone in her sternum, but that was the least of it. Chest x-rays had disclosed a shadow on her lung. Aunt Rose had lung cancer. We had been so focused on her kidneys that the three-pack-a day habit she had maintained until she was seventy-five had completely slipped our minds

Aunt Rose was kept in the hospital for two weeks. All they did there was to give her painkillers—they call it *palliative care*, another way of saying *we are not even going to try*. When I asked why they did not attempt to treat her or control her cancer, their answers were evasive. Soon I was out of the loop altogether. On Christmas Eve, Aunt Rose signed her Health Care Proxy over to Jan despite my advice not to sign anything. I warned her that she would be signing her own death warrant, but, as usual, my words went unheeded. At my urging, a friend of mine from the law office where I worked phoned Aunt Rose and asked her why she had chosen Jan. The response, as interpreted by my friend was this: "She doesn't think you are emotionally mature enough to make the necessary decisions." The phrase *emotionally immature* brought back memories of my first-grade teacher who had originally hung that label on me. Life had brought me full circle.

I frantically searched for allies. The cousin who had visited us at Thanksgiving had resumed his travels abroad. I knocked on the door of my aunt's kidney doctor, but the office was locked and a sign in the window announced that they were on vacation. I called up Adult Protective Services, but they declined to get involved.

From the hospital, Aunt Rose was discharged to a nursing home, for rehabilitation. I urged her to come home instead, recalling the half-empty coffee cup on the table. The hospital refused to send her home unless she committed to a home health aide, and I hoped that Aunt Rose would accept that option now that there was no feasible alternative. However, when it was explained to Aunt Rose that Medicare would pay for 100 days in a nursing home, but the home health aide must be paid out of her own pocket, she chose the nursing home. Jan signed her into the home and listed herself as the contact person although I was right in the village, and Jan lived an hour away.

Nevertheless, I visited Aunt Rose each day that she was there, and I even brought the dog up to see her several times. At first, she seemed to regain some of her strength and feistiness. She renewed her acquaintance with an old friend from the neighborhood who had broken a leg and was recuperating in a room down the hall. Aunt Rose spoke more and more frequently of going home and appeared finally ready to concede the need for a home health aide.

The one day I did not visit her was the day she suffered a setback. Apparently, the tumor had pressed against the crack in her breastbone, causing her to wake in the middle of the night with extreme pain. The facility called Jan who did not, of course, relay the news to me, but instead telephoned both her ex-husband and a third cousin who lived a few miles away. The first I heard of the crisis was two days thereafter when Aunt Rose greeted me by throwing things and screaming that I had abandoned her in her hour of need.

The situation came to a head a few days later. It was a Saturday morning. Jan had come to the house with an entourage of other cousins and in-laws. They planned to spend the day working on the house, cleaning it up and doing repairs for Aunt Rose's expected return home. In fairness, they had invited me to join them, but I decided to stop by the nursing home first. Truth be told, I was becoming increasingly uncomfortable with the number of relatives coming out of the woodwork.

It was 11:00 am when I arrived at the facility and found Aunt Rose seated in a wheelchair in the lobby of the fifth floor. This was Aunt Rose as I had never seen her before. Her head was lolling, she was drooling and mumbling incoherently about being in Hell and surrounded by devils. As if that were not bad enough, her lungs were so congested that she could hardly breathe. That galvanized me into action. An off-duty nurse had come to visit the neighbor with the broken leg and I persuaded her to examine Aunt Rose. She advised that Aunt Rose be taken back to the hospital. I spoke to the staff at the nursing home and insisted that they call a doctor immediately, even if it were a weekend. I phoned back to the house and one of the in-laws came up. We discovered that Aunt Rose had been given an overdose of morphine and that her lungs were filling up with fluid.

The nursing home made plans to send Aunt Rose back to the hospital where her lungs could be drained and she would be given her necessary dialysis treatments. However, at 5 pm Jan arrived with her entourage to take Aunt Rose home. Now, in spite of the health care proxy that had been given to Jan, the staff refused to release my aunt unless she personally signed a Do Not Resuscitate order. That scene from twenty years before at the home of Aunt Liz was eerily repeated, with Jan seated on the left side of Aunt Rose and I on the right. Instead of a supporting cast of aunts and uncles, the room was full of cousins and—me being the sole exception—they were all of one mind. Nonetheless, for a half hour, Aunt Rose refused to sign the DNR order. Even in a drug-induced haze, she had enough presence of mind to know what that paper meant. All the while, Jan was urging her to sign it and I was saying, "Aunt Rose, you don't have to do it. You can think about it a while. You can go back to the hospital and be treated." Finally, Jan got down on her knees and begged: "Aunt Rose, if you don't sign this, you will spend the rest of your life in the hospital hooked up to machines." I wavered, and I surrendered. Maybe Jan was right. Maybe it was better to come home and die rather than live in a hospital bed hooked up to machines. Aunt Rose placed her signature at the bottom of the DNR and my cousins took her home.

It was truly a weekend in the inferno. As soon as Aunt Rose arrived home, Jan had her sign another paper, this one giving Power of Attorney to Jan. Then, as soon as Aunt Rose fell asleep, she and an in-law began to rifle through Aunt Rose's personal papers. Oh, yes, it was all quite improper, but I let it pass, suspecting that my aunt would not survive long enough for it to matter. She was scheduled for dialysis on Monday and, although Jan assured me that she would be taken there, I had my doubts. The following day, Jan downloaded a will form from the internet and attempted to have Aunt Rose sign it. The Will would not have given Jan the entire estate—no, that was too brazen, but it would have made Jan the executor, with all the power that entails. I was able to quash that scheme, but only because neighbors had come to visit, one of whom was the local police chief, and he had seen that Aunt Rose was no longer competent to make a Will.

Jan hardly left the house that weekend, and she never closed her eyes. When she did have to leave for a short errand—to go to the bank, for example—she made certain that one of her minions was left behind. They feared, I suppose, that, I might carry Aunt Rose out to my Toyota subcompact and whisk her off to the hospital.

That first night Jan and I wheeled her into the bedroom, but Aunt Rose refused to get into bed. We escorted her back to the music room where we sat her in her favorite armchair in front of the TV. In a morphine-ridden sleep, she had visions that were truly blood-curdling. She pleaded for help from her sister, my Aunt Carmela, who had passed away a decade before. She repeatedly cried out the name of one of our dogs that was also deceased. I brought our sole surviving pup, Buffy, in to stay with her, but it brought her no solace. On Sunday night she had trouble breathing and we thought she was dying right then and there, but she fought through. By Monday morning, Aunt Rose was awake and coherent and able to joke with Jan and myself and the other cousins who had returned to the house. However, I was watching the clock as the dialysis appointment neared and no mention was made of it. Finally, I exploded. Jan told me, that if I preferred, she would call in a nurse. I jumped at the offer, for I believed that any nurse would insist that Jan take Aunt Rose to dialysis. In my naïveté, I was wrong, so terribly wrong.

An hour later, a nurse and a social worker from a nearby hospice arrived at the house They sat down in the kitchen with Jan and the other relatives while I waited with Aunt Rose in the next room under the illusion that something good was about to happen. Finally, I beckoned them into the music room, saying "Aunt Rose, you have visitors." That was the last statement I was ever able to make to her.

The two newcomers immediately took possession of the bottle of liquid morphine that Jan had brought home from the nursing home and began squirting it into my aunt's mouth, without introducing themselves or telling her why they were doing this. Aunt Rose kept shaking her head and trying to keep her mouth closed, but she was eighty-five, frightened and gravely ill while they were healthy, young and determined. Despite that, she put up a good fight. In a panic, I cried out, "Leave her alone! Leave her alone!" to no avail. When the hospice workers had forced sufficient amounts of morphine into her mouth, they physically assaulted her and carried her into the bedroom. It was like a scene from a B horror flick. She was still resisting with all her strength and crying, "No! No! No!" I tried to reach her, but I was prevented from doing so. The nurse and the cousins formed a tight circle around Aunt Rose on the bed while I was detained by the social worker in the kitchen. Jan telephoned Aunt Rose's primary care physician, the one she had so loudly complained about, and he verbally gave permission for the hospice workers to administer a series of drugs that would effectively put Aunt Rose down. For a while I could still hear her terrified screams, and then there was silence. Aunt Rose had slipped into a coma from which she would never awaken. She died on Tuesday evening.

But first, I had to deal with another surprise. My brother unexpectedly appeared at the house on Tuesday afternoon. Jan had summoned him, probably with good intentions, and he had made the long drive from Massachusetts. After all, Jan's own brother was her pal. He would have lent her strength and solace in her darkest hour. She may have imagined my brother would do the same. Or perhaps she just wanted to get me out of the house while she and her allies made Aunt Rose's strongbox disappear. It might have been a little of both. In any event, here I was, imprisoned in a nightmare, the very earth slipping from beneath my feet. My heart was breaking and I was compelled to go on a blind date.

Brett made a request that was so strange that I had to honor it. He asked me to drive him across town to the Real Me's house. I had passed by our old house, a hundred times since returning to Croton. On summer evenings and at Christmastime I often drove along that street, hungry for the comfort that the mere sight of my childhood home could provide. It had never occurred to me, however, to knock upon the door. That my brother had come up with the idea amazed me. He had only been a small child when we had gone into exile. Nevertheless, we journeyed to our lost home, and finally met the people who had purchased the house from our parents. As it turned out, they knew Aunt Rose and were pleased to give us a little tour. Once again, I walked through our front door and visited my old bedroom with the window which overlooked the L-shaped ranch where Alexis had lived. The very night I lost the last remnant of my family, I went back to the beginning, the Alpha and Omega.

Afterward, my brother suggested we get a bite to eat, and I took him to the diner. We ate, mostly in silence. As usual, we had nothing to say to each other. He would not hear anything against Jan, and that was what was on my mind. I struggled instead to make small talk, not an easy task for either of us under any circumstances. By the time we returned to Aunt Rose's house, it was all over.

Do you ever wonder what became of the schoolyard bullies of your youth? I found myself besieged by them again, now in the guise of my paternal cousins. The cousins insisted that I immediately vacate the premises, and that the house on Grand Street be sold right away. They set about dismantling what remained of the Toy Garden. Several of the cousins wanted to tear the entire place down and market the empty land. However, the rules of the village proved too stringent for that. Of course, I was the chief impediment to their plans. I planted my feet and refused to budge. The cousins had retained a lawyer even before Aunt Rose died. On the day following the funeral, Jan filed papers to become the administrator of the estate. I could not let that happen. That was my one small victory. That post was awarded to one of the out-of-state cousins, at least in name. In reality, the out-of-stater was so besotted with Jan that he let her do whatever she wanted. On the day of the funeral, she had presented this cousin with a box filled with old photos of his mother who had died a half century before, when I was a toddler and Jan not even born. She must have been collecting them for years against the odd chance that I would seek his assistance. That's when I realized I was up against a pro.

Have you ever heard someone use the expression *buying time?* During the year following the death of Aunt Rose, the meaning of that phrase was made clear to me. I literally bought time, both for myself and for our 16-year-old dog, Buffy, the one I called "Mr. Speaker" because he looked like Newt Gingrich and barked incessantly. Aunt Rose, who had seen no reason to provide for her human heirs, had nonetheless blurted out two verbal instructions on the weekend before her death. While she was fading in and out of consciousness in a drugged haze, she suddenly sat up and exclaimed, "Don't put me to sleep! Don't put my dog to sleep!" I had been unable to spare her that fate, but I did my best to save Buffy. I insisted the dog should be allowed to live out his natural life in the only home he knew. Unfortunately, the law does not recognize any rights in the pet of a deceased owner. Buffy was a chattel of the estate, like my aunt's car or jewelry. Even though I had taken care of him for years, I had no more right to Buffy than I did to my aunt's home. Stubbornly, I hung on to both as long I could. My parents had left me a modest inheritance which seemed like a great sum at the time. Certainly, it was more money than I had ever had before, and I foolishly spent a large chunk of it holding my cousins at bay. I paid the operating expenses of the house, and for Buffy's food and medications. I took him to the vet and groomer. While he was still strong enough for walks, I put the leash on him and paraded up and down the street. After his arthritis made walks unfeasible, I would carry Buffy out to our fenced-in yard and let him putter about until he took care of his business. When he grew incontinent, as old dogs do, I purchased puppy training pads and spread them about, much to the horror of the cousins who were focused only on the poor market for half fallen-down, smelly old homes.

Jan wanted to take Buffy to her home. She promised to take good care of him. I had my suspicions from the beginning, but eventually I had no choice but to turn over custody of Buffy to Jan. For three months, she did take very good care of him. Then she put him down. I know someone who works at the vet's office. I was tipped off. On the appointed day, I met them there. Buffy looked old and frail, but he was not sick. He was walking about the lobby, sniffing the furniture and wagging his tail. I fed him a slice of turkey I had left over from lunch. My heart told me to sweep him up in his arms and run out of there, but I was no longer in a position to take care of him. Helplessly, I said my goodbyes and walked out alone.

Two weeks passed in an utter funk until one day I lost control and found myself in a stupid road-rage incident. I was hauled into village court and charged with a misdemeanor. It took another dip into my parents' money to get me off the hook.

There was one other companion animal I did manage to hold onto. A late season snowstorm blanked the town shortly after Aunt Rose died. I went out to shovel the walk, and there was the kitten Boots standing on the porch. I opened the door and he walked in. I closed the door behind him, and rescued us both.

Boots offered me cuddle therapy, and that had to suffice, until a real therapist came along. For hours upon hours, all through that endless winter, I would sit in Aunt Rose's rocking chair holding Boots on my lap, burying my hands in his fur and snuggling into the cocoon of familiar surroundings. I found old photos of Aunt Rose at her wedding, read faded invitations and postcards that had been sent to my grandmother many years before, materials that my cousins had deemed of no importance when they pillaged the house. If I looked out the window and saw a Para transit bus waiting for a disabled neighbor, I would burst into tears. Twice during that summer, my cousins came by while I was at work, opened the front door and out Boots went, but both times he loyally returned after dark. The French have a word for it, *matagot*—a magical cat, who brings his human good fortune as did his namesake, the legendary Puss 'n' Boots. If staving off the wolf of my despair can be considered good fortune, then that was the gift Boots brought to me.

I now live with Boots and another kitty in a small apartment on the poor side of town, half a mile away from the house I once shared with Aunt Rose. It is stifling in the summer and, in the winter, the wind seeps right through the walls. Comes a storm, we are the first to lose power and the last to have it restored. Still, the rent is modest and it is located right down the street from the police station. Should the cops want to arrest me, they will not have far to go. Although I remain a resident of Croton-on-Hudson, the village no longer brings me a sense of warmth and safety. It has ceased to be my Smallville, the one place on earth where I am not a stranger. I'll never find *my gang* here. Perhaps I should leave, but where would I go? There are no return flights to Krypton.

As for my cousin Jan, I fear I have lost her, too. I might forgive her for Aunt Rose who, after all, gave over her health care proxy when she was still in her right mind. Against my warning, she signed her own death warrant, so little regard did she have for my counsel. Buffy, on the other hand, had no say in the matter. Yes, I was quite angry at the time, but as the months lengthen into years, anger loosens its bite and turns into sorrow and regret.

One night last summer I caught a glimpse of Jan at an outdoor concert down at the riverfront. My cousin did not see me there; it was dark, noisy and crowded, and she was occupied with chatting up a handsome hunk. The tight shorts she wore showed off her exquisite legs, the tome of her voice was cheerful and perky, and her face radiated all the confidence in the world. Yes, even at fifty, she is drop-dead gorgeous.

Redemption of an Outcast

•

He who learns must suffer
And even in our sleep
Pain that cannot forget
Falls Drop by drop upon the heart,
And in our own despite,
Against our will
Comes wisdom to us by the awful grace of God.

Aeschylus, from *Agamemnon*, quoted by
Robert F. Kennedy in his eulogy
of Martin Luther King, Jr.

Just taking up space. That was the assessment of one of the members of my bereavement support group as she described her 94-year-old uncle who suffered from Alzheimer's disease. She could not understand why the Angel of Death had taken her virile, youthful, motorcycle-riding sixty something husband while passing over the elderly bed-ridden relative who could not even recognize her. When she said that, I cringed and turned my head away. Was that not what my own life had become, just taking up space? Truth be told, I felt more worthless than the 94-year-old Alzheimer's patient, forty years my senior. At least he had a niece who would visit him in the nursing home each Christmas, if only out of a sense of familial obligation.

Within six years, I had lost both my parents and Aunt Rose. During that time, two uncles who had been sources of emotional support had also passed away. Neither was very old. They were both in their mid-seventies. One uncle had been ill for some time, but the other's death was completely unforeseen, the result of a minor medical procedure gone awry. These losses only added to the apocalyptic feeling of those years. It seemed as though Atropos, most dreadful of the Fates, had gone wild with her shears, cutting the thread of life of everyone that I had ever cared for. When she snapped the thread of Aunt Rose's, she nearly dealt me a mortal blow. The earth slipped out from under me and I was swirling on a dark churning sea, a sea of heartbreak.

I had learned to tolerate the lack of a *normal life*, so long as I could come home each night and chat with Aunt Rose or phone my parents when my solitude became unbearable. With this firewall gone, a feeling of abandonment and loneliness crashed down upon me. There seemed no point in going on. The Wolf of Loneliness, after lurking by my door for forty years, now found that the lock was broken, the barricades were down, and he rushed in, jaws apart, ready to devour me.

"Lotsa people lose their families," one grief counselor told me, "and they manage to cope. They rely on their friends." She was trying to make me feel better, I suppose, but her words reminded me of my mother's old harangue, *other kids move.* I had known only a few close friends in my life, and by now, each had drifted away. The only reason I had a family in the first place was because I was born into one. Now that, too, was gone.

For several months following the death of Aunt Rose, I spent my days stimming and weeping under a black cloud. At other times I would rage and throw tantrums. I stumbled blindly into corners. If, by chance, someone did talk to me, I responded by babbling incoherently like an autistic child. My mind ran away from me. I committed thoughtless acts of vandalism. A series of minor automobile accidents sent me spinning into snowdrifts, backing up into parked cars, or colliding with curbs, trees and cement walls. It was a wonder I did not do grievous injury both to myself and to innocent pedestrians. My depth perception, never the best, had further diminished, and I simply could not see the obstacles in my path.

All that was left, it seemed, was to drown myself in the river as the Lady of Shalott had done. However, before I could follow through, someone else went before me and committed suicide in my place. Her name was Annie Morrell, and she was an attractive divorced mom in her late thirties. One warm September evening she took her life by jumping off the Tappan Zee Bridge. It was the final act in a suburban high tragedy that made my own troubles, by comparison seem scrappy and small.

They say that people in San Francisco put an end to despair by throwing themselves from the Golden Gate Bridge. If this is so, the Golden Gate must be the California version of the Tappan Zee. The Tappan Zee is a massive span that crosses the Hudson at its widest point, three miles wide, linking the Village of Tarrytown with Nyack in Rockland County. I dislike the Tappan Zee for any purpose. It is one of those vertigo-inducing bridges that go up, up, up and then down, down, down. Returning home from a prom in New Jersey one Memorial Weekend night, I was trapped for forty-five minutes on the span of the Tappan Zee, my Suzuki hatchback wedged tightly between a pair of eighteen wheelers. Two inmates had escaped from a nearby facility for the criminally insane and the police had set up a roadblock. For three quarters of an hour, I fought vertigo, anxiety and the rising certainty that one of the eighteen wheelers would slip its gears and crush both me and my Suzuki. It was an aspie's nightmare. Had this occurred, not at midnight, but in daylight with the bright sun blazing in my window, I should have become completely disoriented.

To cap it off, the toll on the Tappan Zee is three times more than that charged to cross the flat, two-lane, scenic Bear Mountain Bridge, a short ride up the Palisades. However, few choose to throw themselves from the Bear Mountain. One glance downward would tell you why. It would be a very long drop indeed from the span of that little bridge to the surface of the water below, and the impact would hurt, really hurt. It would not be the sweet, painless death by drowning that suicides seek. Thus, they all go to the Tappan Zee.

One of the more celebrated Tappan Zee suicides in living memory was that of Scott Douglas, age 38, on New Year's Eve of 1993. Only a few years before, Scott had been a struggling house painter with a dubious past. He then became the recipient of some undeserved good fortune. A beautiful, wealthy newspaper heiress, several years his senior, fell in love with him and took him home to live in her palatial residence in the pretty town of Bronxville. Anne Scripps Douglas already had two grown daughters from a previous marriage, but she soon gave Scott his own, Victoria (called 'Tori'), a child who would also be entitled to the label of *heiress*. In short order, the former nobody had been elevated into a man of property and status, a husband and father, with a home and family. His money troubles were behind him. He had access to the country-club scene and vacations in exotic places. You would think that Scott Douglas would have fallen on his knees each night and thanked God for the treasures that fate had bestowed on him, but, no. He threw it all away.

On that New Years' Eve of 1993, Scott Douglas fatally beat his wife with a claw hammer and disappeared, leaving his own three-year-old daughter behind with her dying mother. When the police came looking for Scott, all they found was his car parked on the center span of the Tappan Zee and, in the passenger seat, the bloodied murder weapon.

The story received a lot of press here in Westchester County, and that is no surprise. Since the days of the ancient Greeks, nothing has so fascinated the public as tales of wealth, sex and violence. There were also important legal issues involved. Anne Scripps Douglas had previously sought an order of protection against her husband and the court had turned her away. Jeanine Pirro, our D.A. at the time, who later became a pundit and TV host, took the opportunity to proclaim that domestic violence was not just for the poor and working class. (*A fact she could have ascertained by reading Aeschylus*).

You might wonder how this story is relevant to my life, but I felt an eerie connection to the crime. A few months before the death of Anne Scripps Douglas, I had been flipping through the pages of the *Pennysaver,* when this ad caught my eye: "THE HUDSON: New York's only holy river. Throw your body in!"

I turned to Aunt Rose, and asked, "What do you make of this?" Aunt Rose did not think it was so much romantic gibberish. She saw it as a coded message from one mobster to another, providing instructions on how to dispose of the evidence. The more she thought about it, the more convinced she became, and then Aunt Rose did what she deemed right and proper. She called up the media and raised a firestorm. The local Gannett paper even did a write up on the incident, something in the nature of "Homeowner Makes Frightening Discovery in Shopper's Weekly!"

It was a very cold winter that year, and parts of the Hudson were frozen over. It was not until March that the body of Scott Douglas washed up downriver in Yonkers. During the interim, the police suspected that he might have faked his own suicide. However, I never had a doubt. I knew that the prophecy had been fulfilled.

Annie Morrell was the younger of the two daughters of Anne Scripps Douglas by her first marriage. On the fateful New Year's Eve, she had been home on Christmas break from college. Her friends had invited her out to a New Year's Eve party. Her first instinct was not to go. She knew that there was trouble in the marriage, that Scott had been drinking heavily and become abusive. Her mother told her she must go. "You are young, you are on the brink of life, you should be celebrating, and I will be all right." (*This is exactly what my mother would have said to me had I ever been lucky enough to be invited to a New Year's Party. She said, in fact, something in that very vein two days before her own death when, through my tears, I drove out to Rhode Island to visit her in the hospital. "Go back to New York and live your own life. Forget about me."*)

So Annie, against her better judgment, went off to her party. When she returned in the wee hours of the morning, her stepfather's car was no longer in the driveway. The house was locked. Annie, who had forgotten her keys, knocked and knocked in rising panic and yelled to be let in. In the end, the fire department was summoned and had to break down the door.

Several years ago, the story was made into a TV movie. As I watched it with Aunt Rose, I turned to her and nodded. "Remember that *Pennysaver* ad? *Throw your body in?*

Annie made a bid for custody of her orphaned half-sister, but the child was sent to relatives in Vermont who adopted her. The baby sister she adored drifted out of her life as my own brother had out of mine. Annie married, but the marriage lasted only a few years. She squandered her inheritance and buried herself in debt. There were part-time jobs, but none that worked out. She drank and battled depression. According to one magazine article, she even consented to undergo electroshock therapy. The electroshock erased many of her memories, but left intact the one she most wanted to forget.

Annie Morrell was lonely, but certainly not as lonely as I. She had friends. She had relatives. She had a teenage son, although she eventually lost custody of him as well. Best of all, she had an older sister and best friend named Alex who lived only a few miles away, and who was always there to watch over her. However, none of this could save her. When Annie had attained the age of thirty-eight, the same age her stepfather had been at the time of his death, she drove her SUV to the center span of the Tappan Zee and parked it in the same place that Scott had left his vehicle. The police found a suicide note on the front seat. One line was addressed to the kid sister who had been adopted out. *Tori, I wished you loved us.* So I might have written, *Brett, I wish you had loved me.*

Annie's suicide received only a fraction of the coverage that the original affair had inspired, but I was seized by an intense fascination with the saga. I buttonholed people at my own bereavement support group and tried to discuss the case, but each time I brought it up, the facilitator changed the subject. I was left to surf the internet for any and all facts that I could find.

One of the newspaper websites had an open thread for readers to post comments. It was the simple logic offered by one anonymous poster that stopped me in my tracks and caused me to shelve my own plans for suicide.

Foolish girl, to take your own life! Don't you know that time will do it for you?

So true. No need to bother myself with the gory details of plotting my own demise. All I needed to do was wait a little while. While I was waiting, I might put the time to good use. Through therapy and diagnosis, I might find out why I had always been a stranger on earth.

I had also decided that the time had come for me to take drugs.

Except for a brief period in high school when I had been prescribed a medication which I believe to have been Ritalin, and the occasional marijuana joint in college, I had never, prior to the death of Aunt Rose, taken any psychotropic drugs, legal or illegal. Individuals with Asperger's Syndrome are particularly susceptible to anxiety and depression, and I had certainly experienced these disorders since adolescence, but I had never thought of them as medical problems, which might be treated like the flu or an ear infection. If I were sad and if I were frantic, it was the natural outcome of a life lived in bitter loneliness, social isolation and inexplicable misfortune. My mother believed in the supreme power of reason. She was convinced that, due to my superior intellect, I could will myself to be happy, normal and prosperous. That I did not was proof of my recalcitrance, and there were no pills for that. My father, as proprietor of a convalescent home for disabled veterans, held a dim view of the medico-pharmaceutical field. Many of the veterans in his charge had been prescribed psychotropic medications to keep them calm and manageable. He gave me the impression that the primary goal of psychiatric medicine was to turn people into zombies for the convenience of those that had to deal with them.

Now, however, I was so consumed with desolation and despair that I lost all control over my emotions and became a hazard, both to myself and all who came into contact with me. If I were to go on living, even for a little while, I knew I would need some help. Several of the women in my bereavement support group had been widowed after long-term marriages. The loss of their husbands of 40 years or more had completely immobilized them with grief. They spoke candidly about the beneficial effects of antidepressants and swore that such medications had given them back the capacity to cope with everyday problems.

Being without medical insurance, I had no regular physician, and made a practice of avoiding doctors altogether until it became a matter of life and death. Now I called up the local physician who had treated Aunt Rose for her kidney problems. He had been the one truly kind person I had met in the long run up to Aunt Rose's death, and he generously agreed to see me on a sliding scale. His nurse gave me a sample of Lexapro, a medication that many of the widows at bereavement had sworn by. I was eager to try it. The Lexapro, however, had rather bizarre side effects. I became numb below the waist, and when I rubbed myself between my legs to see if I were still alive, I felt no sensation whatsoever. That was scary. Even more frightening, was the catatonia. I could not wake up. I struggled to open my eyes, and once they were open, I could not get to my feet. It seemed that my father's view of psychotropic drugs as *zombie-inducing* was all too accurate. Two weeks into my Lexapro regimen, I dragged myself into the doctor's office and collapsed on the sofa.

The doctor then wrote me a script for Buproprion, another type of anti-depressant which goes by the brand name of Wellbutrin. The prescription was not for a strong amount, just the regular starter dose. Nevertheless, the Wellbutrin acted strangely as well. What is the opposite of zombie? The Wellbutrin was an upper. I could not sit still. I could not go to the bathroom. I could not fall asleep and obtain the only solace that was left to me. My mood had indeed been elevated, but far too quickly. Now I was climbing the walls and freaking out at every little thing.

What was I to do? Should I return to the doctor and request a third alternative? I hesitated. Perhaps he, too, would ascribe it to character flaws. He might conclude that I was so weird that medications that benefitted others did not work for me. Suppose he threw up his hands and turned me away?

On my own, I cut down the Wellbutrin to every other day. With the reduced dose, I was less manic, but I still had trouble sleeping. One day I ran into a neighbor who was a registered nurse. She assured me that if I took a little bit of Wellbutrin each morning, and a small dose of an anti-anxiety medication called Klonopin in the evening, I would be fine. I returned to the doctor and begged him to prescribe Klonopin. The Klonopin worked like a charm. I was able to sleep during the night and function during the day.

However, Klonopin is what we in the legal field call *a Controlled Substance*. That is, it has addictive properties and so the government places strictures upon it and discourages its use even by prescription. The danger of addiction meant little to me; nothing was worse than the relentless hurt which had me in a death-grip. The doctor was more concerned, and, after a few refills, he advised that if I wanted to keep taking the medication, I would need to consult a mental health professional. The kidney doctor did me a favor, pushing me down the road to a long-delayed date with self-discovery. *Know Thyself* was the motto engraved above the ancient Temple of Apollo, and deservedly so. Without self-knowledge, all my education proved of little value.

Diagnosis helped me to unravel the mystery of my past. Once I came to understand who I was, the burden of shame that I had borne all my life slowly slipped away. *Tout pardonner est tout comprendre*. My heart opened up and was touched by a gentle rain. It must be akin to what the Church calls *a state of grace*.

My psychiatrist gave me several books to read, including memoirs by two other adult aspies: Michael John Carley's, "Asperger's From the Inside Out," and Liane Holliday's, "Pretending to Be Normal." Although both these individuals are nowhere near as impaired as myself, their stories comforted me and made me feel less alone. The enigma of my past began to unravel. I raided the local libraries and bookstores and spent many hours on the internet conducting research on autism and Asperger's Syndrome, their causes, their treatments, their signs. I discovered online forums for adults on the spectrum. At the time of my life when I felt most dispossessed and uprooted, I gradually became grounded again and regained some pride in myself. The need to constantly apologize was gone. Character defects did not cause my shortcomings. My brain was wired in a different way.

Since that time, I've spoken with several young aspies who were diagnosed as children at school. They were often unhappy with their diagnosis and rebelled against it. Being told at an early age, that they had Asperger's Syndrome, seemed akin to a life sentence. For me, it was just the opposite. Finding out the truth about myself was empowering. I could finally understand why so much misfortune had befallen me and why life had tossed me aside. I recognized those of my behaviors that alienated others, and set my mind to modifying those behaviors that I could. As to those I could not change, I accepted them and stopped resenting others for reacting the way they did.

I also bought a horse. It is called *hippotherapy*.

You may remember that, during my early days in the Kingdom of Frost, my Dad had purchased a black gelding named Perhaps to assuage my loneliness, and that my mother quietly gave him away to a local horse farm eighteen months later. I never spoke of Perhaps again, but I never forgot him. A spectral Perhaps pranced through my dreams for decades, haunting me in much the same way as did Alexis and my childhood friends. As an adult, I was compelled to take up horseback riding again.

I cannot recall where or when I first began to ride as a grown-up. For many years I would spend each weekend on the trail. At one time, there were several public stables in the northern suburbs of New York City which offered Western style horseback riding. For a modest fee, you could ride the trails for an hour or two, commune with Nature and enjoy a bit of socialization.

By the mid 1990s most of the nearby public stables had either shut down completely or become private boarding stables. Those that remained open raised their prices so exorbitantly that I gave up riding for many years. It was only when my Dad passed away that I turned to horses again.

After Aunt Rose died, I bought Silverado from a ranch in New Jersey. He is an undocumented immigrant, a refugee from the cattle ranches south of the border. Mexican horses are short and stocky, and well broken to the trails. He did not even have a name. At the stable they called him, *the gray gelding*, and advertised him at 15 hands. That proved to be a bit of an exaggeration. I measured him at the withers. Silverado is 14 hands and an inch. A horse under 14.2 is called a *pony*.

It took another bite out of my dwindling inheritance, but this time I felt no guilt. I was naïve, of course. I had no appreciation of just how expensive owning a horse would be. The cost of farrier visits, vet calls, worming, boarding, fly masks, fly spray, not to mention saddles, blankets, halters, and all of the other accoutrements a pony requires, turned out to be any eye-opener. Moreover, learning to tack up Silverado proved to be every bit as difficult as learning to tie my shoelaces had been. The art of putting on the bridle, in particular, I found most baffling. There were plenty of times when we rode out with the reins crisscrossed or with Silverado's chinstrap in his mouth.

You might expect me to claim that there was an instant bonding between myself and Silverado. That was not the case. It took time for us to grow together, but as we each struggled to deal with our new lives, a bond was forged. Horse back riding is good for autistic people. The rhythmic movement of the horse beneath me takes away stress and builds muscle tone. When I am seated in the saddle, I no longer feel helpless. My feet take wings as I canter down the trail. There is also much to be said for sharing your special interests with others. If you have an obsession, and most aspies do, it is a good idea to hang around others who have a similar preoccupation. Now I spend my free time at the local barn where I board Silverado. There are other horse owners there with whom I can casually socialize. Are they my best friends? No, but we make horsetalk and there are always chores that need to be done around the stables.

Perhaps, above all, it was my job at Kykuit which saved me.

Kykuit is a wonderful place. *It's where God would live if He had the money.* That is what newsies said when the house was first built. John D. Rockefeller, Sr., mogul and founder of Standard Oil, was a lover of the great outdoors. On top of one of the highest hills in Westchester County with large cascading views of the Hudson River and the Palisades, he found a haven from a world which had provided him with amazing wealth, but hated him for it. If the art created by God was not fabulous enough, it was augmented by art created by man, thanks to son John D. Rockefeller, Jr. and his son, Nelson, Governor of New York in the days of the Real Me. People at Kykuit have grown old and died, and some have perished in accidents, but none have been known to take their own lives. No matter how hostile the world has become, no matter the despair and pain that enshrouds you, the sight of Kykuit will make you want to live.

In the winter of 2002, I came upon an ad in the *Pennsysaver* seeking weekend tour guides at Kykuit, the Rockefeller Estate, in Sleepy Hollow, New York. Now I recalled quite a bit about Nelson as I remembered each detail of life before the Fall. History and politics had been special interests of mine from early childhood when Aunt Rose first pinned me with a JFK button. Working in the field of criminal law, I had become quite familiar with the Rockefeller drug laws and their consequences. Nevertheless, Governor Rockefeller had died twenty odd years before, and had gradually faded from my memory. I needed a new part-time job, however. My attorney-friend in Connecticut had notified me that she was closing her private practice and taking a full-time job in the New Haven court system; *a real job, with benefits.* Several years before, she and her husband had adopted a child. Now her husband was out of work and it had fallen to her to be the breadwinner. The tour guide position sounded like fun, like the kind of quirky offbeat kind of work that Aunt Rose had sagely suggested I might be most suited for. So I sent in my application and stumbled into paradise.

How did I ever pass the screening process? I had persuaded one of my attorney-bosses to write me a recommendation. It held up long enough to land me the job. Everyone I work with at Kykuit has all the social graces I lack. The other guides are well-spoken, neatly dressed, poised, sophisticated, self-assured and highly educated. They all read the *New York Times*. I am highly educated myself; otherwise, I stood out like a black sheep. That was the allure that drew me to them. I wanted to be a member of the troupe.

Guide training provided me with a sense of camaraderie I had not enjoyed since junior high. My fellow guides fancy themselves as "artsy" types and are obliged to be tolerant of other people's quirks. My brother discovered this early in life. It is why he associates only with musicians and music followers.

I was already conversant with much of the history and politics; as to those subjects that were heretofore unfamiliar, I quickly gobbled up names, dates and facts. Soon I could spout off Chinese dynasties and 20th century artistic movements like a PhD. Landscape theory came easily enough. I devoured books on garden design, and was delighted to find that the gods and goddesses of ancient Greece and Rome, close friends from childhood, often masqueraded as garden ornaments. In fact, I fell in love again. On one of the terraces at Kykuit, there stands a beautiful sculpture of Apollo and, when no one is looking, I surreptitiously run my hands over his perfectly contoured limbs. He is made of cast stone and, unlike the others, he cannot flee from my embrace.

Nonetheless, guiding did not come easy. During my first season, my supervisor constantly criticized me for speaking in a monotone and having a *flat affect*, for the inability to project my voice and failure to follow the prescribed schedule. Certain of my colleagues, artsy or not, tattled on me each time I committed a minor infraction.

I often gave visitors the wrong information without intending to. As a trainee, I had followed veteran guides around. At one point, we reached the Music Room which features Ming Dynasty ceramics, a 17th century Chinese rug, a painting by Miro, a portrait of Governor Rockefeller's maternal grandfather, Senator Nelson Aldrich, for whom he was named, and two modern porcelain elephants holding up a Chinese screen to form a coffee table. The guide turned to me and said, "The Governor must have bought those elephants from Pier One." She was making a joke, as I would later discover, but at the time, I took it as gospel truth. Throughout my first year, whenever I led a group into the Music Room, I would say, "Here are Ming Dynasty ceramics, here is a portrait of Senator Aldrich, there is Miro's *Hirondelle Amour*, and those elephants are from Pier One." One day my supervisor heard that and placed me on probation.

I was desperate to keep this job. Midway through my first season I lost my Mom who I adored despite her Snow Queen persona, and my heart was petrified with grief and shock.

I had hoped that Kykuit might finally provide an opportunity for my mother and I to bond, just as working on the legal troubles had brought me closer to my Dad. Under ordinary circumstances, Mom would have been highly impressed that I was working at the Rockefeller mansion, even without any great salary or status. Yet each time I telephoned her that spring, excitedly babbling on about my wonderful new job, the magical site and my alluring fellow guides, I was met by sheer disinterest. Mystified when my enthusiasm went unshared, I ascribed it to my mother's unyielding disappointment at my failure to land the high-powered legal position that, in her eyes, was my just due. Here I was, settling once more for low-paying part-time employment. Aunt Rose suggested that her indifference might have a more sinister cause. "I hear your mother keeps seeing doctors," she whispered. "Something must be terribly wrong."

She was a mere earthling; I had realized this long ago. She must die someday, but surely, I thought, not until she had attained an age like 102. Even at seventy, she had appeared young and beautiful. Rhode Island had rejuvenated my Mom. She led an active life, ate healthy foods and, amazingly, acquired a circle of adoring friends. Yes, she smoked a pack a day, for as long as I had been alive, and probably for some years before. There had never been a serious attempt to quit. Cigarettes were so much a part of her personality, that I was inclined to give my mother a pass on the general rule that smoking is hazardous to your health. Even when I learned that she did indeed have lung cancer, in my naïveté, I supposed it was treatable or that its worst effects could be staved off for years. I saw Mom on Independence Day. She appeared to be in decent physical health, although mentally exhausted. By the end of July, death had crept upon her like a thief and stolen the breath from her body.

My co-workers witnessed my sorrow. They comforted me, lent me their shoulders to cry on and talked me through. In order to keep my job and remain in their company, I forced myself to look visitors in the eye, project my voice and speak with inflection. I dragged myself out of bed at a decent hour and reported to work on time. I looked at my watch and hurried my groups along. Speaking for two hours was not difficult; like many aspie girls I can talk a blue streak on a subject in which I am interested. The trick was to talk so that people wanted to listen. I practiced my new techniques before Aunt Rose who was not in the least interested. She asked me why I cared so much; I was being paid barely more than the minimum wage at Kykuit. I could earn far more as a paralegal. Neurotypicals never understand that there are riches which cannot be encapsulated in a paycheck. Kykuit had become the touchstone which would carry me through the rough waters ahead.

It was there I found the long-sought antidote to the Kingdom of Frost. The Rockefeller mansion reminded me eerily of the old manor house my parents had purchased. There had been a dumbwaiter in the kitchen there. At Kykuit there was a dumbwaiter as well—a feature that I had never come upon in all the intervening years. There were long driveways, hidden paths, outbuildings, back stairways and chandeliers at both places, but here was the difference: Whereas my parents' estate had been cold, dark and scary, a winter place, devoid of love or laughter, Kykuit was spring, summer and fall. It radiated peace and wonder. Kykuit heralded the return of the Real Me. When I was leading a tour, I could feel my lost self begin to stir from that deep-down place where she had lain dormant for so many years. I developed skills I never knew I possessed and, with them, a new confidence. Guiding has become so much a part of me that I have already chosen my occupation for the afterlife. I will be a psycho pomp leading the newly arrived souls of the dead on a tour of the underworld

Many of my colleagues at Kykuit are bedazzled by the more dynamic characters of the Rockefeller saga, John D. Rockefeller, Sr. or Governor Nelson Rockefeller or Nelson's mother Abby, co-founder of the Museum of Modern Art. I find myself drawn to the often overlooked John D. Rockefeller, Jr. We share a lot of traits in common, Mr. Junior and I. Like me, he never quite fit in. Like me, he was fascinated by history, natural splendor and classical art. He felt so out of place in the twentieth century that he would build Colonial Williamsburg and spend a portion of each year at his home there. Jr. believed that you could see the hand of God in the beauty of nature, and he bought the land atop the Palisades, those sheer glacial cliffs lining the west bank of the Hudson, to give to the States of New York and New Jersey as parkland. He helped create many National Parks including Grand Teton National Park in Wyoming and Arcadia in Maine. While the image of the I.B.M. cubicle was dangled before me as the iconic workplace, Junior had always been expected to follow in his father's footsteps and take the reins of Standard Oil. After a lot of false starts and disappointments, he realized that he was not cut out to be a corporate executive. Like me, he could not find the words to tell his parents that he needed to chart his own pathway. While I helped mine out of the legal imbroglio they found themselves entangled in, Junior built his Mom and Dad the house on top of Kykuit Hill. In order to do so, Junior hired Italian stonemasons who, like my paternal grandpa, immigrated to the Hudson River Valley in the early 1900s. Both Junior and I struggled our whole lives to find inner peace.

During my second year at Kykuit, I gave a tour to the Superintendent of Schools for the Croton-Harmon School District. When I learned her identity, we got to talking. I mentioned that, although my father had gone to Croton High, he had left in his senior year to join the Marines and had never had the opportunity to graduate. She informed me that the School District was issuing special diplomas to honor *the boys of '42'* who had dropped out after Pearl Harbor. I submitted my Dad's name and was able to send him his high-school diploma, sixty years past due.

It was through Kykuit that I found Alexis again. I have bonded with so few people in my life, that each one has left an indelible print on my heart. Although she was gone, Alexis continued to haunt my dreams. Ironically, the one time she did return to Croton, for a twenty-fifth high school reunion, I ran and hid. At that time, I was still undiagnosed and carrying a crushing burden of shame as the little savant who had fallen flat on her face. I had supposed that my childhood-best friend was living happily ever after down in the Carolinas. I could not face her.

Last summer, a Christian tour group from the South visited Kykuit and I was assigned as their guide. One of the ladies wore an identification tag with the name of the small town in North Carolina to which Alexis' family had moved. Just on a lark, I mentioned her name. Another visitor suddenly chirped up, "Alexis? I work with her!" This was Terry, a nurse at the very hospital where Alexis was the chaplain. That was a surprise, indeed—Alexis, a chaplain! The Alexis I recalled had been far from chaplain material, but there was a tale behind it. Far from living happily ever after as I had imagined, Alexis had been left a widow with a small child at forty. Her opera singer husband had died of a heart attack onstage at the Metropolitan Opera during the premiere of *The Makroupolos Case*, an opera ironically about the search for a philter of immortality. Following this traumatic experience, Alexis heard a calling and enrolled in theology school. I gave Terry my e-mail, and I soon heard from my long-lost friend. As fate would have it, she also has discovered the wonder of horses. She e-mailed me her photo, and she has hardly changed a bit. Perhaps, one day, if fate is kind, we will meet in person.

My Dad's baby brother, Uncle Ralph, was too young to serve in World War II, but he was drafted and sent to France during the American Occupation. While in Paris, he fell under the spell of a twenty-something Frenchwoman, the daughter of White Russian émigrés. She was several years older than the young draftee and a whole world more sophisticated. Uncle Ralph did not stand a chance. However, when he brought his new bride back to the States, she was not given the warmest of welcomes by Dad's family. They viewed her as a gold digger, perhaps, and as a foreigner, for certain. Surprisingly, it was my Mom who befriended her when the others turned a cold shoulder.

This aunt is quite elderly now, and not in the best of health. Soon I will lose her as I have lost everyone who once was part of my life. However, each time I have spoken with her since my parents passed away, she has repeated one thing to me, and always in an adamant tone. "You know your mother loved you very much. Jacki always told me how very proud she was of you. You must know that." At first, I put her insistence down to incipient dementia, but she has spoken of this several times as if she feels bound to deliver a message.

It may be true, then. My mother did love me in her own way, although she could not express it. I was a riddle she never solved. That knowledge will have to sustain me as I continue my journey through this world all alone, a castaway on a fathomless sea with no anchor. When one has a family, the passing years are marked by Christmases, birthdays, vacations, anniversaries, births and deaths. With no family, the world spins by without you. It is an ache in my heart that the years cannot erase.

Still, receiving a late diagnosis of Asperger's Syndrome or, as it is now also called, Autism Spectrum Disorder, did much to dispel the despair and aimlessness which had engulfed me following the death of Aunt Rose. Once I had supposed I would depart this world leaving nothing behind me but a pool of frozen tears. I now found a sense of purpose. I realized that, by telling my story, I might bestow the gift of solace upon others who, like myself, have wandered the world in shadows, fighting off the Wolf of

Loneliness, and dogged by the question which had taunted me for years: Why am I not like other people?

In college, we were given a poem to read by Samuel Taylor Coleridge called *The Rime of the Ancient Mariner*. It told of an old sailor who, in his youth, had served upon a ship which became lost in a fog down near the Antarctic. An albatross, a bird of good luck, appeared out of the mist to guide the ship into safe waters with a good wind in its sails. Without any just cause at all, the Mariner took his bow and shot the albatross. Thereupon, the winds died and the ship became becalmed. The sun blazed down; the crew exhausted its water supply and became delusional. Eventually, everyone on the ship except for the Mariner would die, but before that occurred, the sailors hung the dead albatross around the mariner's neck as a reminder of the misfortune he had brought upon them. Soon the Mariner was adrift with the dead bodies of his mates on a boat infested with creepy, crawly water snakes. He reflected upon the errors of his past. Instead of killing the nasty snakes, he blessed them and, as he did, the dead albatross fell from his neck into the ocean.

As the poem begins, the Mariner is old, weather beaten, and, like me, quite alone in the world. He hails the Wedding Guest and tells his story. That is how he finds his redemption, and how I will seek mine.

Addendum

Not One of Us?

It happens each time a horrific crime is in the news. Commentators characterize the perpetrator as "The madman," or "the deranged individual," or announce that "a person suffering from mental illness" walked into the school . . . the mall. . . the movie theatre . . ." Each time I hear that I cringe, not because of any sympathy for the guilty party or because it is a slur against the mentally disabled, but because of the smugness of the speaker. To call someone "deranged" or "mad" is to marginalize them, to declare that they "are not one of us," and, indeed, not really human at all. As an adult with Asperger's Syndrome who has been marginalized all her life, I feel very uncomfortable when anyone, even someone quite unsavory, is summarily written out of the human race. I wonder if these sanctimonious pundits realize that most instances of mass carnage (a.k.a. "wars") have been planned and executed by neurotypicals just like themselves who were perfectly sane, unless you consider "drunk with power" to be a cognizable mental disorder.

Now, with the news that Adam Lanza, the shooter in the Connecticut elementary school massacre, may have had Asperger's Syndrome, it is the autism community's turn to recoil in horror and declare that no, he could not have possibly been one of us. The Autism Society issues a press release stating that, "it is imperative to remove autism from this tragic story. Alex Plank, autism self-advocate and founder of Wrong Planet.net pleads on CNN to leave autism out of the discussion of mass shootings, "The speculations are needless, untrue and hurtful" he says. The well-known author Joe McGinniss, father of an aspie son, told the *New York Times*, "The suggestion that Asperger's might be a clue as to why this happened is offensive to me." The Asperger's Association of New England (AANE) complains that "it is painful and frightening to feel associated by virtue of a diagnosis with someone who has committed such a horrific crime."

The press release put out by Susan Moreno, CEO of OA-SIS@ MAAP, a website for families affected by high functioning autism boldly declared:"We at MAAP wish to state that the vast majority of individuals with autism spectrum challenges (this includes Asperger syndrome) are not capable of the detailed planning and completion of the diabolical plans reportedly involved in this tragedy."

"There is really no clear association between Asperger's and violent behavior," echoes. psychologist Elizabeth Laugeson, an assistant clinical professor at UCLA. "It must have been something else," as though it would protect us to shovel him off onto another persecuted minority, as though there were a "something else" which would compel a person, not only to pump four bullets into the head of his mother as she lay in bed, but to then pack up the car with military gear, drive five miles to the elementary school and methodically gun down twenty first-graders and a handful of adults who got in his way. Perhaps he had a demon, riding alongside him, loading ammo into those high-capacity magazines?

Lost in the rush of autistic advocates, educators and experts to disassociate themselves from Lanza, are the remarks of Dr. John Constantino, an autism specialist at Washington University in St. Louis who stated on LA Times.com that "the social detachment and withdrawal associated with the disorder can accentuate other psychiatric conditions that are connected to violence."

The details of Adam Lanza's formal diagnosis, if any, may never be known. It does appear, however, that Lanza's behavior, up to the date of the shooting, was very aspie-like: shy, remote, highly intelligent, but fidgety, nervous and always alone. So we will assume that Lanza likely did fall somewhere on the autism spectrum and we may further assume that like many adolescent and adult aspies—myself included—he may well have suffered from co-morbid disorders such as depression and anxiety. None of these conditions caused him to commit such a despicable and irrational crime, but to say that his autism had nothing to do with it may be too much of a stretch. Rather than rushing to publish disclaimers, is it not possible that we might learn something about ourselves through this one horrific exception to the general rule that autistics only harm themselves and those that are close to them?

There were three kinds of violence involved in Lanza's rampage: murder of self, murder of a family member and murder of two dozen strangers, child and adult. If we were honest, we might admit that it is only the third sort of violence that confounds us.

I actually knew someone who killed his mother. I lived next door to his family for many years. Jason was not on the spectrum and, as far as I know, he had no mental disorders. He was just an ordinary kid. Yes, as a teenager he was a bit wild, but, by the time he reached his early twenties, the young man appeared to have turned his life around. He took responsibility for his life; he dressed well and was gainfully employed. In truth, I admired him immensely. Like many aspies, I myself had experienced a world of difficulty making the transition to adulthood and foundered about for many years in a limbo of dysfunctionality.

The young man disappeared from the neighborhood. I supposed he had gotten his own place, moved to another town, perhaps even married. His mother told me no, that he was jailed on a drug charge and asked me to say a prayer for his release. Eventually Jason was freed, and one night, apparently in an alcohol-fueled rage, he bludgeoned his mother and stepfather to death. He's back in prison now, locked away for life, and trapped for eternity, or what will seem like eternity, in his own private hell of remorse and regret, more intractable than the steel walls of his cell.

When I heard what Jason had done, I not only mourned for the victims, I shuddered, crossed myself and murmured, there but for the Grace of God . . . This was the kind of tragedy that I, as an autistic individual, could relate to. Had I not myself, in times of stress, flown into blind rages, and lashed out at loved ones or anyone who might be nearby? Had I not lost control of my behavior and caused damage and harm? I had never flipped out to such a degree, of course, but the realization of what rage might do caused me to reexamine my own tendencies and thenceforth I held the reins a little tighter whenever my emotions threatened to run away with me.

Nonetheless, Adam Lanza's criminal rampage was not a crime of passion; he did not just "snap" one night and strike out blindly like my young neighbor. No, it took planning and it took deliberation and it took a degree of cold-bloodedness to assemble that combat gear, a bullet-proof vest, and numerous clips of ammunition, to pack that arsenal into the family car and drive to town, not aimlessly, but directly to the local elementary school. That was the very unaspie-like thing he did, a deed which was not only evil, but seemingly inexplicable. Individuals on the autistic spectrum almost never commit preplanned premeditated violence against strangers. That is why so few autistics *go to soldiers*. We on the autism spectrum are so inner-directed, as the very word "autism" implies, that we cannot understand why anyone should be hell bent on mowing down strangers, be they children or be they grown-ups, be they neighbors or be they residents of a country halfway around the world.

About a week after the incident, I met with my therapist. She suggested that perhaps Adam Lanza was envious of the children. Perhaps he believed that he had been deprived of his own childhood, perhaps he had felt shunned by his own classmates and locked out of their world, and the very existence of these present day first-graders wrenched his heart with excruciating pain. A light went on in my head when she said these words.

It was a coincidence, but while sitting in the waiting room, I had been scanning a *New Yorker* article on Michael Jackson. Jackson certainly had some quirky, eccentric ways, and he was unquestionably obsessed with children and his own lost childhood. Although never the perpetrator of violence, the singer did express his obsession in ways that many people considered inappropriate and wrong.

I recollected my own past. It was not my childhood that I had been robbed of, but adolescence. The summer I turned thirteen, my parents sold our house in my hometown and moved to a rustic area in upstate New York. Life as I knew it was ended. Left behind were my childhood friends, my school, three grandparents and numerous aunts and uncles. Once a spunky street urchin, I suddenly found myself abandoned on the frozen tundra with no one to talk to and nowhere to go, unbearably lonely and homesick. High school was a nightmare from start to finish. I was bussed to a large impersonal campus full of bullies and strangers. My grades which had once been exceptional now plummeted. I made no new friends to replace those I had lost, nor did I have an adult mentor. There were a few good teachers there who might have taken me under their wings, but they were overwhelmed and far too busy. My parents were convinced that I was only making believe, pretending to fall apart in order to punish them for tearing me away from my hometown. Dragging myself out of bed in the morning was sheer agony; sleep, my only solace. All the while I was well aware that, all around me, the other students were having fun, dating, going to parties, dances and football games It's not that I did not want to join them; My nose was pressed tightly to the windowpane, but where was the key?

Long after those days were passed, when I was an adult in my twenties and thirties, and, yes, in my forties, my heart would sink whenever I happened upon a group of teenagers chatting, flirting, and enjoying themselves. An unreasoning envy would seize me, and I would curse them under my breath and wish them misfortune. I knew that my reaction was irrational, that these young people had done me no harm, that they were not the bullies who had tormented me and locked me out of their world. Logic could not dispel the anger and pain that seethed within.

Now, I might have wished them misfortune, but would I have ever taken steps to inflict it? No, of course not. I turned and walked away. If I had come upon the teens in a diner, I got up and left. If we were on a train, I moved to another car. Then I did what aspies commonly do. I turned and sunk my claws into my own heart, scorpion-like. I gave myself up to the slow suicide of desolation and despair.

If Adam Lanza had only destroyed himself, no one would have noticed. He would have silently departed this world, leaving "few footprints in life," as The *New York Times* put it. If he had only killed his mother, well-meaning people would have shaken their heads and said exactly what they said about my neighbor, that here was another troubled young man who "snapped." It is because Lanza exploded in such an unusual and almost apocalyptic way, that we are so shaken. If there is a silver lining to this horrific event, it might be that now the autism community will take a candid look at the dark side of living on the spectrum.

Aspies are "prey animals" say Tony Attwood and Temple Grandin. We are much more likely to be victims than villains. Wounded prey may, however, grow desperate and strike back. A lifetime of being bullied, rejected and relegated to the periphery of life can give rise to anger and bitter fantasies of revenge, especially among lonely young autistics that have grown up in a culture where violence is glamorized and who may turn to perfecting their skills at violent video games in lieu of a social life.

Advocates prefer not to address these negative aspects of autism. The reason for this is easy to understand. First of all, scare no one. That is rule number one. Better to portray us as shy, gentle, quirky geniuses. That is the safer depiction, but is it complete? Yes, we want acceptance, but must we sacrifice some inconvenient facts? Pretend all aspies are saints and the one who is not a saint, who carries the scars of unbearable pain, must hide himself in shame.

This is not to excuse Adam Lanza or anyone else, on or off the spectrum, who commits a terrible crime. In the end, I believe in free will. Unless a person is truly insane and has no control whatsoever over his or her actions, one must ultimately be held accountable. An ordered society could not exist unless there were laws against wrongdoing, and most aspies respect the law.

It has been written that courage is not the absence of fear, but the strength to overcome it. Perhaps choosing to be a good person entails not the absence of anger, but the presence of mind to channel that anger in a constructive way. Rather than sweep it under the rug, would it not be wonderful if aspies who have succeeded in that endeavor could give back to their community by lending a helping hand to those who are still challenged by the darker emotions and temptations that the autistic experience may imprint upon the heart?

Charli Devnet

•

For questions or comments regarding
The Snow Queen's Daughter,
please contact info@bramblebooks.com
or write to:
The Snow Queen's Daughter
P.O. Box 465
Crugers, New York 10521